Adult Children
of
Abusive Parents

Adult Children
of
Abusive Parents

*A Healing Program for Those
Who Have Been
Physically, Sexually, or
Emotionally Abused*

Steven Farmer, M.A., M.F.C.C.
Director of the Center for Adult
Children of Abusive Parents

Lowell House
Los Angeles

Contemporary Books
Chicago

Library of Congress Cataloging-in-Publication Data

Farmer, Steven.
  Adult children of abusive parents.

  Bibliography: p.
  Includes index.
  1. Adult child abuse victims—Mental health.
I. Title.
RC569.5.C55F37   1989   616.85′82   89-2451
ISBN 0-929923-01-4

Lowell House
1950 Sawtelle Blvd.
Los Angeles, CA 90025

Design: Brett Palmer
Manufactured in the United States of America
10 9 8 7 6 5 4 3 2

To Nicole and Catherine.
I love you with all of my heart.

Although stories in the book are based on actual incidents, names have been changed out of respect for privacy.

CONTENTS

PREFACE

Like you, I was abused as a child. I grew up with an alcoholic father and a hysterical, co-dependent mother. One of my earliest memories is from age three, watching in horror while my mother burned my brother's fingers with matches as he cried out. I hid in a closet, terrified that she might find me and burn my fingers too. Crazy, wild scenes like this punctuated my growing-up years. Many, many nights I lay in bed, knotted up with fear, as my parents and my brother screamed and fought in the next room. How I often yearned for someone to be there to take away the pain, to hold me and tell me that everything would be all right.

But no one was there. To survive, I learned to deny my feelings and to be as quiet, as invisible, as good as I could. I hoped that by my being good, somehow everyone would be happy and the abuse would stop. But it didn't. I felt powerless to influence the chaos and found that the best I could do was to help others feel better after one of these scenes.

I became so good at helping others that by the time I was 10 years old I had become our family's "counselor." This disposition plus an intense curiosity about what made people tick prompted me 15 years ago to become a real counselor.

In my first years as a therapist, clients came to me seeking relief from depression, anxiety, relationship problems, and a host of other difficulties. Seldom did they attribute any of these problems to childhood abuse. The more therapy I did, the more I found that most of these men and women had common issues and considerations stemming from their abusive childhoods. Many of them were also adult children of alcoholics, but most were not. Some had been abused dramatically; others had been "only" emotionally abused or neglected. Whatever the particular form of abuse, all experienced the torment of shattered emotions and the betrayal of childhood innocence.

In looking around my community and in examining popular and professional literature, I found precious little geared toward the problems of adults abused in childhood. The literature that was available contained much discussion of the problem but few solutions.

That is why I opened the Center for Adult Children of Abusive Parents and that is why I wrote this book. I trust that it will help you in understanding the connection between your past maltreatment and your present-day difficulties and that by following its recovery program, you will find a way to heal your emotional and psychological scars.

When we as Adult Children heal ourselves, we create a safer, more loving place, starting in our hearts and radiating outward to our world and to our children and our children's children. May this book serve you lovingly and purposefully.

I welcome your letters. You can write me at P.O. Box 9192, Newport Beach, CA 92658.

Steven Farmer

ACKNOWLEDGMENTS

I have been generously assisted in writing this book by many colleagues, clients, friends, and family members. I would like to express my special gratitude to the following people:

• The participants in my Adult Children of Abusive Parents groups, for their courage, insight, and honesty.

• Joanne Arns, Karen Bow, Julie Brown, Steve and Teresa Caldero, Joan D'Ardenne, Martha Hellman, Cori Herzig, Jeanne Hood, Michael and Dorothy Hyde, Pauline Jackson, Joyce Joseph, Melinda Kuhr, Victoria Maddock, Cheryl Onofrio, Pamela Orozco, Suzanne Peebles, Paula Proske, Melanie Silvers, Pat Soileau, Diane Sparkling, and Scott Van Druff for their personal advice and encouragement.

• Marilyn Murray, M.A., and her Scindo Training for some valuable ideas about the "three lost children."

• Tom Bell, M.A.; Paul Fairweather, Ph.D.; Eliana Gil, Ph.D.; M. K. Gustinella, M.A.; Bonnie Hesse; Suzanne Long, L.C.S.W.; Bill Lyon, Ph.D.; Lee Madigan, Ph.D.; Robin Powell, M.A.; Roland Summit, M.D.; Susan Watson, M.A.; and Dick Wilson, Ph.D., for their professional expertise and support.

• Steve and Patricia Tashiro, Michael Exeter, John Gray, Rev. Casey Gryba and Dr. Peggy Bassett for their consistent spiritual focus and leadership.

• Jack and Nancy Artenstein for giving this book a start.

• Amy Rudnick for always sounding so cheerful whenever I called.

• Janice Gallagher for her tireless inspiration and outstanding editing, and Derek Gallagher for his production assistance.

- Lise Wood for putting on her marketer's cap.
- Cindy Cashman and Erick, for their friendship, love, and guidance.
- My parents, Richard and Helen Farmer, for listening.

PART ONE

GROWING UP ABUSED

I

Beyond Survival

Norma has no close friends, seldom goes out, and discourages her husband, George, from going out as well. Her possessiveness makes George feel trapped, so he's joined a bowling league to have an excuse to be away from home. Each time he gets ready to leave for his night out, Norma asks and nags and begs him not to go, and usually he complies. George is getting more and more resentful of Norma's clinging and is withdrawing from her more and more. As Norma senses his withdrawal, she clings all the tighter. Norma is an Adult Child of Abusive Parents.

Art owns and operates his own accounting firm. He has built it into a very successful business over the last ten years. Although he now has others working for him, he still puts in 15-hour days. His stomach is constantly in knots, he complains about feeling tired and run-down, and he eats antacid like candy. His wife has been trying to get him to slow down for some time but has just about given up. Every time she threatens to leave him, he slows down his frenetic work pace, but only for a short while. During what little time he spends with his daughter, he usually gets frustrated and ends up yelling at her. Art feels depressed much of the time, and no matter how well his business does, he feels like he has to do more. Art is an Adult Child of Abusive Parents.

Patty haunts happy hours and singles groups, looking for love. She feels empty, lonely, and depressed most of the time. Once in a while she meets a man who looks like a good prospect. There's a feeling of electricity and a lot of intensity between them. She goes home with him, they end up having sex, and typically he's gone the next day, never to call again. Patty is left once again feeling empty, lonely, and depressed. To feel better, she resumes the hunt. Patty is an Adult Child of Abusive Parents.

Greg moved in with his parents after his second divorce. He is quiet, shy, and inhibited, but he has learned to smile easily at others. Very little communication goes on in his parents' home, and he is not close to his parents. He has no friends and doesn't go out, spending much of his free time in his room reading or working on various projects. Greg has worked as an engineer at an aerospace company for more than 12 years. When he's been offered promotions, he has turned them down, saying he doesn't want the "headaches." Even though he says he's happy and may even look happy to the casual observer, deep inside he is very lonely and depressed. Greg is an Adult Child of Abusive Parents.

These Adult Children were all abused when they were growing up. They may want to minimize the issue and deny the effects, but the conclusion is inescapable: The abuse they suffered in childhood continues to substantially affect them. They long for a break from their cycles of repetitious, self-defeating patterns of behavior, yet they cling to familiar habits because they know no other way. Conflict and struggle dominate their lives, as do persistent feelings of being victimized, exploited, and betrayed by others.

Statistics suggest that millions of adults today were victims of childhood mistreatment. In *Healing the Child Within*, Charles L. Whitfield, M.D., summarizes:

> Not everyone was mistreated or abused as a child. No one really knows how many people grow up with a healthy amount and quality of love, guidance and other nurturing. I estimate perhaps 5 to 20%. This means that *from 80 to 95%* [italics added] of people did not receive the love, guidance and other nurturing necessary to form consistently healthy relationships, and to feel good about themselves and about what they do.

This means millions of people today are grown-up victims of some form of abuse. Often the "symptoms" of abuse are not obvious to others or even to themselves—no broken legs, no damaged tissue. They seem fine, with no physical signs of having been injured. They are ordinary people, just like Norma, Art, Patty, and Greg are ordinary people. Yet they continue to feel anxious, depressed, and lonely. They continue to be trapped by their past, yet only vaguely aware that their present-day difficulties are substantially related to their childhood history. At some level, they realize there has to be something more to life.

Although the particular type of childhood abuse each received was different—Norma was sexually and physically abused, Art was emotionally abused, Patty was sexually abused, and Greg suffered from neglect—there was a common thread: the thread of emotional abuse.

Emotional abuse is always part of any form of child abuse, since it is during childhood that we are particularly vulnerable to emotional and psychological scarring from trauma or mistreatment. James Garbarino and Anne C. Garbarino in *Emotional Maltreatment of Children* elaborate on this point:

> Emotional damage is often the underlying problem in many, if not most, cases that first appear as other forms of abuse and neglect. Thus, in most cases of physical or sexual abuse, it is the emotional scars rather than the physical ones that must receive special attention. . . . Unless emotional maltreatment is considered an essential piece of the puzzle, efforts to protect and nurture children are incomplete at best and doomed to failure at worst.

Whether it is your body or your mind that is assaulted, your heart and spirit are always wounded in the process. While injuries to the body heal relatively quickly, emotional injuries leave more permanent but less obvious psychological scars.

Emotional abuse does not occur only as a by-product of other types of abuse; it is significant and damaging in its own right. You may never have been hurt physically by your parents and made it through childhood without so much as a scratch, yet still have been abused. The old saying about "sticks and stones" needs to be revised to reflect the truth: Words *can* hurt. Words, as stated in a recent advertisement for the National Committee for Prevention of Child Abuse, "can hit as hard as a fist."

The authors of *Emotional Maltreatment of Children* stress the need to recognize emotional abuse as a tragic and very real problem:

> As surely as one can break a child's bones, one can break a child's spirit. Society is coming to grips with the physical abuse and neglect of children, and that is a major accomplishment. But physical assault is not the only form of abuse; nor is nutritional starvation the only form of neglect. Emotional assault and psychological starvation are of equal, if not greater, importance as social problems.

When you are a child, rejection, fear, and constant humiliation take their toll emotionally and spiritually. When you become an adult, the effects of this emotional devastation are still with you.

Perhaps you, like many others, are an Adult Child of Abusive Parents. If so, you have survived your abusive childhood, but at great cost. Your spirit was shattered and your emotions disregarded and discounted. Something was lost along the way, something precious and real that you yearn to retrieve but may not know how.

This is the purpose of this book: to help you recover what you have lost—the natural state of innocence, your real self that was buried long ago behind the psychological barriers you constructed to cope with abuse. *Adult Children of Abusive Parents* will help you understand how you were affected by the abuse in childhood and how you still carry your abusive past with you. It will also present a recovery program that can help you at last to put the past behind you.

THE PAST BECOMES PRESENT

No matter how else you may have been abused, it is the effects of *emotional* abuse that are at the core of the problems that still plague you as an adult. The difficulties you face today most likely include an inability to trust, low self-esteem, depression, relationship problems, eating disorders, and alcohol or drug problems. The emotional abandonment you experienced as a child—the lack of consistent nurturing, protection, and guidance—not only was frightening and painful, but also left you in a constant state of internal deprivation, with feelings of emptiness and isolation. It is likely you have tried to fill up this emptiness, to replace the love and security you lacked, with something from outside yourself—alcohol, drugs, food, sex, gambling, or relationships, to name a few—yet find they provide only temporary respite from the pain of deprivation.

Still, since you feel a desperate need for relief from pain and emptiness, you have turned to these substances or activities again and again. This is the basis for all addiction: an attempt to replace missing love and security with something external. As an Adult Child of Abusive Parents, you are especially susceptible to addictions.

This statement may be alarming because it conjures up an image of someone in a dark room sticking a needle in his veins. However, that particular form of drug abuse is not the kind of addiction that you as an Adult Child are most likely to contend with. There are many things that one can become addicted to. Ann Schaef, author of *Co-dependence: Misdiagnosed & Mistreated*, describes two broad categories of addictions. The first is *substance addictions*, involving any chemical that, when ingested, produces a change in the natural body chemistry. This includes alcohol, drugs (prescription and nonprescription), caffeine, nicotine, and sugar. The second type of addiction she calls *process addictions*, which means a compulsive attachment to an activity. These include such things as love and romance, sex, work, eating, relationships, and religion, to name a few.

If you are addicted to one or more of these substances or processes, you did not start out with the intention of becoming addicted. Yet you find yourself compelled to continue; you literally cannot stop yourself. What started as a means of distracting yourself from emotional deprivation, of numbing the pain of your loneliness and isolation, has become an obsession.

Ellen's addictions began when she was teenager. "In high school, I used alcohol and drugs to numb myself just so I wouldn't have to feel anything," she states flatly. "I just couldn't deal with the pain, with the insanity of it all. I'd walk around all the time depressed. I took a bunch of pills in high school, so my mom and dad took me to the family doctor. He gave me something to make me throw up, and nothing was ever said about it again. The communication was just never there. The pain . . . you know, you just want to die. There's no reason to want to hang around and feel that depressed, that crazy, to feel like you don't even belong on the planet. After I left home, I just kind of took all of these feelings with me. I sure hadn't changed. I felt like I was 'bad' when I was a child, and when I became an adult, I still thought of myself as 'bad.' "

It may have taken a while after you left home before any of the problems that stemmed from abuse began to surface. You were just glad to be away from home. As you entered adulthood, you focused on getting a job, finishing school, establishing a career, and perhaps on dating, getting married, and having children. You were too busy with these concerns to pay much attention to the aftereffects of your childhood abuse. Once you left home, life seemed to promise new beginnings and greater happiness away from your abusive family.

It didn't take long for you to become disillusioned with your idealized vision of adulthood. Things weren't working out as you had hoped with your education, career, or relationships. You were lonely and depressed much of the time. You started noticing the same characteristics in yourself that you detested and feared in your parents—perhaps you were drinking more than you liked, perhaps you were being mean with your own children. You were aware of a vague sense of discomfort and emptiness that nothing seemed to truly satisfy. You started asking some difficult questions that do not have immediate answers, such as "Why do I feel so alone? Why am I drinking so much lately? How come I can't seem to be in a relationship that lasts? Why am I so angry all the time?"

Paul describes how he first became aware that something was wrong. "I thought I had it made. We had just bought our first house, Meg was pregnant with our second child, and I had just gotten a nice promotion at work. I was on top of the world, or so you would think. That's when the fights started. I was probably drinking a little more than I should have, and Meg seemed to need a lot more from me than usual. After one particular fight I slapped Meg, and really felt horrible. That's when it struck me: This was exactly how my parents' marriage was—*I was turning into my dad!*

I had decided long ago that there was no way I was going to treat my wife and children like my dad treated me and my mom, but here I was doing it. It was frightening!"

For answers as to why your life isn't working out the way you had expected, you must first look back into your childhood. By doing so you can see how you did exactly what was necessary to adapt to your abusive family. You will begin to see how your past has formed your present-day behavior and attitudes and how it continues to have a hold on you as long as you remain unconscious to that fact. You will see connections between specific decisions you made very early in life and rigid beliefs you still hold about yourself, about others, and about how life works. You will rediscover your own Inner Child and all the joy, innocence, and spontaneity that you had long ago forgotten.

As you remember, so begins your recovery and healing from the abuse. This will be a gradual process, and throughout you must pay close attention to your feelings and needs. It will require a strong and persistent commitment on your part to become emotionally healthier and spiritually integrated.

It may be painful at times, especially as you remember the buried hurt and anger from your past, but stay with it. It will be worth it. You're taking a step toward living a life in which you feel whole and complete. You *can* live a life free from the destructive influences of your past. In my own life and in my psychotherapy practice, I have seen many Adult Children who have been able to make dramatic changes in the way they see themselves and the way they carry on their lives.

Your recovery depends in part on your finding other ways to fill the emptiness inside you. If you're trying to fill it with a substance or an activity in an addictive way, it won't work. Addictions, whether to drugs or alcohol or to work or relationships, are only short-term, immediate solutions. They will never work with long-term problems. You will never find true happiness in anything external. Your happiness is an inside job.

My own recovery has been a long, steady journey. I have recovered from a few different addictions, each of which I can now see was an attempt to cover up the intense loneliness and isolation I felt. I had to grieve for my missing childhood, blame my parents for not giving me what I thought I should have had, and then forgive them for being nothing more and nothing less than who they were. Finally, I had to forgive myself for what I saw as my immense failure to make my parents happy. I realized that for years I had carried the blame for not having made my mom and dad feel better about themselves. Now the internal emptiness I once felt is more and more consistently filled—filled with the spirit of life and love, with a –

childlike quality of innocence that I once knew naturally and have now been able to recover. This to me is what recovery is all about.

THE MANY FACES OF ABUSE

To understand your past, it's helpful to understand the different kinds of abuse that children can suffer. The National Committee for the Prevention of Child Abuse defines child abuse as "an injury or pattern of injuries to a child that is nonaccidental." This includes physical and sexual abuse, neglect, and emotional abuse. In 1985, the American Humane Association reported that there were 1.9 million cases of child abuse and neglect, and the figures have been steadily on the rise. And this is only reported cases. We can only surmise how many walking wounded have not been reported.

Physical abuse is any nonaccidental physical injury, including ones that result in bruises, welts, broken bones, scars, or serious internal injuries. It's estimated that approximately half a million children each year are physically abused, though the actual figures are probably much higher.

In September of 1988, an eight-year-old boy testified in court that his father and stepmother made him spend time in a cage in the house and sleep on a piece of cardboard under a car outside. Examination revealed many injuries, and the boy said he was often struck "everywhere" with a belt, a golf club, an extension cord, and a long stick. His parents were arrested for felony child endangerment after the boy ran next door to a neighbor and asked, "Can I live with you for the rest of my life?"

Although this may be an extreme example, if you were physically abused you can undoubtedly relate to this little boy. If you were physically abused, you came to associate touch with pain. You learned to associate feelings with hurt and to be constantly vigilant for the open hand or the switch. The very people you turned to for love and protection became your tormentors. You could find no safety with your parents.

Debbie, an Adult Child who was physically and emotionally abused, carries herself with a slight bounce and a ready smile, but her sad and wary eyes betray a caution that comes from years of keeping a safe distance from others. She talks about her childhood in clipped, rapid sentences. "I was the scapegoat of the family," she states matter-of-factly. "I was the one who got it all the time—physically as well as verbally. The worst time I remember was when I was about five. I asked my mom what some words meant, some words I thought were kind of neat that my older brother told me never to say. She took all my clothes off and had me lie on the couch and beat me with a belt. I had blisters all the way from my neck to my feet. I remember just lying there crying and she just kept hitting me, screaming. It was awful! When I talked to her about it later, she denied that what she had done was wrong. She was a real strict Christian and believed the Bible said to do that if your kids did stuff like I did. I didn't understand the beatings, but I just figured I must be really bad."

Sexual abuse means any exploitation of a child for the sexual gratification of an adult. The American Humane Association estimates that approximately one in three girls and one in eight boys under the age of 18 will be involved in some sort of forced sexual experience with an adult, and that most of these cases go unreported. Sexual abuse includes exhibitionism, fondling, intercourse, or using the child to produce pornographic materials. There are millions of Adult Children today who have been sexually abused.

If you were sexually abused, your body was treated like an object to be used. You could not feel safe being touched and caressed. Touching meant sex rather than affection. You had nowhere to turn with your simple needs for being held and cuddled. You were robbed of your innocence, robbed of the right to discover your sexuality gradually, to become sexual at a time when you were psychologically and emotionally capable of assimilating the experience.

Michelle, one of my clients, is an attractive woman in her forties. She speaks of the childhood terror she lived with for a number of years: "My mom was lonely after my dad left—that's why she let Arthur move in." Michelle proceeds slowly, deliberately choosing each word. "Then my mom started working nights, and . . . that's when it all got started. I was ten years old at the time and was watching TV when he came and sat down next to me. Then he started touching me—his arm around my shoulder, his hand on my knee. When it first was happening, it felt kind of good, but eventually it felt real strange. This went on just about every night after my mom went to work. Then one night it happened. He touched me—my private parts—and made me touch him. It felt good but felt wrong at the same time. Then he took me into the bedroom and forced me to have sex with him. He told me not to tell my mom because it would break up the family. This went on for the next four years. What a nightmare! One day Arthur moved out—I was so relieved, but I've never to this day told my mom what happened."

Any time the caretaker fails to provide the basic necessities of life, including food, water, shelter, medical care, attention to personal hygiene, or adequate supervision required for optimal growth and development, the child suffers *physical neglect*. If you were neglected, your parents were simply not there to provide the basics you required to survive, so it's through good fortune that you are alive today.

Hal reports, "My mom used to date a lot after she left my dad. I must have been six or seven years old, and she'd leave me alone most of the evening. I'd play with my toy soldiers and keep the TV and all the lights on in the house. Sometimes it got pretty scary, so I pretended that I had a friend there with me. That made it a little better."

Emotional abuse includes unreasonable demands put on a child that are beyond her capabilities and may include persistent teasing, belittling, or verbal attacks. Natalie was constantly told that something was wrong with her, that she was defective. She could "never do things right," suggesting that her parents' expectations were often unreasonable. Emotional abuse also includes failure to provide the emotional and psychological nurturing necessary for a child's emotional and psychological growth and development.

It's difficult to estimate how widespread emotional abuse is because it is more difficult to define than other kinds of abuse. The signs are not as visible; the emotional scars are usually inside. Many of its victims deny that they were ever abused—after all, they weren't beaten or sexually molested.

The difficulty in concretely defining emotional maltreatment as child abuse was highlighted by the tragic story of 10-year-old child actress Judith Barsi. In July of 1988, the bodies of Judith, her mother, and her father were found in their Los Angeles home. It was determined that the father had shot his wife and daughter and then himself. In the preceding months, several family friends, the child's agent, and her therapist had reported that Barsi had threatened his family. The county child-welfare department dropped its investigation shortly before the slaying.

The headline of an article in the *Los Angeles Times* read: "Panel Scolds Agency in Girl's Death." An investigating panel, the Commission for Children's Services, reprimanded the county's child-welfare department but apparently could do no more. Helen Kleinberg, a member of the investigating commission, said that one reason the county did not act was that the abuse was emotional rather than physical. "But emotional abuse can be as threatening to a child as physical abuse," Kleinberg stressed. "This is part of the whole problem: It's easy to focus on physical abuse because we can see it." As Eliana Gil, Ph.D., author of *Outgrowing the Pain,* observed on the ABC television show "Nightline," "Emotional abuse is usually considered the lesser of two evils."

Another dramatic example of emotional abuse is illustrated by the story of Mary Bergamasco. In August of 1988, she put her seven-year-old son on public display in a pig costume in front of her home to punish him for stealing. She tied his hands behind his back, put blue fingerpaint on his face, and taped a fake pig nose on his head. A sign on his chest read, "I'm a dumb pig. Ugly is what you will become every time you lie and steal. Look at me squeal. My hands are tied because I cannot be trusted. This is a lesson to be learned."

Charged with misdemeanor child abuse, Bergamasco denied there was anything wrong with what she had done. "My mother did it to me," she said, "and it didn't affect me." We can only guess how the effects of this incident may remain with this young boy into adulthood. Perhaps he, like his mother, will "not be affected" yet will perpetuate the cycle of abuse by passing it on to his children or others, or keep it alive by abusing himself.

"I *THINK* I WAS ABUSED"

You may be wondering whether or not you were really abused. Some of my clients wonder about this from the start. Others describe very cruel treatment on the part of their parents, including beatings and verbal assault, yet deny that it was abuse. Still others discover their childhood abuse only after beginning to explore gaps in their earlier memories.

Like some of my clients, you may be saying, "After all, it happened to lots of other people, too. And it really wasn't all that bad. In fact, many other people have had it a lot worse." If you have told other people about your mistreatment, they may have thought it was just standard child-rearing practice—not really abuse. They may have said or implied that you were making too big a deal out of it, that it couldn't have been all that bad, or that most parents treat their children that way. Many people want to minimize the fact that child abuse has been much more common than we have acknowledged; they excuse cruel child-rearing practices as being "for the good" of the child. Many people ignore the fact that the damaging effects of child abuse remain into adulthood and are passed on to the next generation.

No matter how abuse is defined or what other people think, you are the ultimate judge: If you think you were abused, you were. If you're not sure, you probably were. It's often a matter of the degree to which you were abused rather than whether or not you were. By acknowledging the fact of your abuse, you begin your healing and recovery. Even if you were abused by someone other than a parent, much of what is contained in this book applies to you. The reason I focus on abusive parents is that 80 percent of child abuse is perpetrated by the child's parent or guardian.

As I reflect on my own childhood, I can see how the emotional deprivation I have felt through much of my adulthood stems from the emotional abuse I received. My father was an alcoholic, and my mother was addicted to getting my father to stop drinking. Because of their individual addictions, they weren't there for me much of the time emotionally, so I became a "little adult" very early and tried to take care of both my parents. I remember crying myself to sleep on occasion because when they were fighting, there was nowhere that felt safe. When my dad drank, he could say some pretty nasty things and get quite violent. My older brother frequently got involved in the fray.

I learned to rely on myself for comfort and eventually stopped looking to my mom or dad for the safety and protection that parents usually provide. Yet, like most people, I found it easy to deny that I was seriously affected by this emotional neglect. As a result, I spent much of my early adult life believing I didn't need anything from anyone and I could handle anything without becoming distraught. I wasn't affected by this abuse—or so I thought. But if that were true, why did I feel so empty, so isolated from others and from life?

Alice Miller, in *For Your Own Good,* describes what happens when we downplay our past abuse:

> I have discovered that we are less a prey to . . . . the repetition compulsion if we are willing to acknowledge what happened to us, if we do not claim that we were mistreated "for our own good," and if we have not had to ward off completely our painful reactions to the past. The more we idealize the past, however, and refuse to acknowledge our childhood sufferings, the more we pass them on unconsciously to the next generation.

Your abuse was not unusual. A philosophy of child-rearing has been handed down for many generations that is best captured in the familiar saying, "Spare the rod and spoil the child." According to this philosophy, children need to be trained early to be passive and obedient, and whatever a parent has to do to control the normal outbursts of childhood emotions and limit the child's natural unruliness is permissible.

Obedience to parental authority took the foreground, while empathy and respect for the child's feelings and integrity were often slight or nonexistent. Parents treated their children like possessions with which they had a right to do whatever they pleased. It was not until 1871 in New York that a battered child was first given protection from her abusive parents. There were no child abuse laws at the time, so the Society for Prevention of Cruelty to Animals brought the case on the grounds that the child in question was an animal and thus was entitled to protection.

It was not until 1964 that the first modern child abuse reporting law was passed. Within five years, every state in the union had passed a reporting law. Since that time, there has been increasing public recognition of the extent and far-reaching implications of child abuse.

BEYOND SURVIVAL

You have survived abuse and are to be congratulated. You have developed some remarkable skills that helped you adapt to the craziness in your family, and those skills continue to serve you today. You have developed a great deal of strength and emotional endurance, as well as an incredible tolerance for upheaval, chaos, and uncertainty.

The only problem is that you're still operating on a survival level. It's been hard to relax your need to be in control, to trust that you can protect and take care of yourself, or to let other people close to you, to be vulnerable with others. To do so would seem threatening at a very deep level. So you remain isolated, doing your best to "handle" your life. You stay alive, but you don't thrive.

You have an opportunity to move beyond survival into a fuller, richer life—to truly *live* rather than just exist. You begin when you start accepting and dealing with the fact that you were abused, when you realize that you can free yourself from the chains of the past, that you can forgive yourself for any imagined "badness" or wrongdoing as a child. Then you can recover that sense of innocence, vulnerability, and realness that is an important part of being a child and let the child live on inside you as an adult. As the familiar saying goes, "The journey of a thousand miles begins with the first step."

THE ROAD TO RECOVERY

My program for your recovery has two parts. In the first part, *Growing Up Abused,* you will gain a better understanding of your past and what life was like for you as a child. In the next chapter, "Growing Up in an Abusive Family," you will see how your upbringing contrasts with that of children in healthy, functional families. The third chapter, "Surviving the Abuse," will help you recognize how you chose to survive and how you decided what you had to do in order to survive. In Chapter 4, "The Roles That Bind," we will look at how the strategies you used in childhood have turned into roles, and how these roles now limit your growth and keep you rigid and emotionally and spiritually isolated.

In the second part of the book, *Your Recovery,* you will take steps to heal the wounds you suffered. Here you will have an opportunity to work a specific three-step recovery program that will help you free yourself from the burden of the past. With your participation, patience, and perseverance, this program will help you go beyond survival.

Before you proceed with your recovery program, it's important to take a hard look at your use of alcohol or drugs and to ask yourself honestly if you are addicted to one or both. If you are, you *must* deal with these addictions first. If you keep using them, they will screen out any progress you make in recovering from the effects of abuse. They are an excellent way to continue denying, to temporarily ease your internal deprivation and numb your pain. Continued use will merely sabotage your recovery. For help in this area, please see the Resources list in the appendixes section.

The first step in the program of recovery from abuse is Chapter 5, "Healing Your Inner Child." You must mourn the loss of the childhood you never had. You must create an internal mother and father that better meet the needs of your Inner Child. It will be like childhood all over again but with a different set of parents—ones you create!

The second step in recovery is outlined in Chapter 6, "Growing Up Again." Here you will find some specific skills that you will need in going through your "second childhood," including how to play and how to touch and be touched. This is a way to reconstruct your childhood in a healthier, more functional way.

The third step is "Integration," detailed in Chapter 7. This is where you will begin to feel "together" and experience personal power and self-esteem. The various parts of you that you had disowned will come together in a cohesive statement of life called "you." Here you begin to express your spirituality as a natural outgrowth of this integration.

Finally, in Chapter 8, "Breaking the Cycle," we will talk about how you can break the pattern of abuse being handed down from generation to generation. Here you will find some tested tips on dealing with your children that will interrupt the cycle of abuse in specific ways, making room for greater love and respect with your children and in your life.

We'll start by examining abusive families and how they compare to healthy, functional families.

2

Growing Up
in an
Abusive Family

*D*addy's home!" shouts five-year-old Angela Harrison as she races toward the front door. As soon as the door opens, Angela jumps into the arms of her father, Jack. He gives her a squeeze, tousles her hair and tells her how happy he is to see her. He sets her down gently, gives her one more kiss on the forehead for good measure, and then proceeds to the kitchen, calling, "Sweetheart, I'm home!"

Charlotte, his wife, greets him with open arms. "Hello, darling," she says softly as she plants a kiss on his cheek, "how was your day?" As Charlotte finishes preparing pot roast, Jack's favorite, Angela sits quietly on her daddy's lap as he tells of his triumphs at the office. Then Jack carries Angela to the garage to see how his nine-year-old son is doing fixing his bike.

Smiling at the sight and sound of his dad, Todd continues working on the bike as they talk. "I'm having a little trouble getting the wheel to line up right, Dad," Todd says as he puts down the wrench. Jack tells Todd how happy he is to see him, then explains how to put the wheel on straight, being careful not to do the job for Todd but instead to provide him with appropriate guidance.

Within a few minutes, the job is done. "Thanks, Dad. I couldn't have done it without you!" Jack tells his son how proud he is of him and how he likes the way Todd does things for himself. They go into the house together and sit down at the dinner table.

Dinner is a time of togetherness, laughter, and sharing. There is a lot of love in the air. After dinner, Dad and the kids clean the dishes while Mom rests in the living room, reading a book. When this is done, all gather in the family room for a rousing game of crazy eights. Angela and Todd take turns dealing the cards; between hands, Jack and Charlotte exchange playful nudges and caring glances.

Jack tells the children it's time for bed, and they go to their rooms and put their pajamas on. They return, having brushed their teeth and washed their faces, and they snuggle with their parents on the couch while Charlotte reads a bedtime story. After the story, the children go to bed. Mom and Dad come in to say their final good-nights.

Jack and Charlotte spend the rest of the evening talking about the trip to the park this Saturday, where they will join some other friends and their children for a day of play. In the middle of the discussion, Jack looks affectionately at Charlotte and says, "You know, I'm a lucky man. I have two great children who get along well almost all the time. We never fight, and I'm always delighted to be with you and the children. You're a fantastic wife and a great mother. I couldn't ask for more. I love you."

After a while, they go to bed. They snuggle together and hold each other through the night, as they have nearly every night for the last 12 years, and drift off into peaceful slumber. Thus ends another wonderful day in the lives of the Harrisons.

You might think of the Harrisons as a healthy family, but they aren't. They are a perfect family—one that never has existed and never will exist.

Television has provided lots of models for "perfect" families in such shows as "Father Knows Best," "Ozzie and Harriet," "Family Ties," and "The Cosby Show." You may have found such shows discouraging to watch because they made your family seem all the more dismal by comparison. On the other hand, they gave you hope that someday you too might have a better family than the one in which you grew up.

These TV families, like the Harrisons, are a myth, the product of writers' imaginations. What you mistook for healthy, functioning families were idealized versions of family life.

As you grew up, you were disappointed that your adult life was not nearly as warm and wonderful as life on these situation comedies. You felt guilty that you had failed to do better than your parents, and today you still find it hard to forgive yourself for being less than ideal. Like many other Adult Children, you do not have a true, realistic model of a nonabusive family, one that operates reasonably well as a unit while respecting the integrity of each of its members.

PORTRAIT OF AN ABUSIVE FAMILY

To give you a more accurate basis of comparison and to help you understand how your family contributed to your present-day difficulties, let's take a closer look at eight specific interactional elements found in all abusive families and compare them to healthy ones.

"Let's Pretend": Denial

Jerry walks in from work with a scowl on his face. Carrie, his 14-year-old daughter, is setting the table. She asks what's wrong and he replies, "Nothing" rather tersely. Carrie comments on how his frown and wrinkled brow are giving him away. Jerry mutters something, and Carrie shrugs. Melinda, his wife, breezes into the kitchen, starts to greet Jerry, then notices that something is wrong. She asks what's bothering him, and although at first reluctant, he blurts out, "Hal Wilson got the promotion that I thought I was going to get. I'm still reeling from the news, and I keep wondering how I screwed things up."

"Aw, c'mon, Dad," Carrie says cheerfully, "It couldn't be all that bad."

"Damn it, Carrie," Jerry shouts, "I know it's not the end of the world, but I'm really angry and disappointed right now, and it doesn't help when you tell me to cheer up. I know you're just trying to help me out, but for right now, I need to stew a bit. That promotion meant a lot to me!"

Carrie finishes setting the table in silence. Melinda reaches out to Jerry and gently massages his shoulder while he sits with his arms crossed and one hand on his chin. "I'm sorry for yelling at you, Carrie," Jerry says in a more subdued voice. "It's just been a rough day, and I'm in a lousy mood."

Tears well up in Carrie's eyes. "I was just trying to cheer you up, Dad. That hurts my feelings when you yell at me that way. I'm really sorry you didn't get the promotion, because *I* think you deserve it!"

In healthy families, like the one above, parents encourage the sharing of thoughts and feelings and respond to their expression, even when the feelings are unpleasant. Not only did Carrie's father feel free to express his annoyance, he supported Carrie's reaction to him. This is one of the hallmarks of a healthy family—members talk about what's going on.

In your family, however, feelings were often too painful to acknowledge, so the family members refused to admit what they plainly knew to be true. Not only were the feelings painful, but the silence and the put-downs kept everyone from acknowledging what was going on. Everyone pretended, and your parents lied to you so often, you ended up believing the lie. Or, if you weren't convinced, you at least learned to keep your mouth shut about the truth.

One of my patients, Kevin, remembers: "Whenever my dad went on one of his rampages, all of us were hurt and scared and didn't know what to do. My mom would always come up with some sort of explanation for his behavior: a bad day at work, he didn't feel good, we were a burden. Meanwhile, she'd be shaking and crying herself, saying she was okay. It got to the point where I sometimes believed her!"

When you were a child, your parents kept telling you that what you felt, what you saw, and what you heard were wrong. It didn't take you long to figure out the message: Lie, pretend, fake it, but whatever you do, be sure to deny your thoughts, feelings, and perceptions. Don't trust others, and certainly don't trust yourself. As Claudia Black summarizes in *It Will Never Happen to Me,* "Don't talk, don't trust, don't feel." Better to not see anything, say anything, feel anything. How could you do anything else but turn off your feelings and shut down?

You learned to deny the truth, first to your parents, then to others, and finally even to yourself. If mother and father were fighting violently, you knew better than to interrupt. If you were sexually abused, it remained a secret between you and the abuser. Most likely, instead of telling, you pretended nothing was wrong. So did everyone else in the family.

"I learned to keep quiet and keep smiling," states Roberta, smiling of course as she shares this. "My brother Tommy was coming into my room just about every night from the time I was nine or ten until I was fourteen, reaching under the covers and touching me and putting his finger in me. I'd pretend I was asleep, because I didn't know what else to do. I dared not tell Mom and Dad, because I thought it was my fault, that I was bad, and they would punish me if I told. So I didn't tell anybody, and finally one day just told him to stop it, and he did. Nothing was ever said about it again."

Just like Roberta, you learned the lessons of denial very well. It served a purpose: It helped you survive. To understand why you would deny in order to survive, it's important to fully appreciate the significance of your relationship with your parents. As a child, you were completely dependent on their love and nurturing, their caretaking. They provided you with the home you lived in and the food you ate. They were far bigger and much stronger; in your young eyes, they were all-powerful. Since you saw your parents as the keys to your survival, you did what you had to in order to remain alive. You endured a great deal of mistreatment, mainly because you saw no other choice. In order to endure this mistreatment, you made some compromises. The main compromise was to play along with the family game of denial.

Kimberly describes what happened when she tried to confront the reality of her mistreatment. "When I was about thirteen, I couldn't take it anymore—my stepdad always touching me, molesting me whenever my mom wasn't around. He had threatened that he would beat the living daylights out of me if I told her, so for three years I didn't say anything. But finally I figured that anything would be better than having to live with this kind of fear. So one day, I took a deep breath and told my mom—right in front of him—what had been going on. She slapped *me*—I couldn't believe it—she slapped *me,* and they both told me I was a liar."

Life as a Perpetual Roller Coaster: Inconsistency and Unpredictability

Leslie plays tag with a couple of friends from her third-grade class, waiting for her dad to pick her up from school. They are laughing and giggling so hard that she doesn't hear the horn of her dad's car. When she finally sees him, she says goodbye to her friends, grabs her tote bag, and walks swiftly toward the car. She knows that her dad doesn't like to be kept waiting.

In the car, Leslie and her dad exchange pleasantries about each other's days, and he tells her that her mom has called and will be a little late for dinner tonight. Leslie briefly expresses her disappointment without words, staring blankly out the side window for a few seconds.

"She'll be home before too long. She's still finishing up with one particular account that she's had some problems with. I've made us a great spaghetti dinner. Besides, Friday night is our family night, and you and I and Richard and Mom will all have a chance to be together. I'm looking forward to Friday."

Leslie is reassured by her father's words. Friday nights are always fun. She knows her mom has been extra busy lately, but Leslie still misses her. Then Leslie remembers that she is going to have her "day with Mom" next weekend. This is something that started before her last birthday. She and her brother Richard each get to have one day alone with Mom and one day alone with Dad every few weeks. Leslie thinks this a great idea and takes full advantage of it whenever it is her turn. It makes her feel better to remember that this special day is just around the corner.

Healthy families like Leslie's provide a steady and dependable environment for the children. Parents are there when children expect them to be there. They pick up their children when they agree to do so. They come home from work when they are expected, or if they don't, like Leslie's mom, they phone. Parents are there not only physically but emotionally to provide for their needs. The children don't need to do a lot of guesswork about their parents' whereabouts physically or emotionally.

Children receive consistent reactions to their behavior. Leslie knows that if she makes her father wait, he will not like it. It is predictable.

In healthy families, when children smile, parents smile back. When they cry, they can usually expect to be comforted. When they misbehave, their parents discipline them clearly and fairly.

In a healthy family, there is a regularity to events. Routines and family rituals emphasize the continuity of the family unit. Leslie is looking forward to the new ritual of having a day alone with either parent every few weeks. There may be family home evenings once a week, regular religious or spiritual activities, or a game night in which everyone participates. These routines and rituals offer consistency and predictability for the children, yet do not become so inflexible that the practice in itself becomes oppressive.

In your family, however, there was a great deal of inconsistency and unpredictability. Rather than serving as a source of stability for you, your family was a source of turbulence and chaos. Rather than providing a safe refuge from the external world, it often seemed like the worst place in the world.

Your parents provided poor leadership. Rules were often unclear and often broken. Your parents' behavior fluctuated wildly from day to day. One moment they would be calm and peaceful; the next, they would explode into shouting and screaming.

Since your parents tended to react readily to upsets, you often had to guess what Mom or Dad would do next. Although you may have picked up warning signs sometimes, such as Father's drinking, very often the abuse came about suddenly and unexpectedly. Did that look in Mother's eye mean that she was about to get angry and start screaming at you? When you disagreed with Father, would he beat you up?

"I hated coming home," declares Robert as he takes another slow drag on his cigarette. "I wasn't sure if Mom would be there, and if she was, whether she'd be drunk and start spouting all over the place about what a no-good son I was. One time I got elected class vice-president, and I wanted to tell her about it. When I got home and walked in the door, she didn't even say hello before she started cussing at me for being home fifteen minutes late, then went on to berate me for my messy room, my loud stereo, and the fact that I hardly stayed around home anymore. Even though this kind of thing happened before, I was still stunned. I went straight to my room after this harangue, and I don't think I ever did tell her about my election."

You were unable to predict with any certainty whether your mom or dad would be there for you at all, either physically or emotionally. Dad sometimes may have "forgotten" to pick you up from the movies, perhaps because he had had too much to drink. Mom may have often left you at home alone before you were old enough to care for yourself. No one was there for you when you most needed the loving comfort of a trusted adult. Because of this inconsistent caretaking, you learned to rely on yourself in order to gain a sense of predictability or certainty.

One of my patients, Gary, describes how unpredictable his mother's behavior towards him was: "Living at home was like a bad dream. Everything would be going along just fine when all of a sudden, wham! She'd hit me. One time I was doing my homework and she asked me something. I didn't answer—I was involved in my work. And then with no warning, she slapped me on the side of my head. 'Don't you ignore me!' she shouted. 'When I'm talking to you, you listen to me!' I started to explain, but she didn't want to hear. She grabbed the ruler that was on my desk and started hitting me some more. Later that night I went out of my room for a drink of water, and she asked me if I had finished my homework, like nothing had happened. The next day, everything seemed calm and peaceful and nobody ever said anything about it again."

"I'll Give You Something to Cry About!": Lack of Empathy

Five-year-old Darrel is playing a video game with his older cousin Scott. Aunt Sylvia and Jean, Darrel's mom, are visiting in the living room, catching up on the latest gossip. Jean hears her son cry out, and he comes into the living room with tears streaming down his face. "What happened?" she inquires.

"Scott wouldn't let me have my turn!" Darrel says between sobs. "And then he hit me!"

"Ouch! I bet that makes you pretty angry! Here, let me see where he hit you." Darrel's sobbing begins to subside as he approaches his mother and shows her his left ear. "Well, it didn't leave any marks, but I'm sure it hurt." She kisses the side of his head where Darrel had pointed, puts her arms around him, and speaks soothingly as she rocks him for a few moments.

Empathy is the ability to be sensitive and responsive to another's feelings and needs, as Jean is with Darrel. It is not sympathy, which is pitying someone, nor is it agreeing with the other person. It is the ability to "walk in another's moccasins," to feel what the other person feels. It's only when you truly have empathy that you can recognize another person as a human being just like yourself, one worthy of being treated with respect rather than as an object. When you have empathy, you can share in another person's feelings without becoming enmeshed in them.

In a healthy, functional family, parents have empathy for their children. Jean does not ignore Darrel's feelings or tell him they are wrong; she validates them. When Johnny fails a test at school, his parents may be disappointed, but they want to know how he feels about having failed. When little Catherine falls off her bicycle, the first aid her mother gives includes comfort and compassion.

Parents in a functional family understand that their children are capable of different things at different ages. Typically, the younger the child, the more self-centered he is. At age three, he may literally not be able to control his crying or his temper at times. Parents make more allowances for this type of behavior at that age. Nor would they expect "adult behavior" from their five-year-old, such as entrusting the child with the care of a younger sister while the parents are absent.

Empathic parents can relate compassionately to what it is like to be a child and can appreciate how a child's needs differ from an adult's. An empathic adult recognizes the child's need to know his limits, to know the boundaries of acceptable behavior. If a child's behavior is unruly or unmanageable, parents in a healthy family may send him to his room until he behaves appropriately. And, although a mother may completely understand her teenage daughter's feelings and reasons for violating her curfew, she may "ground" her daughter from outside activities for the next few days. Consequences such as these help a child understand where his limits are and can be imposed with complete respect and empathy for the child's integrity.

In your family, your parents did not empathize with you. They expected a great deal more from you than you were capable of giving. At age seven, for example, you may have looked and acted quite mature, yet you still had your moments of whining and crying, you still needed considerable comfort and guidance. Your parents, not taking into account that this was to be expected, struck out aggressively against you because you were not acting according to their expectations.

Tyler recalls the following incident that took place when he was seven: "I had seen my father digging in the garden just the day before and figured I would help him by taking out some of the weeds. Little did I know that the 'weeds' were really new tomato plants. He was really upset and spanked me until I had blisters. I was very upset and crying and all that, probably as much from his not understanding that I was trying to help him. He kept saying to me, 'You're so stupid sometimes! Stop your crying, or I'll really give you something to cry about!' I had a hard time not crying— until he came over and slapped me. At that point I vowed no one would ever see me cry again, and I kept that promise for thirty years."

Your parents did not know how to empathize with you because their parents did not empathize with them when they were children. If your mother was scolded as a little girl when she cried, she believed that is the proper way to treat a child who cries. If your father was whipped for disobeying, he undoubtedly came to believe that is the way to discipline a child.

Your mother and father had difficulty relating to your feelings and needs directly because their own needs as children were denied and discounted. Your childhood actions triggered at an unconscious level their own memories and fears from childhood, especially the more unpleasant memories of abuse. They projected these feelings of helplessness and powerlessness onto you, while at the same time identifying strongly with the abuser. You then became victim to someone more powerful, just as they had been. Thus your parents perpetuated the cycle of abuse without any conscious awareness of their hurt, fear, and sense of helplessness. Instead, they got angry and expressed it by assaulting you or withdrawing from you. You represented to them all that they feared and at one time experienced themselves as children—powerlessness, vulnerability, and lack of control.

There you were, a vulnerable child, having feelings and needs no one understood. It is not so much the hurts and pains of childhood that remain with you, it's the memories of not having someone there—a trusted, responsive adult, to help soothe those pains, to kiss the hurt and make it better.

David remembers running the 50-yard dash in fifth grade and losing: "My mom—she could be so cold. I came home from school that particular day, still reacting to losing the race. Deep inside, I had really wanted to win. I was in my room crying when she came in without knocking and asked rather gruffly, 'What's wrong?' When I told her, she said, 'Don't be such a bad sport. No wonder you didn't win. You're a bad sport and a baby to boot.' Then she turned and left the room. My anger choked down the hurt I had felt. I'd like to have strangled her just then."

Knowing Where to Draw the Line: Lack of Clear Boundaries

Seven-year-old Allison and four-year-old Mary Jean are playing with their daddy, roughhousing in the living room after dinner. Both girls tackle his legs, and he "falls" to the floor and lies there as if he is out cold. Allison claims out loud that he is faking it, while Mary Jean goes up to his face and tries to open his eyes. Suddenly he awakens, grabs both girls, wrestles them to the ground, and starts tickling. Mary Jean manages to wiggle away, so he puts in a concentrated tickling effort on Allison. In just a few moments, Allison is laughing hysterically, but says in the midst of her laughter, "Stop it, Dad. *I mean it!*" This is the family's agreed-upon signal to cease any bodily contact, especially tickling. Dad immediately stops the tickling, only to be invited by Mary Jean to tickle her. Mary Jean giggles and giggles at his tickling, and finally blurts out between chortles, "Daddy, stop, and *I mean it!*" He curtails the tickling as soon as she says it. The giggling continues as the two girls start to tickle their daddy. He obligingly surrenders to this double tickle-force, until he finally tells them to stop it and that *he means it.*

They realize that their father is going to take some time out from play, so the girls go to their room and resume active play with each other. Soon Mary Jean's voice is heard: "Daddy, Allison's using my crayons and coloring book, and she didn't ask me!" Their father comes in and determines that Allison has in fact been using Mary Jean's crayons, so he instructs Allison to stop using them until and unless she has Mary Jean's permission. Allison pouts for a couple of minutes, then takes out her own colored pencils to finish her drawing.

In healthy families like the one above, each member has distinct boundaries, both physical and psychological. The physical boundaries include the body and material possessions such as toys and clothes. The signal words, "Stop it, I mean it," in the above scenario encourage each family member to establish his or her own physical boundaries. When Dad told Allison to give Mary Jean's crayons back to her, he was giving both girls a message that their boundaries included what was rightfully theirs.

The psychological boundaries, invisible yet very real, include the sense of "self" or "me" as being separate from another person and territorial boundaries—the immediate space around one's body. Psychological boundaries develop as children gain an awareness of their physical boundaries. In functional families, each member has an awareness of both his physical and psychological "self" and sees himself as distinct from others in the family. Putting someone down or calling someone names tend to violate these psychological boundaries.

The family's rules, and the consistency with which these rules are applied, help determine the individual's boundaries within the structure of the family. The rules may be spoken or unspoken, but they are generally understood by all family members. The rule about saying, "Stop it, I mean it," is an example. Other rules include whether family members close the door when they go to the bathroom, whether adults walk around the house naked, and when and how the different family members can touch each other. Boundaries change as children get older, but they change gradually and according to the needs of the family members, not because of parental whim. For instance, parents may let their child sleep with them when he's one year old, but not when he's nine.

A child learns about her own boundaries depending on how these rules are defined and whether they are honored. In a healthy family these physical and psychological boundaries are consistently respected. If the rule is that no one else comes into the bathroom when the door is shut, then no one does.

  In your family, however, you were never quite certain what the family rules were—they seemed to keep changing. Sometimes when you fought with your brother, your mom would get angry, and at other times she would laugh as if to encourage the fighting. You never knew whether the things that you called "mine" were truly yours. You were never quite clear about your physical and psychological boundaries. They were sometimes respected but often disregarded. Your parents forced you to hug Aunt Martha even if you didn't want to. You were beaten with little regard to the pain it caused you—and often with little regard to the offense. If you were sexually abused, even your bodily boundaries were violated. You seemed to have no right to say, "Stop it, I mean it" and have your words listened to and respected. If someone was teasing you, belittling you, there was little you could do because there was no consistent regard for your psychological boundaries.

  Gretchen lived in terror much of her adolescence because of her emotionally abusive stepfather's teasing and sexual innuendos. "I was never sure if he was going to try something or not," she says hesitantly. "He would always make remarks about my body, make these disgusting comments, comparing me to other women. The only thing he ever did as far as touching me was to pat my rear a couple of times, but my mother made him stop doing that. Then he would do this creepy thing of coming into my room after I had gone to bed and just stand there chuckling to himself. I was terrified that he would somehow hurt me, or rape me, or something. When I told my mother, she shrugged and told me to tell her if he tried anything. That wasn't very reassuring, and I went through years of worry."

  There was little respect in your family for your personal belongings, either, which are an extension of your personal boundaries. Your parents may have sold, thrown out, or given away without your knowledge or consent things that belonged to you. This lack of respect left you with an unstable sense of identity, an uncertainty about where to draw the line between yourself and others.

  When Elliot was nine years old, he had a bicycle. "I used it quite a bit," he says, "so it just floored me when I came home one day and found out my dad had given it away. At first I refused to believe that he would do such a thing. But yes, he had, and all because he got drunk and got mad because I hadn't cleaned up the backyard to his satisfaction. I hated him for that—and I still do."

"Will the Real Mother and Father Please Stand Up?": Role Reversal

"Come on, Tim. Come and pick up your clothes off the floor. We have to go soon!" Mom says with some urgency and exasperation to her ten-year-old son.

"Yes, Tim, we have to go if we're going to be on time for dinner and the movie!" Dad adds as backup for Mom's plea.

"Okay, okay! But I want to go to McDonald's," Tim declares as he proceeds to pick up his clothes, "or I won't eat anything!"

"Yeah, let's go to McDonald's," seven-year-old Suzie chimes in.

Dad, obviously irritated, states crisply, "No, we're not going to McDonald's. We're going to a Chinese restaurant. If you don't want to eat, that's up to you, but there'll be no popcorn or other treats at the show if you don't eat any dinner."

Tim and Suzie both groan their disapproval, but their father holds firm. At the restaurant, they eat.

"Let's go see *Friday the 13th Part VII!*" Tim proposes. "It's supposed to be really good! Lots of my friends have seen it." Mom makes a face, as does Suzie.

"No, absolutely not," Mom declares. "That one is not on the list of choices tonight. We already talked about it. We can see *Big* or we can see *Who Framed Roger Rabbit?* Those are the choices. Let's take a vote."

This vignette illustrates how the parents take a clear leadership role in a healthy family. The children are involved in the decision-making process to the extent appropriate for their age and the nature of the decision, but the ultimate authority rests with the parents. Tim and Suzie are given some choices regarding both dinner and the movie. Mom and Dad have already determined where the family will eat dinner, but the children have their choice of anything on the menu or can choose not to eat. At this particular outing, the children are offered two choices of movie, apparently determined during a previous discussion involving the whole family.

Studies of leadership patterns in healthy families have found some interesting tendencies. First, either the mother or father usually takes a more prominent role in leading the family, but that parent does not rule the family like a dictator. Second, leadership tasks, such as finances, discipline of the children, recreation, and education, are shared according to who is best suited for each task. Third, leadership in specific areas changes over time as need dictates. For example, after several years it may become more workable for the mother to assume greater leadership in the financial management of the family. Regardless of these shifting patterns, both parents in a healthy family are responsive to their children's needs.

The appropriate roles for parents in a healthy family are to provide guidance and support for their children and to set limits when needed. It's also appropriate for parents to "delegate" increasingly grown-up responsibilities to their children to help them prepare for adulthood, yet never give too much responsibility too soon.

In your family, the parent-child roles were reversed. Your parents did not know how to take on adult roles and responsibilities since they were not properly parented themselves. Because they did not have the nurturing and guidance they needed when they were young, as parents they were like children themselves. They turned to you to meet their unfulfilled needs, heedless of the fact that you were just a child. Your mother may have lacked affection from your father, so depended on you for these needs.

This was the case in my growing-up years. Since my father was away a lot, my mother looked to me to provide what she did not get from him. When I was twelve and we had moved from Iowa to California, my father was unable to find work, so he returned to Iowa for three months to work to support us. I was left in California with instructions to take care of my mother. I remember feeling helpless and lost but trying to do my best to live up to my father's expectations. As I view it now, it was a tremendous weight to place on a twelve-year-old.

Your parents, like mine, may have been anxious and uncertain about how to fulfill the responsibilities of parenthood. This uncertainty led them to be inconsistent and to place expectations on you that were totally unrealistic. Forced to become a "little adult" very early, you could not express many of your naturally childlike qualities for fear of being abused, abandoned, or both. This "pseudomaturity" further prompted your parents to expect you to be a "little mother" and take care of their needs.

At an unconscious level, this is what the daughter is doing in an incestuous family. If you were the victim of incest, you were obviously taking care of father's sexual needs. But you were also meeting mother's needs. It has been observed in incestuous families that the mother is often in passive agreement with the incestuous relationship between father and daughter. At some level she knows what's going on but denies it. She may secretly feel relieved that somebody else is fulfilling her husband's sexual needs. Or she may fear that her husband will leave her; wanting to keep him at all costs, she lets the daughter become the sacrificial lamb. In rare instances, some mothers have supported the incest overtly, though it is seldom talked about or confronted.

Georgia portrays how this was in her family: "When I was about eight, Mom told me to go sleep with my dad to 'calm him down' while she slept out on the couch. I was thrilled to be able to do that, and it was pretty neat at first. After the first couple of times he started rubbing his penis up against me until he came, then eventually he started having sex with me. It got so that whenever Mom was gone, he'd come to my room and have sex with me. He told me not to tell Mom or he wouldn't love me anymore, but I'm sure she knew anyway. I really felt at the time like I was keeping the family together, and I never even questioned it. Now I'm angry at her for letting this happen to me. She had to know! She had to!"

Even if the abuse was more purely emotional, you took on the role of "little mother," tending to your parents' emotional well-being. You learned to act like an adult even though you were still a child. If you did act like a child, or were expressive at all of your true feelings, you risked punishment or abandonment. You never had a childhood. As a result, you never had a chance to develop emotionally like children in functional families. You were too busy paying attention to adultlike responsibilities in order to simply survive your childhood.

As Jan, one of my patients, says, "I was always taking care of my mother. She was always sick or upset or drunk, and my dad was usually working or out messing around with other women. My mom would come to me and we'd talk about the fact that she was upset and didn't know what to do about my dad. She'd feel better, and I would too. It felt good to make her feel better. Sometimes she would get so depressed she wouldn't get out of bed. Those times I would feed her and take care of my brothers and sister and clean the house. This went on for a long time, starting when I was about six years old."

Us Against the World:
The Closed Family System

"You kids go out in the backyard to play! It's so noisy I can't hear myself think!" Joan hastily waves Brian and Nancy, her seven-year-old and nine-year-old, and their two neighborhood friends out of the house so she can continue her phone calls without distraction. It occurs to Joan that she should set some limits about friends and neighbors stopping by so often, yet inwardly she admits that she enjoys the company and friendship.

Joan picks up the phone and dials the next number on her list. She's pleased with the response to the Neighborhood Watch Program and the upcoming meeting, and feels certain that it will help reduce the crime rate in the surrounding neighborhood.

A healthy family is an open system in that its members interact with the larger community and are involved with a larger world than just that of the family. Mom coaches her daughter's soccer team; dad is involved with the YMCA Indian Guides program with his son; both parents are active participants in their children's school activities; and the children are involved in recreation programs or music lessons. Friends and neighbors come by to visit, and school friends sleep over. Through these and other involvements, the children gradually see that they are not isolated and separate but are connected to an increasingly larger community of people—they are in fact connected to the world.

Your family was much more of a closed system. Your parents maintained few ties, if any, with the larger community. You did not bring friends over, nor did your parents share their home with their friends or neighbors. A sense of isolation pervaded your home. You felt no belonging or connection to anything larger than your own family.

Walter comments on the isolation in his family: "We never had anyone over to visit. My friends used to ask me to sleep over, but I'd say no because I was afraid that they would then want to stay over at my house, and with all of the drinking and the fighting, I just couldn't let that happen."

Walter captures what was true for you and many Adult Children: There were secrets to be kept. You didn't want anyone to know how your family operated. You didn't want to risk the embarrassment of an abusive parent yelling at you when one of your friends was there. You felt ashamed and very guarded about your family. Since you imagined that your friends had perfect families, or at least better ones, your situation seemed all the worse by comparison.

Just as you could not let anyone into your family, you could not let anyone into your private world. You felt alone and isolated, like everyone else in your family. If you were being sexually abused, whom could you tell? If you were being emotionally abused, you didn't want others to think you were feeling sorry for yourself. Your conclusion often was that it was better to continue with the denial, because to let people into your world, into the secrets of your family, would be more painful than keeping people out.

Judy recalls a particularly devastating experience, when she told her best friend about the incest with her father. "She spread it around the whole school," Judy says. "I was so hurt that I decided I would never tell anyone anything about myself ever again. I couldn't face anybody at school and started keeping to myself a lot after that. I couldn't trust anyone."

So you and your family went along, denying and self-contained, maintaining the illusion that you were somehow separate from the larger community of people.

Mixed Messages: Incongruent Communication

Dad crosses his arms, furrows his brow, looks directly at thirteen-year-old Kyle, and says in an irritated tone of voice, "Look, I want you to sit down, put the magazine away, and tell your mother and me what happened over at Jeff's house yesterday. His father just called and was really upset."

Kyle sits up straight in his chair, clears his throat, and pleadingly looks at his father. "I tell you, it was nothing, no big deal," he says. "We used some of the lumber in the backyard to get started on a soapbox racer. How was I to know that his dad was planning to use it? It looked like stuff they were going to throw away, because it was on the side of the yard. I'll give it back to him."

Mr. Glasgow ponders this for a few seconds, then says more softly, "Well, I don't like you taking things that don't belong to you, so I want you to take it back right away and apologize. And you'll be on restriction for forty-eight hours for taking something that's not yours without asking."

"But, Dad," Kyle pleads, "I didn't think there was anything wrong with it! I thought his dad was throwing it away. Besides, Jeff said it was okay!"

His father responds, "I'm sure he did, and I'm sure you didn't think about there being anything wrong, but the restriction still stands."

In healthy families, communication between members is reasonably straightforward and clear. The messages are congruent. What the parents say in words is matched by their body language. If mother is happy because her son won first prize in the spelling contest, her face and smile show it. If dad is angry about the children tracking dirt on the rug, then he looks, sounds, and acts angry. If mom is pleased with how the children behaved at the supermarket, she lets them know by words *and* actions.

Like Kyle and his father, when members of a healthy family communicate, they usually make eye contact and face each other as they talk. Although conversation may take place while some other activity is going on, activity does not serve to avoid communication. When a question is asked, it is answered rather than ignored. When a member of a healthy family communicates, his facial expression, body posture, gestures, and voice match the content of what he is saying.

In your family, you had difficulty deciphering your parents' real message. They often said one thing while their body language showed something different. This was especially difficult for you to understand as a child, since you were still relatively new at language. When confronted with mixed messages, you had to guess what the actual meaning was—and hope that you were right.

When your mother was tearful and frowning and you asked her

what was wrong, she smiled blandly and said, "Nothing." Even though you knew differently, you could not say anything further. If your father spanked you and then said he was doing it because he loved you, adding, "This hurts me more than it hurts you," you must have been terribly confused.

Chip recounts how his parents conducted "silent fights": "I would walk into the room and they'd be sitting across from each other, staring. The atmosphere was thick with tension, but as soon as I walked in, Mom would put this vacant smile on her face, and Dad would just stare at her for the longest time. She'd act like nothing was wrong and immediately ask me how I was. If I'd ask them if anything was wrong, Mom would deny it and Dad would start reading his paper. But *I* knew."

Like Chip, you may have known that something was going on by the incongruent communication but were afraid to break the pattern of silence. One strong arena for denial and incongruent communication is sexual abuse. If you were sexually abused, you received many mixed messages that were extremely difficult to decipher. Your father may have told you he was having sex with you because he loved you. If this was true, you asked yourself, why couldn't you tell anyone, especially Mom?

Harriet recalls the difficulty she had untangling what her parents' messages really meant: "When my father smiled at me, I wasn't sure if he was just happy or if he was making his move to have sex with me. It was always hard to tell what was really going on with him. And my mom, when she told me to keep Dad company or to go and give him a back rub, did she really know what was in store for me?"

Confused by the mixed messages, you learned not to trust what was said and instead to be alert to *how* it was said. Harriet had to watch her father closely to determine what his motives were. You learned to become acutely aware of all the nonverbal signals your parents sent, because these were far more reliable than their words. You learned to be watchful and cautious when you listened to communication. You may have responded very slowly when something was said to you, because you had to take time to figure out the real message from the garbled ones you received.

Too Little or Too Much: Extremes in Conflict

Heather walks in at 1:00 A.M. to find her mother, Marie, waiting up for her. "Where have you been?" Marie says. "I've been worried to death about you! I'm mad at you for not calling to let me know you'd be late."

Heather looks at her defiantly and groans, "I'm not a baby,

Mother! I'm fifteen and old enough to take care of myself! We just got out of the show late, and I figured it was better to come straight home than to take the time to call you. So don't have a crisis about it!"

"Don't talk to me that way!" huffs Marie. "You didn't show any respect for my feelings or my concern."

Heather stands firm, reiterating that she has made her choice about not calling. Marie grounds Heather for a week. Heather goes to her room and barely talks to her mother for the next two days. During this time, they have a few more discussions, a few more arguments, and eventually settle down.

In healthy families, while it is not the primary mode of interaction, conflict does occur, and it is out in the open. Members discuss disagreements, angers, and resentments in an effort to resolve the conflict. There may even be out-and-out arguing, as with Heather and her mother. While conflict is not welcomed, neither is it feared or avoided. The family recognizes that resolving conflict takes time and attention and may require lots of discussion.

The parents in a healthy family provide leadership in resolving conflicts. By modeling openness of expression, they teach their children that conflict is a fact of life. While it is not the most desirable interaction between people, it does happen. The children learn that disagreement is okay and that people can have differing points of view. Most important, they learn that things can be worked out, that conflict need not signal abuse or abandonment.

In your abusive family, there was either too much or too little conflict. In the first case, conflict provided a fertile setting for emotional and physical abuse. The atmosphere was often tense, and you never knew when the next explosion would happen. There were never simple disagreements, only fights. Fighting became a way of life and seemed perfectly normal for your family. You learned to be hypervigilant, always ready for the next attack.

Manny doesn't remember a day going by without some kind of fighting: "If it wasn't with my parents, it was with my brother. There was never any peace. When I was sixteen, my dad got really drunk and started hitting my mom again and again. I got so angry at him, I hit him and knocked him down. He was really surprised, and so was I! I was in a rage, and I probably could have killed him. I don't know if it was because he was drunk or what, but after he got up, he just walked out the door and sat outside for the longest time."

At the other extreme, too little open conflict, everything was kept hidden. Problems and issues were never cleanly discussed, and nobody ever fought. Of course, problems that were never directly handled often festered. But everyone pretended everything was just fine.

In Diana's home, there was little interaction other than what was necessary. "My mom and dad hardly talked to each other. You could just feel the tension. My sister and I were supposed to be good little girls and never stir up any fuss, and fighting was strictly forbidden. There was this code of silence about everything, and my mom's dirty looks kept us from expressing anything that even resembled discord. I learned early on about one of my family's main rules: Don't talk about it!"

YOU, THE ADULT CHILD: TAKING YOUR FAMILY WITH YOU

With her blond hair trailing, Phyllis walks swiftly down the street, looking straight ahead as if on a secret mission. Dressed in her navy blue business suit, she has just left the office, where she has a well-paying job with an advertising agency, and is on her way to lunch with her boyfriend, Derek.

She arrives punctually at the restaurant. Phyllis immediately puts in her name for a table for two, then glances at her watch for the fourth time in five minutes. Noting that Derek is late, she reconciles herself to waiting for him once again. She recalls that this is just one more reason this relationship isn't working out. For eight months now she has dated this man, in spite of the fact that he treats her inconsiderately and has steadfastly refused to make a commitment.

She aches at the prospect of losing Derek, yet because such loss has become a familiar theme for her, she has come to expect it. She hopes to be married and have children someday but knows that if she keeps going the way she has, this will never happen. Her sturdy countenance belies the tears just beneath the surface. She keeps thinking that if she were only thinner, or smarter, or better looking, she would attract the right man. The sad realization hits her that in spite of her attempts to do everything right, she still feels like a failure.

Phyllis is an Adult Child. She is haunted by periodic depression, fears of intimacy, and constant doubts about her self-worth. She may be vaguely aware that these symptoms are all manifestations of growing up in an abusive family, but more than likely she does not see any connection between these problems and her past abuse.

Like Phyllis, you didn't know that you would take your family with you into your adulthood—you thought you escaped it when you left home.

Yet unconsciously you are still deeply affected by the abuse you endured in childhood. There are five main ways you still carry the effects of abuse: lack of trust, avoiding feelings, low self-esteem, depression, and difficulties with relationships.

Always Expect the Worst: Lack of Trust

While writing in her journal, Susan reflects on her meeting with Gail. Susan has only known Gail a few weeks, so she was a bit surprised when Gail asked to move in with her for a month or two. Susan told her she would consider it, yet the more she thinks about it, the more uneasy she becomes.

Maybe it's Gail's neediness—she will probably expect a lot from Susan. Maybe it's Susan's doubts about Gail's ability to get a job and take care of herself. It does seem as if much of their relationship so far has focused around Gail's problems, and Susan wonders if Gail's whole life is one big set of problems. Whatever the reason, Susan's gut instinct is to say no, even though she doesn't want to hurt Gail's feelings. She decides to call Gail the next day and tell her the truth: She just wouldn't feel comfortable having her as a roommate.

Reasonably healthy, functional adults like Susan neither blindly trust nor distrust everyone. Instead, they have learned to first trust themselves and their own senses, and to use these inner signals to decide whether someone else is trustworthy. They have made a few mistakes in the past but have not jumped from these errors to the false generalization that no one can be trusted.

On the other hand, you as an Adult Child have difficulty with trust. Because of the denial that was so common in your family, you learned to discount your own perceptions, feelings, and thoughts. Because of the inconsistent and unpredictable responses you received from your parents—sometimes they were nice, sometimes they ignored or abused you—you learned not to trust others.

Suspicious and fearful of your own feelings, you pretend they aren't even there. It's hard to share your more personal thoughts and feelings with anyone else, even someone close to you, since you don't trust others. You fear that whomever you share these innermost feelings with will either hurt you or abandon you—just like Mom and Dad did.

We find evidence of this basic distrust in almost everything Adult Children say with regard to their relationships. For example, Steve states: "My wife's been after me lately to tell her what's wrong. I keep telling her nothing's wrong, that I'm just in a bad mood, but she keeps asking. I guess I have had a lot of pressure lately at work, but I'm sure she doesn't want to hear anything about that." We can guess that Steve is far more disturbed by events at work than he is letting us know, yet he's reluctant to trust his wife with his vulnerability and fears.

You are cautious and watchful around others, unconsciously fearing that you will be abused or abandoned if you open yourself up. You keep your distance in order to protect yourself. Wary of new situations and people, you hold back until you are absolutely sure it is safe. When you do open up to others, you are so sensitive to any signs of rejection or verbal assault that you are quick to withdraw. You interpret any negative reactions as confirmation of your belief that others can't be trusted and that it's better to keep to yourself.

This extreme cautiousness makes it hard for you to share your feelings. You first test how someone will react to you and then choose what you say very carefully. You find yourself telling people what you think they want to hear rather than how you truly feel or what you really think. You qualify much of what you say with words like "probably," "maybe," or "I'm not sure. . . ." You often ask others for their preference when you really have your own.

"My husband tells me that I never tell him what I like or what I want," says Jeri, one of my patients. "And he's right—I do keep my feelings to myself. I'm afraid he'll get upset if I tell him. For example, he'd be furious if I told him how lonely I get when he's out playing golf." Jeri's distrust and caution keep her safe but terribly unhappy.

Most of what you say is filtered through this veil of cautiousness. Rarely if ever do you make a stand or assert yourself. Ever vigilant, you fear that the next thing the other person says or does might be abusive, or that he will reject or abandon you, so you adapt your behavior accordingly.

You define people in black-and-white terms: either they can be trusted or they can't. If you do let yourself trust, you are always on the lookout for a violation of that trust. After all, your trust was so often violated as a child. Since you are always expecting a lapse, you will, in all likelihood, find it before long.

Lois is typical of Adult Children in that she hopes for the best but expects the worst from others: "My friend Yolanda always keeps our dates and in fact is usually early. The other day I was waiting for her at a restaurant. She didn't show and she didn't show, and I waited. I started thinking that she probably decided our friendship wasn't worth the trouble, that she didn't like me anymore, that she had used me and now didn't need me anymore, that I had done something or said something to upset her and so she was going to stand me up. So I was going to show her, who needs her for a friend anyway? Then Yolanda walked in and apologized for being late, explaining that she had gotten stuck in traffic. We had an enjoyable lunch, and of course I never mentioned to her any of those silly thoughts!"

"You Mustn't Feel That Way": Avoiding Feelings

Kelly takes one shoe off, drops it on the floor, then takes off the other and wriggles her toes. "I'm glad I went for a run—I feel better," she says to Grant, gazing out the window. "I've been bummed out all day about my mom's operation. The doctor made it sound like it was major. I'm just afraid she might not pull through—she's getting old now and isn't as strong as she used to be."

She looks plaintively at Grant, then says hesitantly, "I'm just really scared, Grant, and I'm not feeling so strong. Will you hold me?"

Unlike Kelly, as an Adult Child of Abusive Parents, you still treat emotions as something to be feared. Anger, sadness, even happiness, are to be avoided. You try to control your feelings and even try to control the feelings of others. You have learned to shut down your emotions if they get too intense, for in the past any intensity was punished in some way.

Because of the denial and lack of empathy in your family, you had little support or permission to feel normal emotions and reactions. If you expressed any feelings, they were ridiculed or met with disapproval and anger. How often did you hear, "Stop crying or I'll really give you something to cry about!"? You learned to deny, repress, and minimize your feelings. The message was clear: At all costs, don't feel!

"I refuse to be like my father," Frank says. "He was really mean and mad most of the time. I pride myself in being able to control my anger. I hardly ever get angry—well, I never used to get angry. Lately, for whatever reason, it's been harder. I catch myself putting my wife down, or saying stupid, mean things to my kids. Just the other day I called my five-year-old a stupid jerk, and I was ready to smack him. That really scared me—I sounded just like my dad!"

Frank's story illustrates another problem with avoiding feelings. What do you do with your anger? Frank has tried to control his anger most of his life because of the way he experienced his father's anger when he was young, but obviously he is feeling a lot of it right now. As an Adult Child, you either express anger freely or you try hard to avoid feeling or expressing any anger because it's so intimidating. The problem is that there is no such thing as unexpressed anger. If it isn't acknowledged, it gets expressed in indirect ways such as complaining, gossiping, backbiting, and "forgetting" to do things for someone.

Another indirect way of dealing with anger is to internalize it. There is increasing support today for the idea that internalized anger contributes to disease. One of my patients, Helen, had a history of severe migraine headaches. Her physician had ruled out any physical causes. Through psychotherapy and hypnotherapy, we discovered that Helen's mother had been very cold and dominating. She never allowed Helen to express herself, so Helen learned to put a lid on her feelings. She stifled her rage toward her mother for fear that she would lose whatever crumbs of love she was able to get from her. It was only when Helen began to acknowledge and work through this intense, repressed anger, and learned to express her feelings in her present-day life, that the migraines disappeared.

Another reason you avoid feelings is your fear that if you feel something strongly, you have to act on that feeling. In other words, if you feel like screaming, you have to scream; if you feel like hitting someone, you have to hit them. You experienced this way of dealing with feelings when you were growing up, so you learned that the best way to avoid acting on feelings was to avoid having any feelings altogether. You have come to believe that feelings are the direct *cause* of behavior, rather than seeing feelings as inside information that would help you decide how to act.

Lisa recalls being surprised to hear how her friend Betty handles her feelings: "She [Betty] was telling me how she was angry and upset with her husband and was really tired of his not paying any attention to her, and she felt like taking a long vacation without him. My advice to her was to move out if that's the way she feels. Betty looked slightly aghast when I suggested this and said—I'll never forget her words—'I'd never dream of it!' That surprised me because I usually figure you should go with how you feel. Listening to Betty made me realize that just because somebody *feels* something, it doesn't mean that they have to *act* on that feeling! Major insight for this kid!" It is indeed a "major insight" for most Adult Children that feelings need not be avoided nor acted on, but simply experienced and then released.

You even have difficulty expressing happiness and joy. You may have been punished or belittled when you were young if you expressed some naturally childlike enthusiasm or exuberance. In *Grown-Up Abused Children,* James Leehan and Laura Wilson write: "Two lessons were learned: Joy should not be expressed, or even felt; and happiness is followed by pain. The ultimate lesson was that it is best not to be happy or to express or acknowledge any emotion at all."

You still have difficulty feeling and expressing those "childlike" emotions of happiness or joy. Lisa describes this in her own experience:

"I've never had a problem with getting too upset over things. I've always been the one to handle whatever is needed. What I'm discovering, though, is that while I don't get upset, I also don't feel 'up' much of the time. I know a person can't have the highs without experiencing the lows, but I don't know how to do either!"

"I'm No Good": Low Self-Esteem

Eric is thumbing through the CDs, looking for the latest Huey Lewis album for his girlfriend. He's feeling particularly good today, because he thinks he's aced an interview for the head nurse position at the hospital where he works. "When Wendy hears the news," he anticipates, "she'll be pleased." As he ponders further, he considers that she might be a little bit upset should he get the job, since it will involve his working a few more hours a week and spending less time with her. But he is confident that she will ultimately be supportive. If not, they will still work it out.

Eric is an adult who likes himself. He knows he is not perfect, but he accepts his talents and abilities and is confident about being able to deal with life. Like most healthy adults, he has his doubts yet carries a realistic, generally positive attitude about himself and about life. Eric loves himself without being egotistical about it.

Unlike Eric, you have many doubts about yourself. You carry lots of negative self-statements and wonder how you could ever truly love yourself. Your parents either told you you were stupid, bad, ugly, or worthless, or by abusing or ignoring you they showed they didn't value you. The conclusions you made about yourself still haunt you today in the form of beliefs you maintain about your inherent unworthiness and unlovableness. You hear yourself saying negative things in your mind or out loud that reflect these beliefs, usually stated in the second person (because that's how you heard them originally), such as, "Boy, are you stupid," "What an idiot you are," "You're so ugly," "What a clumsy jerk!"

These self-statements all stem from earlier decisions you made about your own value and worthiness, and in spite of the fact that they may not be true, you believe them. Worse, you *act* as if they are true. Never mind that 90 percent of the time you are graceful and coordinated. It's the times when you trip, or spill a drink, or hit the ball into the net, that you say to yourself, "I knew I was right. I really am clumsy." Your beliefs become self-fulfilling prophecies and constrict you to a narrow definition of who you are.

These beliefs prevent you from being happy in two important areas: relationships and career. You may avoid relationships altogether because you don't believe you deserve to be loved. When you do develop relationships, you never fully accept the fact that someone loves you. After all, how could anyone love someone who's so unlovable? Anyone who loves you must have a real problem—at least that's what you tell yourself.

William describes how this kind of thinking has affected him: "Here I am, thirty-five, and I've never been married. I've had a couple of girlfriends, but the relationships always seem to end pretty lousy—you know, they find someone else or something. I wonder if I'll ever get married. I don't think anyone would want me for keeps." In this state-ment—as in almost everything Adult Children say about their relation-ships—we can hear the voice of low self-esteem coming through.

You may unconsciously choose someone who is abusive just to prove that you really don't deserve to be loved or treated well. Abuse is what is most familiar to you. If someone you care for does treat you well, you may test her to see if she will be mean to you, once again to prove that you are right about not deserving to be loved.

The other area where low self-esteem affects you is your career. One possible outcome is that your fears about lack of competence drive you to succeed. You push yourself to achieve all your goals and to outperform everyone else. Yet you feel dissatisfied because you still have a deep-seated belief in your unworthiness. Although you may achieve wealth and fame, you still have the fundamental belief that somehow you just don't deserve any of it.

Another alternative consequence of low self-esteem is fear of suc-cess: You avoid trying altogether, so that you never have to face success. You believe that you could never really accomplish anything important anyway, so why try? You avoid risks altogether or you start projects but never complete them. If you never complete a project, you never have to deal with your fears about not being good enough.

Doug has just begun to see this pattern in himself: "For years I've had one low-paying job after another—janitor, crossing guard, meter reader. I told myself, 'How neat, I get paid just for helping these kids cross the street,' but now I realize I've been avoiding challenge, avoiding risking failure, avoiding facing the fact I really don't think I'm worth much."

"I Can't Do a Thing About It!": Your Sense of Helplessness

Jody stares at the pile of papers that has just been laid on her desk. It is Friday afternoon, one hour away from the time she usually leaves work, and she realizes that if she does what her manager has asked, she'll be there until nine o'clock that night. She'll have to cancel her plans for dinner with her girlfriends that she has been so much looking forward to.

After her initial irritation, she settles down and begins examining her options. Although her boss might be upset if she were to leave, she really does have a choice. And she does want to be with her friends—she's ready for a break from the office. Jody decides to tell her manager that she will work until six o'clock, then return on Saturday to finish so that the report can be ready by Monday.

Jody, like most functional adults, sees that she has choices no matter what the situation. She does not think of herself as trapped or victimized by the demands or expectations of others. She feels that she can have some influence over others yet does not insist that they give in to what she wants. Jody is a woman who believes she has some influence over her own destiny.

Like other Adult Children, however, you may not fully accept that you can affect situations and other people. Instead you maintain a passive, helpless stance with regard to life. Since you were victimized as a child and experienced a great deal of helpless feelings in dealing with your abuse, it's not surprising that you would unconsciously carry with you into adulthood a strong sense of helplessness and powerlessness.

You have been trained to feel helpless. You decided a long time ago that what you do does not make a whole lot of difference in influencing your environment or people around you. When you are faced with life's trials and tribulations, this conditioned sense of helplessness is unconsciously triggered.

Closely associated with this sense is an unconscious anger, a deep rage. This is the helpless rage of an infant whose needs are not met. One way you express this anger is by striking out verbally or even physically at people or things around you.

It may be too frightening, however, to openly acknowledge your anger and express it because you have associated anger for so long with abuse and destructiveness. In this case you deny that you are angry. You direct your anger against yourself, turning the frustration of feeling helpless and victimized into all-too-familiar feelings of guilt and depression.

A rude awakening was in store for Lila, who learned long ago that it doesn't do any good to get angry: "People only got hurt when I yelled at them, so I just stuffed down my anger my whole life. I used to get depressed a lot of the time, and I used to think that I could never even feel angry. Then one day my girlfriend looked at me when I told her this and she laughed. She was right, because I was getting angry with her! We talked a lot about it, and I realized how afraid I was to even feel angry, let alone get angry."

Since anger has always been such a frightening thing to experience, you may have decided to avoid it at all costs. The only problem is that the more you deny and repress it, the more it builds up, increasing the chance that you will end up acting abusively to yourself or to someone else. If you do act abusively, you will prove yourself right—anger is destructive. The guilt you will inevitably feel will cause you to repress the anger, and you'll begin the cycle all over again. You will feel defeated and helpless, yet still have the underlying anger unresolved.

It took recognizing this vicious cycle for Ken to take action: "I'd always mistaken my passivity for 'being cool' and accepting whatever happened. It took several years for the lid to come off of that. I had lost a job a few years ago, and we had a second kid on the way. It seemed like nothing was going right. That's when I abused my four-year-old son. One day when I was watching him while my wife was out, he got into a drawer he wasn't supposed to. I really lost it. I yelled at him and spanked him so hard. Fortunately I stopped before I really hurt him, but I felt like killing myself. That day I called to get some professional help."

Because of your conditioned helplessness, you believe that you have little or no control over your own life, that your life is controlled by factors completely outside yourself. This attitude frequently leads you to feeling victimized by other people and events. It is difficult to accept that you do indeed make a difference in your world and those in it.

Charles describes his feelings of drudgery at work: "I keep waiting for things to get better, but they haven't. I've been with this particular company fourteen years now, but they aren't treating me much better than the day I started. They are so petty. The other day my supervisor chewed me out because I was fifteen minutes late, when everybody else walks in late all the time. I just think he has it out for me." Robert's defeated tone and passive language reflect his deep sense of helplessness.

Friends, Lovers, and Other Strangers: Difficulties with Relationships

Maria hangs up the phone and heads for the door to keep her dinner appointment with Bob and Caroline. She is looking forward to spending time with these valued friends. The three have shared a lot, especially since Maria's divorce two years ago. She reflects on the phone conversation she just finished with her ex-husband and feels good that they are getting along well now as friends, even though some of the old hurt still surfaces at times.

As she is driving to the restaurant to meet Bob and Caroline, she recalls the vacation they shared on a houseboat last summer. They had a great time water-skiing and swimming, and it was on that trip that Maria caught her first fish. She considers how refreshing it has been to have both of them as close friends. She can count on them, and they can count on her.

There are certainly no perfect friendships or other relationships, yet a reasonably healthy adult has relationships that work well for all parties involved.

As an Adult Child, however, you have had consistent recurring difficulties with all your relationships. Lack of trust, avoidance of feelings, low self-esteem, and sense of helplessness all contribute to your difficulties in relationships. Trust particularly is an essential characteristic in any relationship of depth and closeness.

You isolate yourself to keep others from finding out about your abusive past. Since you couldn't relate to the style of interaction you saw in other, more functional families, and you did not learn any effective communication skills from your parents, you now feel inadequate socially. As an adult, not knowing what to say or how to act, you are exceedingly cautious about saying anything. Others may mistakenly assume that you have nothing to say or are simply not interested in them, and they tend to stay away from you. This, of course, confirms one of your worst childhood fears: that no one will ever love you.

Hiding her past has been one of the main reasons Heidi avoids forming close relationships: "I don't remember much that happened before I was eleven, but I have a pretty good idea of what happened. My mother was really nasty and drunk a lot of the time, and I think she might have let her boyfriends use me sexually—but I don't exactly remember it. I've just recently been putting some of the pieces together. I don't talk about it to anyone. When I'm in a group of people and they start swapping stories from their childhood, I just sit there and listen. If someone asks me about my childhood, I just tell them that it was pretty dull and uneventful. If they only knew!"

You have had such a deep hunger for real human contact for such a long time that when it is offered, you consume it ravenously. Such clinging and highly dependent behavior eventually forces the other person to reject you, and you take this as further proof that you are unlovable.

If you do become close to someone, you may unconsciously sabotage the relationship. At first you idealize the other person and the relationship, clinging to the hope that perhaps you have finally found a friend or lover who will meet your needs and never let you down. Yet unconsciously you expect this relationship to be like all the rest; you expect this person to let you down. Inevitably, this does happen, since no one will ever meet your unrealistic idealization.

Because of your doubts, you test the other person relentlessly in many different ways: If I yell at him, will he leave me? If I refuse to have sex with him, will he tolerate my moodiness? If I call him six times in one day, will he reject me? Behaviors such as frequently being late, forgetting dates and appointments, and calling much too often or at inappropriate times can be ways to test the other person. If they do not reject you, you feel temporarily reassured. But if continued, these methods ultimately *invite* rejection. The type of testing will vary, but it is always designed to prove that you can't trust anyone, that you are not worthy of love.

Lori finally identified this tendency in herself: "I choose these men who seem to be a lot like my dad, in that they ended up being real abusive. My last husband seemed different—he seemed like a nice guy when I first met him. But when I think back on it, there were probably some definite signs. Like he used to put me down a lot. And he even drank quite a bit. I guess I didn't want to notice those things. I kept accusing my first husband of having an affair. I'd yell and scream, call him names. I just didn't trust him, and in the end it turned out he did leave me for another woman. As a parting shot, he told me he had been faithful and had loved me until I kept on accusing him and yelling at him all the time."

Your unconscious testing has much to do with your fear of intimacy. Because of the emotional deprivation in your childhood, you have an insatiable need for intimacy, despite your fear of it. One way you resolve this conflict is by having several distant, superficial relationships. This way you do not get too involved yet still maintain some contact with others. Even with these superficial relationships, your overwhelming need for closeness drives you to make unrealistic demands and to have idealized expectations. As a result, you end up frequently disappointed and rejected, which is what you have come to expect from others throughout your life. Thus you are confirmed in your isolation.

Frances talks about this pattern: "With every man I get involved with, I get out my microscope and look and look to find something wrong, some reason to reject him. Or I pick and pick and pick until he gets angry, blows up, and ends up rejecting me. It's like I can never leave it alone, I can never enjoy it or accept it."

As a child, abuse became your only option for human contact, so you concluded that abuse was a sign of love. As an adult, you continue to equate love and affection with abuse.

People often choose familiar negative situations over unfamiliar positive ones. If what is familiar in an intimate relationship is abuse, you may unwittingly get involved with someone who mistreats or abuses you. Remaining unaware of this repetitive cycle, you maintain the childhood victimization into your adulthood.

As Jill describes it, "Both times I was married, I was beaten regularly. The first guy—our marriage lasted less than a year—started drinking a lot and beating me up just after we got married. It's kind of funny—I think I married him just to get away from my daddy, because *he* used to beat me up. The second guy, Craig, seemed pretty nice at first, but it wasn't too long after we got married that he started giving me a hard time. One night he came home late and was drunk. He bruised me up pretty badly, and I left him. I'm involved with a really nice guy now, and I can't stand it—I'm just not used to it. I test him and don't even know I'm doing it. I think I'm trying to see if he'll be like all the others and like my father was. At least I know how to deal with men who are jerks."

Growing up in an abusive family helped you learn many things about survival. You had to use a lot of natural resourcefulness just to get through childhood. You did whatever you had to do to remain alive—but often at a heavy cost mentally, emotionally, and spiritually. Now that we have examined the characteristics of your family and the effects that remain with you from growing up in it, let's take a closer look at some of the internal adjustments you had to make in order to survive and how these have stayed with you to the present day.

Surviving the Abuse

*P*eggy has been looking forward to going to the movies with her husband, Sam, for several weeks. As they settle into their seats, she makes a mental note to call the baby-sitter during the break. Her youngest son has been running a slight temperature most of the day, and she wants to make sure he is all right.

A few minutes into the movie, Peggy feels a tightness in her throat and catches herself gripping the armrests. The little girl in the film reminds Peggy of herself when she was young. The father in the story constantly berates his daughter, and the little girl becomes more and more withdrawn. Peggy has to remind herself that this is only a movie. Images of her own childhood stream across her consciousness, flashbacks to when her father beat her, verbally and physically. Again and again, she replays in her mind the time her father hit her and called her a whore and a slut while he threw away some of her favorite clothes. She was only twelve years old.

Peggy endures the rest of the movie. Sam notices her tension, but when he asks, she denies that anything is wrong. That night, and for the next several nights, Peggy is depressed and has trouble sleeping.

Like Peggy, you have come through a childhood filled with confusion and uncertainty. You have endured a lot of pain, both physical and emotional. Whether your pain was from bruises and welts on your body, feelings of emptiness inside, or the guilt and shame of a sexual secret, you have survived the trauma of your childhood abuse in spite of it.

Webster's Dictionary defines trauma as "a painful emotional experience or shock, often producing a lasting psychic effect." Trauma is usually associated with events like war, accidents, or the death of someone close. But it also results from abuse at the hands of another. If you were a child who was abused, then you are extremely vulnerable to lasting psychic effects. Peggy's tension and panic during the film was a reminder of the continuing traumatic effects of earlier abuse. These lasting psychic effects constitute a medical condition known as posttraumatic stress disorder (PTSD).

In *Healing the Child Within,* Dr. Charles L. Whitfield writes:

> I believe, as do others, that growing up, or living in a seriously troubled or dysfunctional family or similar environment often brings about or is associated with PTSD. The PTSD is said to be more damaging and more difficult to treat if: (1) the traumas occur over a *prolonged* period of time, e.g., longer than six months; and especially so if (2) the traumas are of *human origin;* and if (3) those around the affected person tend to *deny* the existence of the stressor or the stress.

The more these conditions fit, the more likely it is that you were traumatized and that you will continue to experience PTSD until you start your recovery.

"Waiting for the fights to happen was as disturbing as when they actually happened," recalls Gayle, one of my patients. "I'd watch my dad put down his beers with that glazed look in his eye, and I knew what was going to happen. It got so that I'd make nickel bets with my brother as to whether the fighting would start after the fifth beer or the sixth one."

The emotional battering you suffered when one of your parents was drunk, yelled at you, belittled you, and perhaps beat you, only to forget all about it the next day, had to have been consistently traumatic. Living with the secret terror of sexual abuse, you must have been in a constant state of tension and alert. If you were used to slaps and kicks and beatings, then you surely felt as if you were in a war zone with only occasional periods of uneasy cease-fire. The emotional abuse of being abandoned again and again, of having no reliable adult there to nurture and protect you, forced you to deal with your troubles on your own and to put away your fears and anxieties.

There are a variety of lingering symptoms of PTSD. One is the reliving of the trauma through recurrent flashbacks or dreams. You may have troubling dreams and nerve-racking flashbacks like Peggy's that are painful reminders of maltreatment. The flashbacks may recall specific instances of abuse, or they may be only fleeting, vague flashes of memories, not completely clear in their meaning but nonetheless highly disturbing.

Another symptom of PTSD is unresponsiveness or lack of involvement in the world, evidenced by an inability to feel emotions, feelings of detachment from others, and a lack of interest in any significant activities. You're generally shut down, removed from your own feelings, and emotionally distant from others. This psychic numbing is similar to the reaction soldiers experience during combat. Tim Cermak, M.D., describes this reaction in *Diagnosing and Treating Co-Dependence:*

> Their survival depends upon their ability to suspend feelings in favor of taking steps to ensure their safety. Unfortunately, the resulting "split" between one's self and one's experience does not heal easily. It does not gradually disappear with the passage of time. Until an active process of healing takes place, the individual continues to experience a *constriction of feelings, a decreased ability to recognize which feelings* are present, and a persistent *sense of being cut off from one's surroundings* (depersonalization). These add up to a condition known as *psychic numbing.*

There may be other signs of the PTSD you have carried since childhood. You may feel constantly on the alert for any potential danger. As a result, you may have difficulty falling asleep and trouble remembering or concentrating.

Anything that reminds you of the traumatic event prompts many painful memories. So you avoid your parents, your old home, your former neighborhood, or any situations in which strong feelings are expressed. In fact, you avoid anything that reminds you in any way of the terror and the mistreatment you received.

"Every time I visit my parents," explains Evelyn, "I go into this shell. When they start arguing, I usually find some excuse to leave. I actually break out in a cold sweat—and I'm forty-seven years old!"

Whether you have all or only some of the above symptoms, they have been with you since childhood, when they were necessary for your survival. Had you not reacted as you did, you probably wouldn't be alive today. Your unemotional demeanor, your avoidance, your hypervigilance, all served to help you make it through your childhood. Today these symptoms are remnants, vivid reminders of trauma. They are now automatic and habitual, though they are no longer functional. They actually hinder you more than help you, since you no longer need them for your safety and well-being.

"My doctor said I should see you," Bill announced matter-of-factly in his first therapy session with me. "He said I'm too tense and I need to learn how to relax and have fun. So what do I do?" I found out that Bill had a rather isolated, lonely childhood, with a father who was rarely around and a mother who constantly teased and belittled him. What Bill was experiencing would not ordinarily be thought of as PTSD, yet he had many of the symptoms. His story highlights the point that it is not the objective, observable maltreatment that causes traumatic reactions so much as the child's perception of the maltreatment. Whether or not anyone else would agree that he had been traumatized, the emotional abuse of his childhood was indeed traumatic to Bill.

If we think of the effects of PTSD as separate symptoms, we will treat them separately without ever getting to the more fundamental cause. This is like the drunk who was looking for his car keys near the streetlight when a kind stranger happened along and started helping him. After several minutes of searching, the stranger finally asked the drunk where he had lost the keys. The drunk indicated he had lost them about half a block away but, he explained to the stranger, "there's more light here."

The point is that by focusing on individual symptoms, we miss the larger picture. Instead, we can see PTSD as a cluster of symptoms that relate to one cause—the abuse to which you were subject as a defenseless, vulnerable child.

No child should be subjected to this kind of trauma, particularly without someone to turn to for protection and comfort. Yet human beings can adapt to and survive even the harshest of emotional climates, and you did. In spite of the trauma and emotional deprivation, you succeeded in living through an extremely stressful upbringing.

You survived, but you paid a high price in the ongoing symptoms of PTSD. You still live your life on a survival level. You have not yet recovered from the effects of your mistreatment, and to do so will require you to actively participate in your own healing program.

A MATTER OF LIFE AND DEATH

Not only did you learn to make some adjustments in your behavior to get through childhood, you had to make some important internal adjustments. By understanding more precisely what happened to you psychologically when you were younger, you can appreciate more fully why you, like other Adult Children, continue to operate on a survival level. This understanding can then help you move beyond survival to greater freedom.

When you were a child, though you were not aware of it, you were making major conclusions about life, such as what kind of person you were, what other people were like, and how life actually worked. These early decisions then became unconscious, fixed beliefs—operating principles upon which you based your adult life. You still follow these beliefs today. If you decided early on that you were clumsy, that people couldn't be trusted, or that life was a struggle, then you continue to act as if these beliefs are true today.

For you growing up in an abusive family, some of these decisions were so critical that they were literally a matter of life or death.

To Live or To Die

It's tragic that any child should have to consider life-or-death choices, but when the pain became unbearable, overwhelming, you had to take steps toward making a critical decision. Marilyn Murray in *The Scindo Syndrome* calls these "Death/Survival Judgments." She writes: "When a person endures a Trauma or Deprivation, the person goes through a series of definite cognitive choices of varying degrees, in which the person determines whether he/she will live or die." As we look more closely at the process of making a death/survival judgment, it's important to remember that these choices are usually made unconsciously and quickly—so quickly that the decision seems instantaneous.

When you were abused or neglected as a child, you felt afraid that you were going to die. You may actually recall thinking at some point, "I'm going to die!" or "My mom's going to kill me!" These are more than just figures of speech. They reflect your helpless childhood dread of being tormented by an enraged adult, or being abandoned in time of need by the caretaker you depended on. You had to face the abuse alone, even though you felt overpowered by a tremendous sense of helplessness and futility.

It was like this for Denise whenever her mother's unpredictable temper was directed toward her: "I felt awful. She'd say the most hateful things, and if I looked at her at all or talked back, she'd start hitting me. She was scary. One time, she picked up an umbrella and beat me with it again and again. I thought I was going to die, it hurt so much."

As the abuse continued and the pain seemed as if it would never go away, you stopped being afraid of dying. Instead, you actually *wanted* to die. That way, you told yourself, you would be released from the pain of your physical and emotional suffering and the heartache of parental betrayal. You may even have thought to yourself or actually said, "Please let me die." You wanted out of an intolerable situation.

Glenna saw no other way out of the incestuous relationship with her stepfather."He was a real creep. One time he forced me to give him oral sex; he kept threatening to hurt me if I didn't. I wanted to die, I really did. I felt so humiliated and degraded."

When no one came to comfort or protect you, you felt emotionally and spiritually abandoned. To explain to yourself why someone would hurt you, you concluded that you must be a bad child. You decided you were unworthy to live; not only did you want to die, you *deserved* to die.

This last point is particularly important. When anything happens to children, they typically deduce that somehow they caused it. Since children tend to think in black-and-white terms, if what happened was bad, then the child inevitably thinks it was his fault and therefore he must be bad.

You decided that you were the one who was bad, rather than blaming mom or dad. To have decided otherwise would have been entirely too threatening. When you were young, not only were you totally dependent on your parents, but you saw them as all-powerful and all-knowing. You tended to automatically think that what they said must be true and what they did must be right. Any problems or upsets must be *your* fault.

This self-blame is evident in Chuck's recollection of his past: "I always thought that if I hadn't been born, my parents wouldn't fight as much as they did. My mom so much as said that on several occasions, and I believed her. She was really fat and was eating all the time. I remember one time after a particularly ugly fight, my dad left, and she went for the refrigerator. There she sat, eating bagels, ice cream, and cookies, all the time saying to me, 'If it weren't for you, I wouldn't stay in this miserable marriage and I'd be a lot happier.' It was a ridiculous sight, now that I think about it. But at the time, I felt so responsible, so bad."

At the same time you determined that you were the one to blame, that you were bad, dirty, ugly, guilty, and deserved to die, you determined that you *must* die. So in a relatively short time, you moved from being afraid of dying, to wanting to die, to thinking that you deserved to die, to concluding that you were bad and therefore had to die.

Once you decided you must die, you had two choices: literally to die physically, which was obviously not the case for you; or to die emotionally and spiritually. The more common choice children make is the second one, to kill off and bury deep in their unconscious some vital aspect of themselves.

Some children who have endured abuse do die physically, through illness, accident, or suicide, or as a direct result of physical injury or neglect. The American Humane Association estimates that in the United States, up to five children each day die directly from abuse. In 1945, Rene Spitz studied conditions in an orphanage where infants were dying at an alarming rate for no obvious physical reasons—they seemed to be simply wasting away. He found that the babies were dying due to a lack of physical and emotional nurturing. They were not being held, touched, or loved enough.

Some children die, not directly from abuse, but as a result of the associated emotional trauma. As we've already seen, it is the child's perception of events that determines the severity of emotional trauma. Bernie Siegel, M.D., describes his views on this in *Love, Medicine & Miracles*:

Adults often assume that children are happy when they are actually being traumatized by events, even though they often don't show it. Children have been known to commit suicide over receiving a B instead of an A on a report card, because they internalized their parents' expectations, or reacted to a comment that made them feel unloved.

It's a safe conclusion that many abused children who have died physically have made either an unconscious or a conscious choice to do so. Because of the profound emotional deprivation that accompanies any type of abuse, and since there often seems to be no other way out of such a painful situation, it's easy to see why some children have chosen physical death.

Something in you, however, made you want to stay alive. To live through the abuse, you had to die emotionally and spiritually. Your survival decision—not death, but life—was made perhaps once, perhaps several times in the course of your childhood. This choice exacted a cost. Every time you chose to stay alive, you paid with the repression of part or all of your feelings associated with the abuse. You may have even repressed the memories of the abuse. The more severe the abuse, the more likely you were to repress any conscious recollection of it.

Unfortunately, when you repressed the emotions related to the abuse, you repressed *all* of your emotions. You went on living, but you died emotionally. Your spirit withered deep into the recesses of your being.

Phillip recalls the moment he decided not to feel the pain anymore: "I had been beaten so many times by my father that this time, I remember thinking, 'I'm not gonna cry.' And I didn't. I remember the sound of his hand hitting my flesh, but I didn't make a sound or shed a tear, and I never did cry or feel much of anything after that."

Partial or complete repression is a mechanism that nature has provided for us to use to deal with painful experiences. It is what happens when an experience is so traumatic and so painful that we partially or completely push the memory and the feelings surrounding it out of our consciousness. The memory and feelings are still embedded deep within us and we continue to experience the symptoms of trauma, yet we are partially or completely blocked from consciously remembering the actual trauma.

Splitting Off from Yourself

This repression produces what is called a partial or complete *split*: The part of you that was hurt or abandoned psychologically separates, or dissociates, from the rest of you. Splitting, like repression, is a normal way to deal with abnormal degrees of physical and/or psychic pain. This is what happens when you die emotionally—you dissociate, or split off your feelings surrounding the maltreatment, and perhaps any memories as well.

A split that results from repressing painful memories or feelings should not be confused with schizophrenia or with a "split personality" or "multiple personality." Schizophrenia is a psychotic disorder in which there is little or no contact with reality. Usually its symptoms include hallucinations and delusions. In the case of multiple personality, repression and dissociation have been so massive that most of the different parts of the person that are split off remain largely unknown to each other. This was the case in the movies *Sybil* and *The Three Faces of Eve,* both based on true stories of women who were diagnosed as multiple personalities. They represented extreme, dramatic instances of the processes of denial, repression, and dissociation. Most true multiple personalities were abused severely as children.

Since everyone has experienced repression and splitting to some degree, in a sense we are all multiple personalities. It's more a question of the degree to which you have repressed and split off these different aspects of yourself. Most people have some awareness of these different aspects of themselves, or subpersonalities. A true multiple personality, however, has completely blocked out or is amnesic to most of these subpersonalities since they are so completely repressed and split off from the primary personality.

Because of the abuse, you experienced many splits throughout your childhood. Some hurts produced partial splits, and some prompted more drastic, complete splits. In the case of a partial split, you can remember the trauma and perhaps some of the associated feelings. In a complete split, you have repressed all memory of the trauma from consciousness, or you have some recollection of the trauma but not of the emotions connected with it.

I can recall some examples of partial splits in my own childhood. Growing up in the Midwest, my older brother knew of my tremendous fear of tornadoes, and he used to enjoy terrifying me by saying during the height of a thunderstorm that a tornado was going to blow the house away. I could not express the depth of my panic because I didn't want to be called a baby, so I had to split off this vulnerable, fearful part of me. Another time, when I was about eight years old, I came home from school to find that our family dog had "run away." I was heartbroken at the loss, but more than that, I suspected that my parents had actually given him away and were lying to me (later I found out this was true). In this instance, I buried my anger and hurt and split off these feelings.

Some of your childhood abuse may have prompted more substantial repression and therefore produced more complete splits. Generally, the more severe the abuse, the longer it lasts, and the less support there is for your recovery, the more deeply you bury your feelings and memories of trauma.

One of my patients, Judy, remembers splitting off from herself: "When my dad was having sex with me, it's like part of me would be watching this whole scene from over by the door. I really could see the whole room, and it felt more like he was doing it to someone else than me." Judy's lack of emotion in recounting this story suggests that she still remains emotionally split off from the experience.

As you grew into adulthood, the repression from childhood and resulting internal splits remained. Now, as an adult, you still have inside you the child you once were—your Inner Child, splits and all.

YOUR LOST CHILDREN

Your Inner Child contains the memories, images, and feelings of your childhood, both what is consciously remembered and what has been repressed or forgotten. Your Inner Child actually contains three distinct aspects or "children": the *Hurting Child,* the *Natural Child,* and the *Controlling Child.* As you will see, they are split off from one another because of your childhood trauma and have not been reconciled and integrated with your adult self. They are your lost children.

Your *Hurting Child* is the abused, traumatized, deprived part of your Inner Child that split from your consciousness when you were being abused. Your Hurting Child carries the anger, rage, hurt, and fear that you experienced. This is the emotional part of you that died and was buried. When your dad threatened to hit you if you didn't stop crying, you buried your hurt and sorrow to avoid a beating. The shame and embarrassment you felt when your friends said your father was a drunk were so overwhelming that you hid your feelings far, far away.

When you decided to die emotionally, you buried your Hurting Child. You may even have felt like "you" died, but it was only a part of you—your Hurting Child—that died. Since your Hurting Child carries the overwhelming pain of abuse, you pushed down the pain a little further each time by repressing and splitting it off.

"It seems like the more I tried to please my mother, the more she'd put me down," laments Barbara. "I cleaned the entire house one day from top to bottom while she was laid up in bed with one of her illnesses, and all she told me was that I had forgotten to clean the piano keys! I was so hurt, so angry, but I just swallowed it and proceeded to clean the piano keys. I swore I'd never let her see me upset. In fact, just telling you this gives me a lump in my throat."

Unfortunately, your *Natural Child* was buried along with your Hurting Child. Other writers have called this Natural Child by other names, including the Child Within, the Real Self, the True Self, the Divine Child, the Higher Self, and the Inner Core. By whatever name, it is the creative, expressive aspect of your Inner Child. When you feel the most "real," the most genuine, this is your Natural Child. It is your spiritual self, your connection with the eternal. It is the part of you that shows genuine emotional responsiveness. Your Natural Child freely loves, creatively plays, innocently shares, and spontaneously feels—it is all that a child should be. Your Natural Child is the part of you that dances with life.

Unfortunately, in making the choice to survive, you had to bury your Natural Child alongside your Hurting Child. This was another emotional death for you. It was a wise survival decision, because your Natural Child's spontaneity, honesty, and expressiveness would have been too dangerous in your family. You had to split off your Natural Child at least partially from your consciousness and let it emerge only occasionally, if at all. This allowed you to remain alive but left you in a serious state of emotional and spiritual deprivation, like an emotional orphan. Because your Natural Child was repressed, you felt an emptiness inside.

"When I'm home alone," Katy confides, "I put the music on really loud and dance, dance, dance, until I'm absolutely exhausted. I love to dance so much. That's when I feel the most real. I wish I could do that without worrying about what other people think."

Since your Hurting Child and your Natural Child were repressed and split off, someone had to be there to take care of you. Your *Controlling Child,* the ruling leg of your internal triumvirate known as the Inner Child, came to your rescue. Her sole purpose was to protect you from harm.* It's as if your Controlling Child made an agreement with your Hurting Child, saying, "Look, you've been hurt so badly you're dying. Let's bury you, keep you hidden, and I'll take over and be in charge. I'll protect you, since nobody else does. But you'd better stay buried or you're gonna get hurt even worse. Besides, if you rise from the dead somehow, you might lose me, and then you'd have no one to take care of you. So I'll help us survive by keeping you under control and out of sight. And, by the way, we have to bury the Natural Child with you." Under the circumstances of the abuse, it would have been difficult to argue with this.

For a child, the need for protection and safety is even more important than the need for love. It's only when a child feels safe and protected that she can truly let herself love or feel loved. This need for protection is even more apparent when there is abuse and no adult to turn to for safety.

---

*For the sake of convenience, I refer to each of the three Inner Children as "she" or "her."

You had to provide it for yourself. This internal protection, in the form of your Controlling Child, automatically came forth when needed—an example of the wonder and beauty of the human defense system.

Marilyn, one of my patients, recalls how she was left to take care of her sisters when both her parents frequently got drunk: "I wouldn't have time to feel or to think about things because I had too much to do. Not only did I have to take care of myself, but I had to take care of Holly and Yvette. That's the way it was. They [her parents] just weren't there to do their job as parents."

Your Controlling Child is your built-in survival system. She has done the best she could to protect you and to help you live. To do so she has developed certain roles. These childhood roles progress into rigid adult roles, which we will discuss in detail in the next chapter.

The Roles
That
Bind

*B*obbie's mother always called her "mouse" because she was so quiet and unassertive. Even when her father came home in a drunken rage and screamed at her mother and beat up her brother, Bobbie would be in her room reading.

Bobbie is an adult now, but she's still a "mouse." A clerk at the local drugstore, she goes about her duties so quietly and unobtrusively you'd hardly know she's there. Although she is in her mid-forties, she dresses like an old woman. She seldom talks to customers except to say how much they owe and to thank them as she hands them their change, and she rarely looks them in the eyes. Her conversations with fellow employees consist mostly of asking the price of items. Her boss, she says, has called her a "drone" and has never mentioned any plans to advance her.

After work, Bobbie normally goes home and spends her evenings reading and watching television. Her mother has asked to move in and Bobbie was unable to say no, so soon she will have an unwelcome roommate. Barbara seldom talks to the men she sees at work and never encourages the few who try to look beyond her unsmiling face and get to know her.

Bobbie's life is relatively painless and safe, but it is also barren and emotionally destitute.

Bobbie is an Adult Child who has carried into her adulthood a rigid and controlling behavior pattern called a role. The seeds of this isolated, withdrawn role were planted in childhood, when her existence depended on finding effective ways of coping with the emotional abuse at home. Before long Bobbie had honed the role that remains with her as an adult.

Like Bobbie, you developed a particular role. This role became increasingly fixed and rigid as you moved from adolescence into adulthood. You identified completely with the role, seeing no other way to think, feel, or act, and usually hid your true feelings, your real self, behind this role.

This role was your Controlling Child's attempt to keep the pain out of your consciousness, to control your fears of emotional abandonment, and to protect yourself from further abuse. Somebody had to take care of you, so your Controlling Child did the best she could.

It's not unusual for family members to take on roles. In healthy families, the members typically take on different roles at different times. Claudia Black, in *It Will Never Happen to Me,* writes:

> Children raised in homes where open communication is practiced and consistency of life styles is the norm usually have the ability to adopt a variety of roles, dependent on the situation. These children learn how to be responsible, how to organize, to develop realistic goals, to play, laugh, and enjoy themselves. They learn a sense of flexibility and spontaneity. They are usually taught how to be sensitive to the feelings of others, and are willing to be helpful to others. These children learn a sense of autonomy and also how to belong to a group.

In your family, however, the roles the members adopted became fixed and rigid. In the chaotic or negligent interaction in your home, these roles provided each child in the family with some internal consistency and provided the family with some sense of stability.

A ROLE FOR EVERY OCCASION

There are four major roles that Adult Children commonly assume: the Perfectionist, the Caretaker, the Invisible One, and the Rebel.

Whatever role you adopted, it covered up your true self, your Natural Child, behind a false identity. This role has now become a trap that keeps your naturalness and spontaneity buried under an intricate, rigid system of rules and regulations.

You have undoubtedly grown accustomed to your role but have become acutely aware of its severe limitations. Although it was purposeful at one time, the role now suffocates and stifles your Natural Child. By understanding the dynamics behind your role, you can see more clearly how to free yourself.

"I'll Do It So It'll Get Done Right": The Perfectionist

If you were the Perfectionist, you were the family manager, the one who kept things running smoothly. Since your parents' behavior was so inconsistent and unpredictable, you took on the duty of providing some structure and consistency for yourself and others in your family. As the oldest or only child, you denied your own feelings and needs and accommodated those of others. Rescuing mom or dad from their responsibilities became second nature to you. The words "responsible," "achieving," "mature," and "reliable" describe you very well. You grew up too fast, taking on adult responsibilities and adult worries long before you were physically or emotionally ready. Further, you tried to do them perfectly—to you, your very life depended on it.

Jackie typifies the role of the Perfectionist. She is thirty-five, tall, with dark hair and a deep, penetrating way of looking at others. Jackie is an oldest child, with a younger brother and sister. "It seems as if I've always been older. As long as I can remember, I couldn't wait until I got to be an adult. When I turned thirty, I remember thinking, 'Great! Now I can be as old as I always thought I was!' I don't think I was ever really a child. I was too busy being a little grown-up."

Jackie's mother was often immobilized by depression and could not provide consistent and stable mothering. Jackie readily assumed the role of mother. "There were times when she stayed in bed for several days at a stretch," Jackie says. "It wasn't that she was sick; she'd just be spaced-out and really depressed. Somehow, I figured it was my fault. I ended up doing most of the housework, laundry, and other things, taking care of my brother and sister and taking care of her too. And, of course, I had to do it all just so."

When she was nine, Jackie's father began sexually molesting her. "It started out with what I thought was just playful touching and tickling. He'd touch me accidentally on my private parts. Then one day we were playing around, and he told me he wanted to hypnotize me. Well, I went along with it—he was my dad, after all. I wasn't really hypnotized, but I acted like I was. Then he took me into the bedroom and did it to me. It was really confusing. He kept whispering, 'Don't tell your mother. Don't tell your mother.'

"After that he started 'hypnotizing' me whenever my mom was gone. I just pretended that I was hypnotized, and he would go ahead and . . . have sex with me. I felt like dying!"

Not only does Jackie typify in many ways the role of Perfectionist, her family typified what commonly happens in father-daughter incest. Usually the mother is passive and emotionally distant with her husband and children. She is often unconsciously or even consciously aware of the incest but does nothing to protect her child. The daughter often takes on the role of the "little mother," accommodating her father's sexual needs and caring for everyone else in the family.

Jackie was not only the little mother but also developed into quite a family manager. This role distracted everyone from the family secret, the abuse. Like most who adopt the Perfectionist role, Jackie could never relax her vigilance for fear that the family would fall apart. As a result, she felt constantly tense and anxious. "I was really on guard most of the time, especially around my mother. I felt so guilty with her, and now it makes sense why. I remember one time when I was about thirteen, she started talking about her and my dad and how they just didn't seem to be as affectionate as they used to be. I could feel myself squirming as she was talking, trying not to show her how uncomfortable I was, thinking that she had probably found out about my dad and me and was leading up to telling me. One part of me felt relieved, while another part was terrified. Well, as it turned out, she was just talking, but boy, I felt so guilty! I kept the house extra clean for a long time after that!"

The Perfectionist role extends beyond the family. The attempt to control her guilt, anxiety, and tension drove Jackie to perform outside as well as she performed inside. Serious and determined, she gained some success and popularity in school. "I had plenty of friends, but I don't think I was very close to any of them. I was afraid if I did get close someone might find out. I really did like school. It was the one place where I could feel like somebody, since I got along well with a lot of people and generally got pretty good grades. I was even elected my senior class secretary."

This desire for achievement and perfection followed Jackie through school and into adult life. She settled into a career in accounting and has worked for a large accounting firm for seven years. She was recently offered an associate partnership, and to all eyes she would appear to be quite successful and happy. Yet she often worries that someday others will find out she's not as competent as she seems.

If you, like Jackie, are a Perfectionist, you have had considerable success in life yet are plagued by disturbing feelings and nagging self-doubts. You feel inwardly that no matter what you achieve, it will never be good enough, because you believe *you* will never be good enough. You carry a load of guilt, and your Hurting Child thinks of itself as a "bad child." You remain anxious and ever-watchful for emotional abandonment.

If you have taken on the Perfectionist role, you are experiencing continuous dissatisfaction and restlessness. Though perfectionism can drive you to achieve, it may also be your greatest impediment to achievement and material success. Your attention to detail is an asset, but more of your time is directed to getting others' approval than to getting the job done. You may look good to others, but you don't feel good to yourself. Your fear of being discovered makes you constantly tense and anxious. "I know I work hard," says Jackie, "but I always feel shaky about it. Most everyone tells me what a great job I'm doing, yet I keep thinking that someday they're going to find out that I don't really know what I'm doing, that I've been fooling them all these years. I started getting these headaches a couple of years ago, and I'm sure it's from all the stress."

If you are like Jackie, your Perfectionist role demands so much control, so much attention to detail, that you are unwilling to delegate tasks to others for fear that they will not do as well as you. As a result you make your work much more difficult than it has to be. The term "workaholic" aptly describes you. You frequently feel stressed to the breaking point as you find your work becomes a series of crises to be handled.

Because you are so intense and dedicated, it may be hard for you to keep a balance in your life. There is no middle ground for you—it's all the way or nothing at all. You leave no room for less than 110 percent effort and achievement. "I can never do anything half-assed," Jackie pronounces emphatically. "I took up running, thinking that this would be a good way to exercise and relax. Once I started doing it, I became obsessed. It was like a drug. First 5Ks, then 10Ks, and now I'm preparing to do a marathon. It's a healthy addiction, I suppose, but it's like that with everything. I become totally immersed. It's like I always have to be the best—no, not just the best, perfect." This pursuit of excellence is admirable, and this dogged determination has a lot to do with your success. Yet without a balance of play, rest, and socializing in your life, you are subject to excessive stress.

As for relationships, you maintain such high standards for someone to be your friend that most people don't get to first base with you. Those who do face a continual risk of your rejection. It's difficult for you to be tolerant of others when you cannot be tolerant of yourself. Because of your need to be in control, you often try to "fix" others to make them live up to your standards, yet you usually feel frustrated with your attempts. Your perfectionism regularly costs you otherwise good relationships.

Jackie describes how this has worked with her: "Before I was married, I'd either pick men that I didn't care much for, or when I did get involved with someone I'd find something wrong with him. I liked Allen a lot—but he was too short. Ron had lots in common with me—but he was just a salesman. Don had a good career going—but he was younger than me. It's amazing that I ever got married!

"Rick was no angel, but he didn't deserve the bitter criticism I gave him. Maybe that's what drove him to drink, I don't know. Sometimes when he was sweet, I'd even blame him for not being tough enough.

"Since my divorce," Jackie continues, "I've started dating again, and I find myself acting towards men in the same old critical, rejecting ways. Now I'm thirty-five, with a kid, and some men are starting to reject *me* because *I'm* too old. It's occurred to me that looking for the perfect man has been a stupid, losing game. Like I'll meet someone and say, 'Okay, what's wrong with him?' Then I'll look and I'll look—like I'm a detective. When I've found it, I'll reject him. The problem is, *there always is something wrong,* and thinking like this has gotten me a big fat nothing."

When you do form relationships, you're so used to watching out for everyone else's needs that you don't let anyone take care of yours. If you did you'd be vulnerable, and that is extremely threatening. You get very scared when you even think of letting someone get close. As a result, your relationships are often one-sided and unsatisfying. "I remember," Jackie says, "how Don used to get so bugged with me. I was always cleaning, picking up things at his apartment. It was hard for me to relax around him. He'd call me the 'blur' because I was always on the move. One time he tried to fix me dinner, and he got really upset because I just couldn't let him do it by himself. I kept jumping up trying to help him."

As a Perfectionist, you gravitate toward others who will support your seriousness and rigidity, rather than people who will challenge and stimulate you. That kind of honesty and straightforwardness is unknown to you since you are so accustomed to denial, hiding your real self behind the protective mask of perfectionism. Although you ache for some genuineness in those you care about, you defeat it by keeping yourself imprisoned in this role.

It is difficult for you to relax around others, since you are always on guard lest someone try to hurt you or see you out of control. Better to keep your distance, to always stay a bit aloof, than to let someone get too close and discover your fears and uncertainties. At times you may notice this distance you put between yourself and others. "I was having lunch with one of my friends recently," Jackie says, "and we were catching up on all the latest news. For some reason I felt really removed and could see myself sitting, talking with her, smiling at the right times. I felt like I was in a movie, watching someone else take part in this conversation."

Not only do you keep your distance from others, you cannot let things be. Constantly planning, scheming, manipulating, you try to control life, to get it to conform to your schedule of events. You can get greatly upset when things do not go according to your agenda—and life has a habit of presenting the unexpected. "I drove my ex-husband nuts sometimes," Jackie confesses. "I had a habit of writing my daily schedule on a message board near the kitchen. I usually stuck pretty close to it, but if I started getting behind schedule at all, then I would be a basket case, completely upset. Of course I wouldn't show it to anyone else, but I would feel that way on the inside. Well, you can imagine how many times I was miserable. Poor Rick, he would come home and I'd take it out on him. I'd get angry with him, and we'd argue."

Much of your thinking and your talk is future oriented, with phrases like, "Someday I'll . . . ," "Soon there will be . . . ," or, "Before too long. . . ." It's difficult for you to stay focused in the present moment, because to do so would require you to relax your control. You would like absolute assurance that the future is completely predictable and that events will go your way. You worry, worry, worry. When you don't have anything to worry about, you find something. You envy others who can act so carefree and calm.

If things are calm and your life is going too smoothly, as much as you appreciate this harmony and order, you may unconsciously sabotage it. You're simply not used to things going well, so you may drum up a crisis. Handling crises was your familial function. With a crisis, you have a sense of purpose: You can keep things together and put them back in order.

It's more than likely you have been involved in relationships with others who, like you, were raised in abusive families. They may have been abusive with you either emotionally, physically, or sexually. Perhaps they used alcohol or drugs excessively. If so, as a Perfectionist you became *co-dependent* with them, obsessed with their behavior, constantly trying to change them for the better. They became *your* addiction.

Jackie's husband, Rick, was both alcoholic and abusive. "We'd been married about a year and a half, and up to then I didn't really think much about the drinking. We'd had a couple of fights, and he could get really mean sometimes, but I just figured that married couples did that. Then one night when he was drunk, he beat me up really bad. Even after that, I stayed with him for a few months because he kept telling me he was going to change. He would for a little while, then he'd go back to the way he was, swearing at me and being generally mean. He beat me up once more, and that's when I left him for good."

You inadvertently perpetuate abuse so that you can find some familiarity and a sense of purpose from your role as Perfectionist. Jackie unconsciously perpetuated the abuse with which she was familiar by marrying someone who continued to abuse her. Even though her perfectionistic Controlling Child tried to keep the chaos under control, her unconscious Hurting Child was attracted to the familiar scenario of abuse.

Under all this maneuvering, all these attempts to keep "perfect" control over yourself and others, there is a hurt, frightened, and emotionally starved little boy or girl. Your Hurting Child has never been properly cared for, has never felt completely safe and protected, and is not sure of being loved. All these manifestations of the Perfectionist role are merely the child's way of assuring some degree of certainty in an uncertain world, of offering some order and structure where at one time there was none.

"I'll Make You Feel Better": The Caretaker

If you took on the Caretaker role, you too filled a function that helped keep the family intact in spite of the abuse and chaos. You managed other family members' feelings and made everybody feel better. Since your parents were not consistently responsive to their children's emotional needs, it was inevitable that one of the children would step in to fill this role, and for your family, it was you. Whereas the Perfectionist took care of the physical details of managing the family, you took care of the emotional details. The Perfectionist was the family's mind; you were the family's heart.

Bonnie, a 39-year-old registered nurse, is a model Caretaker. A moderately attractive woman with long reddish-blond hair, Bonnie has a habit of nervously glancing downward when she talks. The third oldest of four children, she has a brother five years older, a sister two years older, and a sister two years younger. Her father was physically abusive to all the children, but he was especially cruel to her and her brother. "One time when I was four, my father came roaring out to the backyard. I thought he was coming after me, but instead he grabbed Ronnie, shouting, 'I'll teach you not to lie to me!' and started hitting him with a stick. Then he took him screaming and crying and threw him into this tiny chicken coop. My heart breaks when I think of him sitting there in the chicken coop. He could hardly look at me after Dad let him out. I hung around him, not knowing what to say or do, but feeling so bad for him. I wanted to hug him and tell him it would be okay, but I was worried that if I did he would have been too upset."

You were undoubtedly the most sensitive child in your family. Your feelings were easily hurt, but you learned to bury them. This was your Controlling Child's way of protecting your Hurting Child from further pain and giving you the illusion you had some influence over an otherwise unstable situation. You gave and gave and gave—your time, attention, energy, and empathy—and felt terribly guilty if you failed to comfort or accommodate everyone's needs. It made you feel good to help others feel better.

"My dad went on one of his wild-man sprees one day," Bonnie shudders as she recalls, "yelling at my brother, my older sister, and me. He had found some cigarettes under the porch and insisted we had been smoking them, even though we told him we hadn't. He took off his belt, made all of us take our shirts off and kneel down next to each other in a row, then whipped us until we had welts all over our backs and arms and legs. As soon as he was out of the room, I went and got some wet towels and cleaned up myself and my brother and sister. My sister Terry just sobbed and sobbed for hours, while Ronnie just sat on the bed and stared.

I felt so sorry for them. Even though I was hurt, too, they needed me more to be there for them."

Your sensitivity extended to any tension in the family, and you did whatever you had to do to dissipate it. If mother was angry, you cleaned the house in the hope that this would make her less volatile. If your brother was sad, you tried to cheer him up. If dad's and mom's tempers were rising, you served as their marriage counselor, trying to get them to calm down and settle their argument.

Bonnie learned the art of listening early on: "I'd rather listen than talk, because I figured if I spoke out at all, I might get slapped or else stir up some trouble. Because I did listen so well, almost everyone in my family came to me to talk, including my mom and dad. I remember a few times when my mom and dad were fighting and things would start getting out of hand, I would often end up sitting down with them and giving them some ideas about getting along together. I remember feeling really good about that, because for a while things in the family did seem to go a little smoother. At the time I didn't think anything of it, but now it seems kind of strange that someone thirteen years old would be counseling her parents."

Your identity was so wrapped up in taking care of others that you became rather selfless and needless and grew into adulthood labeled a "nice person." You rarely disagree with anyone, for fear of conflict. "Excuse me" and "I'm sorry" have become well-worn phrases for you. You constantly apologize, not only to protect yourself but also to protect others. You even apologize for apologizing.

" 'I'm sorry for this,' 'I'm sorry for that'—I've spent my whole life being sorry," Bonnie declares. "I took a communication course once and one assignment was to count the number of times in one day I said 'I'm sorry.' Well, I was amazed. I was apologizing to everyone, including the car repairman who hadn't fixed my car as promised: 'Oh, I'm so sorry my car was so much trouble'—like it was *my* problem that he hadn't repaired it properly!"

As an adult, you more than likely are in one of the helping professions, such as social work, teaching, psychology, or medicine. "I'm used to taking care of everybody else," says Bonnie. "I didn't become a nurse by accident." You're very effective at your job and bestow lots of unconditional love and attention on the people with whom you work. You give to others what you would deeply like to receive yourself, yet you have erected tremendous barriers against accepting emotional support. You never get the love and nurturing you secretly desire, and you feel guilty for resenting this.

Your dilemma is three-pronged. First, you give so much and you do it so well that most people feel they can't compete with your giving. This became painfully evident to Bonnie one day: "My boyfriend looked me in the eyes and said, 'You're smothering me. When you give, give, give to me, I feel guilty. You're always available. You clean my house, iron my clothes, pick up after me, and you're always making me cookies. It's too much! There's no way I can give to you the way you give to me. I end up feeling so obligated to give to you, but I could never give enough.' "

Second, your credo is, " 'tis better to give than to receive." To receive would mean bringing attention to yourself, relaxing your control, and feeling open and vulnerable. Having kept the focus on others during childhood as a way to survive, letting someone give to you now feels downright dangerous, especially to your Controlling Child.

Bonnie had a lot of trouble with a surprise birthday party some friends gave her: "I was so embarrassed. It was really hard for me to relax and enjoy the party. I *don't* like being the center of attention; I'm much more used to being the one to set up surprises like that for others."

Third, you are a magnet for takers. It's as if they can read a flashing sign across your forehead that says, "USE ME, USE ME, USE ME." Many Caretakers find themselves in relationships with alcoholics or drug abusers and, like Perfectionists, unknowingly take on the role of co-dependent. Getting romantically involved with a taker fulfills your need to rescue, but it is a trap: You become obsessed with the relationship and you dedicate your energy to trying to cure your lover. You martyr yourself, enduring your suffering for the sake of giving to this person. You inevitably fail at your mission of making the taker a better person, but at least you feel a sense of purpose in trying.

Bonnie describes how this worked with her first husband: "The first time we had sex—before we were married—he basically raped me. I kept saying no, but he pressed on. He also drank a bit, but at the time it didn't seem like much of a problem. After we got married, things got worse. He drank more often and one day he hauled off and slapped me real hard, then punched me in the stomach. That was the first of a few times that he physically abused me. The funny thing was, I kept thinking that it must have been my fault he got upset enough to drink and beat me up; it must have been something I did or didn't do. Isn't that crazy? I had the notion that if I only loved him enough, then he would be different—he'd stop drinking, stop staying out at night. For the longest time, it never occurred to me that it wasn't my fault, that he just had a real drinking problem."

While the Caretaker role affords you some control in your relationships by encouraging others to be dependent on you, it also keeps you from feeling close to others. You long for real contact, real intimacy, yet fear it at the same time. You do not know how to let others in because to do so is simply too threatening. So you rigidly maintain your Caretaker role and maintain your distance and your loneliness.

It's no wonder you feel depressed and lonely a lot of the time. You make your own needs unimportant while you accommodate everyone else's. Although your strategy helped you survive your abusive family, following the rigid Caretaker role as an adult constricts your ability to love fully, freely, and unconditionally.

"I'll Just Disappear": The Invisible One

If you took on the role of the Invisible One, you developed a great disappearing act. In order to survive in your family and to bury your pain, your Controlling Child opted for you to be as inconspicuous as possible. You learned to deal with neglect and abuse by being unobtrusive, which usually meant adapting to the situation. You felt helpless, so you learned to remain detached and uninvolved with events around you. Your parents didn't notice you, and you did nothing to attract their attention. You gave new meaning to the words flexible and adaptive.

Phil, a forty-six-year-old aerospace engineer, is rather short and diminutive, with a habit of propping his chin on his hand and frequently tugging on his ear while talking with you. Phil had little attention from his mother or father and never made much of a fuss about it. "I can't remember my mother ever hugging me. On the other hand, she never hit me or scolded me either. I figured that if I stayed out of her way, she would never be upset with me. My dad was never there much. He worked long hours, and when he was home he spent most of the time in the garage working on his car. My older brother Robert would do something to get into trouble, and then Dad would calmly whip him with a switch from the old birch tree in the front yard. He'd make me watch. No way was I going to cause any trouble! I learned to keep to myself and never bother anyone."

To remain invisible, you spent a great deal of time in your room or away from the house. You were so detached, so deprived, and so split off that you appeared to be self-centered and unfeeling. You generally didn't pay attention to other people, and they concluded that you were aloof and were ignoring them. At school, you were barely noticed by teachers or schoolmates.

"I don't remember having any real friends," Phil recalls. "During breaks at school I stuck pretty much to myself. I'd usually find a spot somewhere near the fence at my junior high school, take a book with me and read. Sometimes the other kids would tease me about being so stuck-up, but really I was just shy. One time some guys were teasing me and started throwing mudballs at my back. I just kept ignoring them, but they kept doing it. I got up, acting as if they weren't even there, and moved closer to where a teacher was on patrol. That worked, but boy, was I humiliated! I felt like a coward. They teased me for a long time after that, but I just kept on ignoring them, all the while feeling real small inside."

You learned to be very accommodating, considering it your job to meet the needs of others. You never questioned what your mom or dad wanted you to do, you just did it. You didn't believe you could resist—you felt powerless to influence the events around you.

Phil remembers being left alone much of the time: "When my dad would stay late at work, sometimes my mom would leave the house in the afternoon, say she'd be back in a little while, then not show up for hours. I remember one time when I was about eight or nine she did that, and me and Bobby barricaded all the doors because we kept hearing noises outside in the dark. When my dad got home he was really upset and took Bobby by the ears down into the cellar and gave him a whipping."

As an adult, you persist in the same kind of patterning. You have no sense of choice or of personal power. While the Perfectionist and the Caretaker feel they can wield some influence on events and the people around them, you don't believe you have any influence. You feel victimized and subject to other people's reactions. Your life is an emotional roller coaster much of the time.

You keep yourself physically isolated and emotionally insulated. If you do form friendships, they are distant and superficial. You don't talk with others about issues of any depth, nor do you deal seriously with your inner feelings or experiences. Any romantic relationships you embark on tend to be with those who are emotionally unavailable. So you remain shy, withdrawn, and quiet much of the time. As a result, you come off as unapproachable.

"With my first wife, there was a lot of distance," states Phil. "We hardly ever talked to each other after we got married, mostly because we didn't know what to say. It sounds funny to say this, but we never got personal. In fact, whenever one of us would say to the other, 'I love you,' the other one would always say, 'Well, you'll get over it.' It got to be a running joke between us. Isn't that sad?"

Because you are so split off, you walk around looking "spaced-out." Your body is present but your mind is off in the distance. It's scary to be emotionally and mentally present, so you often retreat into fantasy and

daydream. At least these worlds contain no threats of harm or abandonment, while the external world continually presents these possibilities.

Phil remembers one job where he got the nickname "Space Case."
"I just kept to myself and did my work. I don't trust people anyway, and
I figured it was none of their business what was going on with me. So I
tuned everybody out. One day my supervisor said to me, 'Hey, Space Case!
You want to work overtime?' Some of the others heard that, and from there
the name stuck. Soon everyone was calling me that."

Continuing with your habit of not letting anyone notice you, you
avoid any situation where you'd need to take charge. To be the center of
attention is your horror of horrors—for you it's the equivalent of being
"caught" and prompts feelings of shame and fear. Perhaps you have found
yourself drifting from job to job, never staying involved with any one for
long.

Phil describes his first job: "My dad got me a job in construction.
Eventually they made me foreman, but I had a hard time with that. I hated
bossing everybody around. After that there were lots of jobs; I could never
settle on exactly what I wanted to do. I wanted to do carpentry after talking
to my Uncle Art, so I became a carpenter for a while. Then my brother
talked me into going into truck driving. I did that for a while but hated
it. I've had a lot of different jobs, some good, some bad, but still don't feel
like I'm doing what I want."

Because you are noninvolved and passive, others make decisions
for you. To make your own decisions would mean being visible and risking rejection or abandonment. Seemingly unaffected by events around
you, you have a characteristic gesture of shrugging your shoulders, in-
dicating resignation, acceptance, or submissiveness to another's decisions
and desires.

Phil's life has been one of living on the edge of involvement. "Even
though I don't trust anyone, I do like people. I just don't want to have
them calling and coming by. They'd probably get pretty tired of me if I
hung around them too much." If we could peek behind this veil of denial,
we might well find a frightened little boy who has learned to deal with his
feelings by denying them and withdrawing from the world.

The flexibility and adaptability you developed in childhood can be
assets in adulthood. You don't get rattled easily, and you readily accommodate changes. This trait, however, comes at great cost. Maintaining your
role as the Invisible One means maintaining your victimization. The pain
and hurt that you deny and the continuing unhappiness that results may
prompt you to hide away even more. You may find other ways to mask the
pain and remain invisible, such as drinking, taking drugs, or overeating.

These addictive behaviors may temporarily numb the pain of your deprivation, but they also fortify the wall that separates you from others.

"I've always felt 'weird' and 'different,' " Phil admits. "Taking drugs
made me seem okay, at least while I was high. I did a lot of marijuana, acid,
and mescaline in high school and for a long while afterwards. Most of my
friends at the time were into the same things. At least we all had something in
common. Later on it was cocaine. After a while none of the drugs worked for
me. Then one night I overdosed on coke and called the paramedics. They
took me to a hospital and later I ended up in jail. I had almost killed myself,
and I got into all sorts of legal tangles over the charge of possession. That was
a turning point in my life. I took a long, hard look at myself and what I was
doing and decided to stop. Without drugs I've had to actually deal with life,
and I'm beginning to see a glimmer of hope. For the first time in my life I've
faced up to how isolated and lonely I've been."

In an attempt at connecting, you often attract Perfectionists or
Caretakers as mates or lovers. With a Perfectionist, your distance and
isolation at first may seem a good match for his need for order, since you
don't seem to cause any fuss. However, your passive-aggressive behavior or
addictive behavior ultimately wreaks havoc with a Perfectionist's own addiction to routine and organization. You simply won't act according to his
plan. This can be a particularly volatile situation if the Perfectionist also has
a history of abuse, since there is a greater likelihood that this volatility could
lead either of you to act abusively toward the other.

If you attract a Caretaker, it's because your helplessness is irresist-
ible. A Caretaker will be happy to have someone who needs rescuing. The
catch is that you will keep frustrating his efforts to rescue you from your
isolation, drinking, or other addictions. A Caretaker's main purpose is to
make you feel better about yourself, which is ultimately your responsibility,
not his. Although you may look like you agree with his plans for your
self-improvement, you quietly and passively resist the program.

"My ex-wife and I *never* fought," Phil recalls. "In fact, we didn't
even talk all that much. We eventually just drifted apart. During sex was
the only time we could feel close, and even that got to be less and less often
towards the end. Neither of us really knew much about feelings. One day
I told her I thought it was a good idea to get a divorce, and she calmly
agreed. We then proceeded to have a calm, quiet divorce, with neither of
us showing much in the way of regret or sorrow."

What's amazing is that, much as you tried to disappear to avoid
the abuse in your original family, you may find yourself re-creating the cycle
of abuse and abandonment with your mate. Like most Adult Children, you
seek out abusive relationships; even though they are painful, they are
familiar.

"I'll Show You!": The Rebel

The roles of Perfectionist, Caretaker, and Invisible One are all designed to avoid abuse and to bring a certain degree of control to an inconsistent and chaotic family environment. Adult Children in these roles do their best not to draw abusive attention to themselves. If you took on the role of the Rebel, in contrast, you frequently drew negative attention to yourself. As the scapegoat for your parents' tension and anger, you became the primary target for abuse when mom or dad was on a rampage.

Beverly, a rebel *par excellence,* was raised by her mother and stepfather. "I think I got the worst of it. My little sister was hardly ever touched." Beverly speaks in a rapid, clipped pace and looks right through you when she speaks. "One time when I was eight my Mom caught me taking some raisins without asking. She grabbed the spatula, made me put my arms straight out on the table and started hitting my hands again and again. If I moved them, she'd hit me somewhere else even harder. She never did this to my sister. I guess she figured since I was older, I had to be the example."

If you were a Rebel, you were continually getting into trouble. You were the one in your family to overtly point out the denial and to pay the price of further abuse when you did. You were the one to fight back when you felt wronged, to speak up even though you knew you risked punishment. You were the one to express outwardly the anger and helpless rage that everyone else in the family felt. Unlike the other roles that were designed to lessen the turbulence and stabilize the family, your emotional honesty as a Rebel drew abusive attention to you.

Acting out your hurt and angry feelings further damaged your already low self-esteem, because it inevitably prompted derisive reactions from one or both parents. These reactions only confirmed what you had already decided: You were a bad child and deserved mistreatment. To further prove this, you may have run away, stolen, failed in school, or stayed out past curfew. You were a rich source of problems for your parents. As a teenager, you may have tried to numb your bad feelings with alcohol, drugs, and/or sex. Not only did these activities draw your parents' attention, but they also may have brought you into early and frequent contact with police, social workers, probation officers, psychologists, and perhaps institutions such as juvenile halls or mental hospitals.

Beverly was a terrible student. "I got okay grades, but I never studied and I was always ditching classes and going with friends to the beach. Once I started getting involved with boys, there was no stopping me. I was out partying every night. I never did drugs, but I was drinking way too much. If I dated someone, I'd end up having sex with him, so I got a pretty bad reputation. All this intensified my mother's abuse, but it got so she couldn't control me. I even ran away a couple of times when I was fourteen and stayed at a girlfriend's house. My mom and I would get into battles where she'd beat me up pretty bad. My stepdad, if he was there at all, wouldn't do a thing about it. He'd walk out of the room whenever the yelling started, or get in his truck and take off. It still makes me angry when I think about it.

"One day when I was fifteen, I came in late. My mom started yelling at me, I yelled back, and she came at me. I slapped her really hard, so hard I scared myself. Somehow she got me down on the floor and started hitting my face with her fist. My dad pulled her off me—about the only time he did—and I ran out of the house and went to a friend's. When my friend's mom saw my face all bloody and bruised, she called the police. I never went back home after that."

You're not a child anymore, but you continue to be a Rebel. For example, anger was the one emotion you allowed yourself to express as a child. In fact, it was the only emotion you allowed yourself to *feel*; sorrow and pain were not part of your emotional vocabulary. Thus your Controlling Child not only took care of you, it also helped you survive. While this anger once offered you a form of protection against being hurt, now it acts mainly as a wall to keep love, tenderness, and affection from getting out or in. Your anger masks your vulnerability. Your standard operating principle is "the best defense is a good offense."

Beverly describes the consequences of her anger. "My anger has cost me jobs, relationships, friends. My supervisor at work has been really patient with me, but even she has reached her limit. I get into fights with people there because I'm so hot-tempered. My anger seems to get in my way. When I think about it, I'm acting an awful lot like my mother."

Although you control your anger a good deal of the time, it's close to the surface, waiting to be triggered by the slightest misdeed on the part of another. You may even try to create conflict by shouting, blaming, or hitting. You still feel that others are out to abuse you in some way, and your continued victim's stance generates much of your anger.

Your strength and courage in the face of the childhood abuse you received are admirable. You did not stand for the abuse, and you supplied a spark of real life to the prevailing denial in your family. But you may not yet have learned to channel your anger into constructive avenues, or allowed yourself to feel the pain and vulnerability that lurk beneath your tough exterior. As long as you continue in the role of the Rebel, you will perpetuate the abuse. You will either abuse others physically or verbally, turn your anger against yourself and maintain some form of self-destructive behavior such as using alcohol or drugs, or find others to abuse you. As long as you stay angry and hostile most of the time, you have not yet given up your role as scapegoat and victim and taken personal responsibility for your life.

If you have learned to channel your anger into constructive social causes rather than striking out randomly, this can be an effective way to redirect your underlying inner tension. Since the root of your rage is a persistent helpless feeling and sense of powerlessness, you empathize with others who have been victimized, and you express this empathy through social crusading.

If, on the other hand, you have not learned to channel your anger into socially acceptable causes, you may continue to act it out in violent or antisocial activities. Unable to feel compassion for those less powerful than you, you continue to punish others the same way you were punished as a child. Unconsciously you have identified more closely with the aggressor than the victim. If you continue to act out your anger as an adult, you invite other authority figures, such as the police, to control you. If you were institutionalized as a teenager, you are more likely to continue this pattern as an adult. If you drank or took drugs as an act of rebellion during adolescence, this pattern has most likely continued into your adult life. In addition to alcohol and drug use, you may have other self-destructive tendencies, such as driving recklessly or driving while intoxicated. You have never outgrown your adolescence, and although you no longer live with the parents you rebelled against, you continue to find substitutes, such as the legal system, social institutions, or mates, to rebel against.

Because of the intensity of your anger, you have alienated others and remained socially isolated. Because you complain a lot and can be critical and negative, you have particular difficulty with friendships. Any friends you have tend to be like you—socially isolated, critical, and negative.

Says Beverly: "I've had lots of friends, but usually I don't end up keeping them. Sheila was one of my closest friends until a couple of years ago. I think I drove her away. I'd pick, pick, pick at her and at everybody else we would talk about. I hate to admit it, but I must have sounded exactly like my mother. Sheila stopped calling, and eventually we stopped doing things together. Whenever I'd suggest doing something together, she'd always say she was busy with other things. I miss her friendship, but I doubt that we'll ever be that close again."

The consequences of the acting out that went on during your adolescence may have followed you into adulthood. Perhaps you dropped out of high school, failed to learn a trade, or had an unwanted pregnancy. Your past continues to haunt you and make your recovery considerably more difficult, but certainly not impossible. As you become more familiar with the Rebel role, understanding that it's not necessary to continue playing it, you will have greater freedom of choice in your thinking, feeling, and behaving.

DIFFERENT ROLES, COMMON PERSONALITY TRAITS

When we look at the functioning of Adult Children more closely, certain patterns of behavior occur repeatedly. These six patterns, or personality traits, appear consistently in all Adult Children, regardless of the specific role adopted: (1) control, (2) avoiding feelings, (3) guilt from overresponsibility, (4) crisis addiction, (5) guessing at normality, and (6) absolute thinking.

"No Problem": Control

The first issue, control, can best be understood when you remember the instability and unpredictability you grew up with. Chaos and uncertainty reigned in your home. You did not know when the next explosion would occur, when mom or dad might let loose with a strap or a torrent of criticism, or abandon you entirely. You learned to "hang back," to be watchful and cautious. Your Controlling Child, whatever her methods, emerged in order to help you survive. You learned to deny, suppress, and repress your feelings and thoughts as well as your outward behavior. To be out of control is frightening to most people, but for you it is a nightmare. You know all too well what happens when adults lose control. You feel you *must* be in control in order to have some predictability in an unpredictable world.

"I'm a private person," Gina declares. "It's hard for me to mix with other people, because I'm always afraid I'll do or say something stupid. With my work in accounting, now, that's another story. I know my work, and I do it well. I can tell when things are in order and when they're not."

As an adult, you spend a lot of energy maintaining control over both yourself and your relationships. By playing out the role that is most familiar to you, you bring some semblance of order, predictability, and control into your life. The cost of such control, however, is great: the loss of spontaneity, of joy, and of a certain freedom of expression.

Ironically, your attempts to control usually create more tension. As Charles Whitfield writes in *Healing the Child Within:* "Ultimately, we cannot control life, so the more that we try to control it, the more out of control we feel because we are focusing so much attention on it. Frequently the person who feels *out* of control is obsessed with the need to be in control."

"It Doesn't Bother Me": Avoiding Feelings

Not only is this an effect of growing up in an abusive family, as described in Chapter 2, it has become part of the way your personality operates. The training you received as a child instilled a denial of what you felt: Don't trust any of your feelings and ignore whatever your senses tell you. If you cried when you were beaten, then you got beaten some more for crying. You concluded that feelings were an experience to be feared, so you learned to keep a lid on most of them—to not let yourself be emotionally affected and certainly not to express your feelings. Your Hurting Child and your Natural Child, the parts of your Inner Child that feel the most deeply and most intensely, became inaccessible.

Another reason you avoid feelings as an adult is that you learned to associate feelings with actions. What you witnessed as a child was that adults tended to act out their feelings. When mom felt angry, she slapped you or cursed you. When dad was sexually aroused, he abused you sexually. Understandably, you assumed a direct cause-and-effect relationship. You didn't know that feelings are sensory information that *may* help you decide on an action, or are simply states of emotional experience that do not have to be acted upon.

"When I get angry, I eat," Jennifer notes. "That's one way I stuff down my feelings. Lately I've been eating a lot. I'm afraid that if I let my husband know just how angry I am, he'd leave me. So I eat instead."

As a child, you were not allowed to feel. If you were scared, you dared not risk going to mom for comfort, because previous efforts had led to rejection. She may even have told you to grow up and not be such a baby. You blindly obeyed the unspoken rule that you simply did not talk about your abuse or neglect.

In addition to all of these reasons for avoiding feelings, the intensity of the feelings you did have—terror, rage, helplessness, and sadness—was so powerful that it would have been overwhelming to fully experience them. There is just so much that a human being, especially a child, can feel before the person "shuts down." Now, as an adult, you have shut down so much and learned to avoid your feelings so well that it's hard for you to feel anything intensely. In *Grown-Up Abused Children,* James Leehan and Laura Pistone Wilson explain:

Underlying nearly all the other problems of grown-up abused children, and certainly related to the lack of trust, is an inability to identify emotions and express, or "own" one's feelings. Perhaps the most common way of handling emotions is to deny their existence. Many of these adults claim never to feel anger, resentment, hostility or their opposites such as joy, happiness, warmth, and closeness to others.

"It Must Be All My Fault": Guilt from Overresponsibility

The guilt you suffer stems from feeling overly responsible for your parents' actions and for the abuse you or your brothers and sisters received. Children are typically self-centered and usually think that the events around them are the direct result of their behavior. If you were abused in spite of good behavior, then you assumed that the mistreatment must have been because of something you thought or did.

You may have tried extremely hard to be the ideal child so that your parents would not continue with their abuse, but it never worked. No matter what you did (or did not do), the abuse continued—and you continued to blame yourself. Your parents might even have told you it was indeed your fault that they acted the way they did.

Julianne's lifetime of this sort of guilt was exemplified in one particular incident: "Mom ended up in the hospital for her drinking and her crazy behavior, and my grandma called. When I told Grandma that Mom was in the hospital, she said, 'Well, haven't you been taking care of her?' I remember thinking right away, 'Well, I guess I haven't been doing a very good job of it.' Here I was fourteen years old, and everybody expected *me* to be taking care of *her!* I still carry around this tremendous guilt. I'm really cautious around people, and I think it's because I'm always afraid I'll do something wrong or blow it somehow. And I end up always taking care of other people, because I feel really guilty if the relationship isn't going perfectly."

As an adult, you continue to feel great responsibility for other people's feelings and actions. If someone is upset, you immediately blame yourself, feel guilty, and feel obligated to do something to take away the upset. If someone is angry, you immediately assume it is because of something you said or did.

"Things Are Much Too Peaceful": Crisis Addiction

Crisis addiction, too, is an extension of your life as a child. You became so used to inconsistency, surprises, and terror that when things in your adult life are calm and stable, you literally don't know what to do with yourself. Chaos is what you are accustomed to, so to do without it feels unfamiliar and very uncomfortable. When your relationships are working and peacefulness pervades your life, you feel uneasy, like an addict who needs a fix of adrenaline every once in a while just to feel alive.

When life is calm, you may find yourself feeling anxious or depressed. At these times you will do something just to stir things up so you can feel that rush of adrenaline. This allows you to play out your role of crisis manager and makes you feel as if you have a purpose. The main difficulty with "life by crisis management" is that you spend so much energy in managing these perpetual crises, you have little energy left over to be productive or to love and appreciate those around you.

Ron's addiction to crisis has adversely affected his choice of girl-friends: "I have always picked as girlfriends women who are hot-tempered and irresponsible, maybe a little crazy. There's just something I like about the drama, that sense of being on the edge and about to fall off. I think I have an aversion to normal women, women who have ordinary jobs and who like to go to the movies and bake brownies and who are calm most of the time and treat me well. I tell myself, 'This is boring. This isn't how it should be. There's no excitement, no rush.' I grew up with so much craziness that normal, smooth relationships seem pretty blah."

"How Am I Supposed to Act?": Guessing at Normality

What is normality? You have no reference point for this, since your home environment was one of extremes. What was standard for you was abuse and unpredictability. Comparing your family with others was confusing because other families didn't seem to be quite so chaotic. Since you could not talk about the differences, ask questions, or share your feelings about them, it's no surprise that you were left wondering how you were supposed to think, feel, and act.

Janet Woititz, in *Adult Children of Alcoholics,* describes this guessing game, and it is just as applicable to Adult Children of Abusive Parents:

> Throughout life, to keep others from finding out that they don't know what they're doing, they guess at what is appropriate. They get concerned and confused about things that they believe other people do not get concerned and confused about. They don't have the freedom to ask, so they never know for sure.

You probably fantasized some ideal family situation you wished you could have been a part of—like that in "Father Knows Best" or "The

Partridge Family." This imagined standard of normality was so ideal that it could not have existed. It was nearly impossible for you to understand that normality in a family situation can best be thought of in terms of whether a family is functional or dysfunctional, and that even these terms are relative. A functional family is one where children get to be children and adults take responsibility for their roles as adults; where there is a healthy respect for one another both as individuals and as members of the same family. Since your family was not functional but abusive, it gave you no standard for comparison.

Ruth wistfully sighs, "I would watch 'The Brady Bunch' on TV and they seemed so happy and loving all the time. It was so different from my family that I swore someday I would have a family like them. As it's turned out, my present family is nothing like that. I've had a hard time accepting that there is no such thing as a perfect family, just as there's no such thing as a perfect me."

As you grew into adulthood, it became more and more apparent that the events in your family were unusual. You had to watch others and model after them in hopes that *they* knew what they were doing. Perhaps they could supply you with some clues to what normal behavior was. You were frequently too embarrassed to test out any behavior that might be construed as different or in any way abnormal. You did whatever you could to hide from others the fact that you really did not know the "right" way to act, but instead spent much of your time having to guess how to act. Your interaction with others has become somewhat of a puzzle. It is your job to piece together whatever clues you can gather so that you can somehow act "normal."

"It's Got to Be All or Nothing": Absolute Thinking

Herbert Gravitz and Julie Bowden in *Recovery: A Guide for Adult Children of Alcoholics* describe "all-or-none functioning" as a characteristic of adults who have been raised in any type of dysfunctional family. They define such functioning as the "tendency to think, feel, and behave in an all-or-none way. Everything is black or white—there is no in-between. Things are either all right or all wrong, and since things are seldom all right, they are often all wrong."

Children generally see things not in relative terms—in shades of gray—but in absolute terms—all black or all white. Because your need to maintain absolute control expresses itself through the four roles we looked at earlier in this chapter, as long as your Controlling Child is in charge, your thinking and your way of operating in the world will tend to be absolute.

You either trust somebody completely or not at all. As a result, in your relationships someone is either in or out. More realistically, you could decide that trust is often a matter of degree rather than decree.

Success is another area where absolute thinking tends to rule you. You put no value on partial success, not recognizing that ultimate success comes in small steps toward the desired goal rather than in one grand slam. You may never try anything too challenging, because if you fail, you automatically categorize yourself as a failure.

As to your self-esteem, you cannot truly win as long as you maintain this rigid way of looking at your self-worth. You see yourself either as all good or all bad. When the judgment is favorable, you can temporarily relax. But one slip and you judge your entire being as bad.

"I think that's why I'm depressed a lot of the time," Cathy discloses. "It seems I'm my own worst critic. I have friends, a successful job as a graphics designer, but I can never quite be or do enough. After a day at work and an evening with friends, I'll sit at home and go over everything I did wrong!"

It's hard to see life as it is when you perceive it through the unrealistic distortions of absolute thinking. Other people, events, or situations rarely fit convenient "either-or" categories.

These roles were once a blessing that helped you survive your childhood. Now, as an adult, you find they have become a burden. In order for you to recover fully from your abusive past, you must soften the rigidity of these roles and augment your personality traits. You need not discard your role entirely nor rework your whole personality, but you can learn how to let your Controlling Child loosen up and relax.

With a greater sense of how you were affected by abuse, we can now move on to a program for recovery.

PART TWO

YOUR RECOVERY

Before
You
Begin . . .

*E*ach stage of this recovery program presents specific steps for you to take. These steps will include exercises and writing assignments. Starting now, keep a journal as your steady companion. It will be an important tool in your recovery.

One final comment before we begin the journey: The exercises may evoke strong feelings that signal you are uncovering repressed material as a part of your emotional and spiritual healing. If and when the process gets scary and painful, you may need help in getting perspective on this unearthed material. In this case I strongly recommend you find a counselor or therapist. Your medical doctor or a friend may recommend one, or you can interview prospective therapists over the telephone. See the Appendix for guidelines in selecting a therapist.

Whether or not you seek out a therapist, it is extremely important that you develop other sources of support throughout your recovery process. These can be found in the form of therapy groups, support groups, and 12-step programs such as those listed in the Appendix, as well as from friends. Do not hesitate to take advantage of the support that is available. Although recovery is something you do for yourself, it should not be done in complete isolation. That will just make it more difficult and will probably take a lot longer.

Go through the recovery program at your own pace. It will take anywhere from a few months to a few years. Since everyone's recovery is different, do not compare your journey with anyone else's. Consider your recovery an adventure in discovery, a journey to find your Natural Child again.

So grab your journal, and let's get started by taking steps to heal your Inner Child.

5

Healing Your Inner Child

*T*ammy felt depressed and anxious much of the time and didn't know why. She rarely went out of her house and was constantly worrying that other people were silently criticizing her. She came to me with recurring nightmares and severe, debilitating headaches that had no apparent organic cause. In recounting her childhood as the youngest of six children, she remembered feeling completely responsible for everyone else's feelings. From very early in her childhood, Tammy felt caught in the middle of her parents' constant fights, with both parents trying to get her support.

As she was recalling a particularly vicious fight her parents had when she was six years old, Tammy began to feel the same familiar fear and guilt she had experienced then. While reliving this experience she had a new thought: "I'm only a little girl!" This was her six-year-old Inner Child realizing that she was not a "bad child" and that her parents' fighting was not her fault. Sitting in my office, she shook with sobs of pain, sadness, and relief as she unburdened herself of years of guilt and self-blame.

Tammy took a major step in her recovery by acknowledging and releasing the buried pain of her Hurting Child and by relaxing the control of her Controlling Child. This cleared the way for the emergence of her Natural Child.

Like Tammy, you are at the first stage of your recovery: healing the split in your Inner Child. There are five steps in completing this stage: (1) Becoming aware, (2) Remembering the trauma, (3) Grieving the loss of your childhood, (4) Forgiving your parents, (5) Reparenting yourself.

COMING TO YOUR SENSES: BECOMING AWARE

The first step in healing your Inner Child is to become aware of what your senses are telling you. Virginia Satir, noted family therapist, believes that full awareness is critical to the healing process. In *Helping Families to Change,* she puts forth the following as the goal of healing: ". . . to see freely and comment openly on what [you] see, to be able to hear freely and comment on what [you] hear, and to be able to touch freely and be able to comment openly on that experience—these comprise the restorative task."

To heal, it is necessary to *stop pretending* and to honestly acknowledge to yourself the rich information your senses provide. Growing up in your family taught you to do exactly the opposite—to deny what you knew to be true, to mistrust your own senses. Making awareness a habit will set your Hurting Child free. Remaining aware will set your Natural Child free. The key to remaining aware is very simple: pay attention.

To regain this awareness, practice this sequence of exercises in focusing, listening, sensing, and seeing. This will take consistent attention for the next four weeks, but the process of being aware will last you a lifetime.

Focusing Total Attention

Focusing means bringing 100 percent of your attention to something outside you or something inside and simply observing your own experience. This exercise will help you learn to focus:

Exercise: Observe your awareness.

Do not direct your attention; simply observe its course. Finish the statement, "I am now aware of . . ." repeatedly, out loud, each time noting whatever comes in focus at the moment. For example, "I am now aware of my breathing. I am now aware of the sound of traffic in the distance. I am now aware of this book in front of me. I am now aware of tension in my back." Note whether your awareness is of something inside or outside you. Now, take two minutes, set this book down, and focus on whatever comes into your awareness.

What did you notice? What did you see, hear, feel, smell, or taste? Did you notice a "voice override" criticizing you or the exercise in some way, interfering with your observations? That was the voice of your Controlling Child. The best thing to do is to simply notice this voice and be aware of it, just as you are aware of many other things during this exercise.

Repeat this exercise twice daily for the next seven days, once in the morning and once in late afternoon or early evening. Choose a quiet setting until you get used to the process, then you may wish to experiment in settings where there are more distractions.

Journal:

Record your observations once each day. Note *whatever* your experience was, no matter how silly or mundane it might have seemed. A sample journal entry from Bill's experimentation with focusing follows:

October 24: "With the focusing exercise today, I became very aware how sharp and defined the trees I can see out my front window are. I noticed chills up and down my spine as the wind bent those trees way over and blew up the dust in the back patio. I was aware that my stomach was tight through most of the exercise. I noticed my Controlling Child was worried that I was not doing the exercise right."

Hearing, Not Just Listening

Much of the time we listen but don't really hear. Instead we filter what we hear through our fear and prejudice, thus distorting the original sensory information. The following exercise can help you more accurately hear sounds both outside you and inside:

Exercise: Listen outside and inside yourself.

Hear the sounds around you. Notice you may also "hear" your thoughts. Finish the statement, "I now hear . . .," out loud if possible, and simply observe what comes to your attention. For example: "I now hear a bird singing in the distance. I now hear my thought, 'I like this exercise.' I now hear a clock ticking. I now hear ringing in my ears." Now set this book down, and for two minutes, listen closely and hear—whatever draws your attention.

What did you hear? Was it easier to listen to sounds outside you or inside you? What thoughts did you notice? Repeat this exercise two times each day, once in the morning and once at night, for the next seven days. Alternate between quiet settings and those where there are more sounds (although too much noise might defeat the purpose of the exercise).

Journal:

Record your observations of your listening experience once each day. In this sample entry, Nancy describes her observations:

November 2: "I tried listening today at work. Wow! I had never noticed before how much noise there was. Word processors clicking, air conditioner blowing, papers shuffling—I must have learned to shut it all off. What was also amazing was that every so often there were these short pauses where there seemed to be no sound, as if for a tiny millisecond everything would stop, then as abruptly start up again."

Seeing, Not Just Looking

How often do we look at something without truly seeing it? For instance, is it possible to look at a rose without really seeing it? Yes, especially if you are *looking* at a rose but *seeing* your mental picture called "rose" instead of the actual flower. The challenge of these exercises is to more sharply focus your vision both externally and internally by turning your focus outward to your immediate world and turning your eyes inward to your rich mental imagery, your image-ination. The following exercises highlight these two different ways of seeing.

Exercise: Focus your attention externally.

This is an exercise in active looking. Observe items in your surroundings. Try not to see your labels of things, but instead notice the features of the various objects in your environment. Notice color, shading, size, shape, and texture. See each as if you're seeing it for the first time. Even with a familiar object like a telephone, try not to label it but instead *see* it. Set the book down now for five minutes and actively look around you.

What did you notice? What objects attracted your attention? What were some of the characteristics of those objects? Mentally, try describing the object to yourself, not by its name but by its characteristics, as if describing it to someone who is blind and unfamiliar with the item. Do this exercise for five minutes twice each day for the next seven days.

Journal:

Record your observations daily. At least once during the week, write out a detailed description of a particular object. A sample entry from one of my patients, Patty:

November 10: "This has been a revelation. There has been so much I missed seeing in the past, it's as if I've been blind. I took a walk earlier today and did the 'seeing' exercise. Colors seemed so sharp and crisp, it blew my mind!

"Now I'll try to describe something to a blind person. It's cylindrical, about four inches high, closed across the bottom and open across the top. It's about three inches in diameter and is made of a hard, though breakable, substance. It is white, with a loop of the same substance attached to the side. It's a coffee cup! Not bad for a first-timer!"

Exercise: Look inward

This is an exercise in becoming aware of your mental imagery. Close your eyes, sit back, and notice whatever is in your visual field. You may at first notice colors, shapes, movement on the backs of your eyelids. Then think of familiar objects, like your living room, your car, your friends or family, and picture them. Next, use your creative imagination to change these pictures. Change color, shape, proportion, or any other qualities. For instance, picture your car about 20 feet longer than it really is, or all of the furniture in your home painted purple. You may at first feel a little silly doing this, but stay with it. Next, allow your imagination to wander wherever it may, letting the pictures appear spontaneously in your mind. Put the book down for a few minutes and give this a try.

What did you notice? Was this exercise harder or easier than the others you've tried? Were you able to reach the stage of letting images happen spontaneously? Do this exercise for five to ten minutes each day during the same seven-day period that you are doing the previous exercise.

Journal:

Record your experiences of this exercise each day. Here's a sample entry from Mark's journal:

November 11: "I did this exercise a few times before, but today was the first time I was aware of any spontaneous pictures in my mind. At first I pictured my son playing on the swings. Then I pictured him sprouting wings and literally flying from the swings into my arms. As I held him

I could almost feel him breathing. Then I put him down and the picture switched to me floating on a cloud high above the earth. I felt very light, very safe, and I could see the earth below. I really felt quite peaceful."

Your Body Barometer: Sensing

The fourth type of awareness you need to activate is awareness of your senses. Your body is a sensitive and accurate barometer for whatever is going on with you. When you're tense, you'll experience tension through a tight stomach, a pain in your neck or shoulders, or perhaps a constricted feeling in the chest. When you're happy, your body will usually feel light and you may experience an inner fullness and warmth. As you learn to pay close, detailed attention to your body, it will give you specific clues as to what you are feeling. This attention to your body and its senses can be especially helpful if your body has been misused or neglected. Do the following exercise once each day for the next seven days; thereafter do it regularly to sharpen up this vital area of awareness. You may wish to tape-record the exercise and play it back.

Exercise: Body scan.

Sit back in your chair and close your eyes. Notice your breathing. Pay attention to the rising of your chest when you inhale and the falling of your chest when you exhale. Let your breathing get a little deeper each time. Count your breathing in sets of four, then begin with one again. Continue this breathing pattern as you relax with each breath you exhale. If any thoughts come up, simply let them pass on by in your consciousness.

Now, pay attention to your skin. Notice its coolness or its warmth, the differences in temperature on different parts of your body. Feel the weight and texture of your clothes against your skin. Feel the pressure of your body on the surface upon which it rests. Notice anything else about your skin that comes to your attention.

Now, notice any areas of muscle tension, and as you do, simply breathe out the tension and let your muscles relax. Start with your head and face and slowly move your awareness down your body, through your neck and shoulders. Now, notice your upper arms, chest, and upper back. Now your lower arms, hands, stomach, and lower back. Be aware of any tension in your buttocks, genitals, anus. Now your thighs, both front and back. Then your knees, calves, and shins. Now, notice your feet, tops and bottoms. Then your toes. Now, once again notice your breathing.

Next, listen closely to the rhythms of your body. Hear your heartbeat and breathing. Can you feel the blood pulsing through your veins? Pay attention to any other internal sensations, such as a contraction in your stomach or a twitch in your toe—anything at all that's going on inside your body.

Now, gradually bring your awareness back into the room you're in. Be aware of sounds, sensations, and lights around you. When you're ready, open your eyes.

Ask yourself: Was I able to relax? What was the easiest thing about this exercise? The hardest? Where do I carry my tension? As you become more consistently aware of your internal physical senses, you learn to pick up important sensory cues, such as tension, that can tell you when you've been operating in a survival mode. Do this 10-minute exercise once a day for seven days, or longer if you find it pleasant and relaxing.

Journal:

Record your reactions each day you do this exercise. A sample from Ken's journal:

November 15: "I did the body scan. It was really relaxing, though it's hard to keep my attention completely focused on sensing. I keep thinking that I should be doing something else. Oh, well, I don't have to be a perfectionist about it. There was one point when it came to relaxing my chest when I started feeling sad, like I wanted to cry. I kept going through the other parts of my body, but that particular sensation troubles me a bit."

As you learn to consistently focus on your senses, you will begin to mend the split between the different parts of your Inner Child. Paying closer attention to your internal sensations paves the way for healing by gradually lifting the lid of repression, allowing you to remember.

UP FROM REPRESSION: REMEMBERING THE TRAUMA

As you learn to focus on your body's senses, it's inevitable that certain physical sensations and emotions will appear both during and after the exercises. These recurrent feelings are related to sensory memories from your childhood and may be specifically related to your abuse. A particularly dramatic example occurred when one of my patients, Joanna, experienced repeated pain on the left side of her face and torso. As she focused on this sensory evidence during a closed-eye exercise, she was able to spontaneously recall a particularly severe beating where she had been hit several times with a cane on the left side of her body. Although she had not mentally remembered the incident, her body remembered it.

These types of clues become increasingly evident as you pay attention to your body's sensations and to your feelings. These sensory memories may trigger visual and auditory recall as well. You may see in your mind things that remind you of the abuse; perhaps you will remember things that were said to you. As you focus on these feelings and sensations, you will remember more and more of your childhood trauma.

If you remember the abuse but have repressed the emotions associated with it, then you will gradually start to feel the anger, pain, and sadness that have been buried for so long. If you do not remember the abuse or have only sketchy or vague impressions of it, then you will start to remember specific incidents and the feelings associated with them.

Tina recalled how her mother's live-in boyfriend would constantly tease her about her weight, her smile, her clothes—anything. She described this experience unemotionally, as if she were just reporting the facts. During a closed-eye exercise, she became aware of a lump in her throat and a knot in her stomach. An image flashed into her mind of a time when she was twelve and this man saw her in a bathing suit. He kept teasing her and calling her "skinny" and "Twiggy." At that time she had wanted to cry and scream at him. As Tina more fully recalled the incident, her crying turned to deep, deep sobbing.

Whether or not you have any conscious recollection of the abuse you suffered, try the following exercise at least twice after you have gone through the exercises in Step One.

Exercise: Focus your memory.

Find a comfortable place to sit, lean back, and close your eyes. Take five slow, deep breaths, letting yourself relax a little more each time you exhale. Next, take your mind slowly back to your childhood. Imagine yourself getting younger and smaller with each breath you exhale. Let your attention wander to whatever memories arise spontaneously, then notice how old you are at this memory. You may recall happy memories or sad ones. Do your best not to censor any of these images, but simply notice them as they occur. Be aware of any accompanying physical sensations.

Now, choose a particular memory, whether it is fuzzy or clear, and bring that memory to your full attention. As you focus on the image, be aware of any sounds associated with it. Listen closely to the sounds around you at that time and the sounds of your thoughts. Now, notice especially any physical sensations associated with this image and these sounds. Be aware of any areas of tension in your body. Be aware of any other internal sensations, such as warmth, coldness, or numbness. Next, become aware of any emotions associated with this memory. Simply let these feelings come. Do not be alarmed by them. By acknowledging your feelings, you can finally release them. Let yourself go as far as you are willing to with your feelings. It has been a long time since you let yourself feel the hurt and the anger you repressed, so let it go.

Journal:

Record your experience of this exercise each time you do it. A sample entry from Ken's journal:

November 23: "I went back to a time when I was eight years old that I had forgotten all about. Some kids at school had been teasing me and calling me names, and after school they caught up with me. They pushed me around and hit me a couple of times, but I refused to fight them. I went home, and when my dad asked me what had happened and I told him, he said he was ashamed of me and called me a sissy. That bastard! He was always making fun of me. I went to my room and cried and cried, but I had to do it without making noise because I didn't want my dad to hear me. When I did the exercise, I didn't worry so much about making noise when I cried. It felt so good, but even then I could hear his voice faintly, taunting me."

Many of my clients ask if it's necessary to remember everything. The answer is an unequivocal no. It's not as important to recall every detail of your past as it is to have some sense of your personal history. You are the best judge. If there are some blank spots in your memory and you feel it's important to remember these details, use whatever tools necessary to uncover them; for example, ask a lot of questions, talk to relatives, pay attention to your dreams.

Danielle was puzzled by gaps in her memory of childhood, especially from ages six through ten. She used the above exercise, talked with her two older sisters about what they recalled, wrote in her journal about what she discovered, talked with her therapist, and finally talked with her mother. She discovered that it had been a generally unpleasant time at home; her mother had been quite depressed and her dad had been drinking a lot. Her mom was not available emotionally, and her dad was verbally abusive with Danielle and her sisters much of the time. Her sisters told Danielle that she had become very withdrawn at that time, to the point where they had been concerned for her. Danielle was relieved to discover this, as it explained a lot of her shyness and tendency to withdraw. As she discovered more about her past, she began to remember specific incidents more spontaneously.

The purpose of remembering the trauma of your abuse is ultimately to bring out your Natural Child. In order to do so, you must lift the lid of repression. As you do this, you will first unbury your Hurting Child, at the same time reassuring your Controlling Child that she will not be discarded. Since protecting your Hurting Child and your Natural Child has been her lifelong purpose, your Controlling Child needs to know that she is still a valuable member of your internal family.

As you awaken these long-repressed memories, your emotional reactions may be rather intense at times. A student named Hazel recalls curling up on her bed as she remembered some of her childhood: "There was such a feeling of emptiness and loneliness inside. I have been depressed for many, many years, and I think part of the reason is that I never allowed myself to feel anything *but* depressed. When I let myself feel angry at my mother, then I started feeling the hurt at her having treated me like her rag doll. I pounded and pounded and pounded the bed, then crawled up on it in a fetal position. It was painful, but it broke the depression."

You may need to get some support during these emotional times from a therapist or a good friend. If you do not create a supportive environment where you feel encouraged to experience your feelings, you will only maintain the repression and splitting. To the same degree that you let yourself feel pain and sorrow, you can experience increasing depths of joy, love, and happiness.

The emotions that you experience as you become aware and remember your childhood trauma are the consequence of feeling the loss of your childhood. This loss must be grieved before you can let your feelings go, which leads us to our third step.

GRIEVING THE LOSS OF YOUR CHILDHOOD

When you buried your Hurting Child and your Natural Child, you lost an important part of you and a big chunk of your childhood. Though it was a profound loss, you could hardly let yourself feel it at the time: Any emotional honesty would have only invited further abandonment or abuse. As a result of your frequent repression of normal childhood reactions, your emotions became very flat. You may even have developed chronic depression as a result.

As you remember traumatic incidents in your childhood, you may not only relive the associated emotions, you may also begin to face the loss of your childhood. As you feel the loss, you will go through distinct stages similar to the stages of grieving Elisabeth Kübler-Ross describes in *On Death and Dying*. These four stages—Denial, Anger, Sadness, and Acceptance—are commonly experienced by any person dealing with loss.

This grieving process will occur throughout your recovery and will overlap with other steps. You won't necessarily move through each of the stages in a direct, linear manner. Your own unique pattern of grieving may take you to one stage for a while, skip the next, then send you back to a prior stage. Everyone's grieving process is different, so don't hold yourself to any rigid formula. It may take you anywhere from one to three years to complete the majority of your griefwork, but do not let this discourage you—you won't be suffering and miserable throughout. There will be plateaus of acceptance and integration throughout this process.

Breaking Through Denial

In denial, you repress the reality of what has occurred. You continue keeping secrets, pretending you are unaffected by your past and minimizing the effects of your childhood abuse. Denial is so powerful and so familiar to you that you may have been stuck at this stage for years. You may be completely unaware that you've been strongly affected by the abuse, or that you have in fact experienced any loss.

Howard came to see me with complaints about depression and troubles with his girlfriend. When the subject of his childhood came up, he recalled being raised solely by his mother, since his father had left when he was only two years old. He indicated only positive memories about his mother. It was not until well into the fourth month of therapy that Howard admitted that his mother had yelled at him and physically beaten him regularly. He hadn't mentioned it before, he said, because he considered it "no big deal." He figured that everyone had been treated that way when they were young. It was only when he recounted stories of his abuse that he became aware of his anger and sorrow.

It may be rather frightening for you to lift the veil of denial. The scariest part of moving through this stage is experiencing the intense feelings that are lurking just below denial's surface, feelings that can seem utterly overwhelming.

The following exercise will help you explore areas in which you may have denied your feelings.

Exercise: Remember specific incidents.

At the top of one page in your journal, write: "I wish my mom hadn't. . . ." Then write the numbers 1 to 10 on the lefthand side of the page. Next, complete the sentence by writing out at least 10 different things you remember your mom doing *to you* that you didn't like. For example, "I wish my mom hadn't yelled at me in front of my teacher at the school open house." "I wish my mom hadn't burned my fingers to punish me for playing with matches." "I wish my mom hadn't left me alone with my dad."

On another sheet of paper, write at the top, "I wish my dad hadn't . . ." and number from 1 to 10. Once again, complete this sentence 10 different ways. For example: "I wish my dad hadn't put me in the closet that night for fighting with my sister." "I wish my dad hadn't climbed into bed with me that night." "I wish my dad hadn't beat us the night we left our bikes outside."

Journal:

This exercise may stir up some feelings related to the incidents recalled. Write in your journal anything that you became aware of while doing this exercise, including your physical sensations, memories, and feelings. A sample entry from Sara's journal:

June 17: "With my mom, it was fairly easy. I thought of a few things that she'd done that I wish she hadn't, like putting up with my dad all those years, and crying every time I tried to talk with her. I didn't feel any particularly strong feelings. But with my dad it was different. I was more intimidated by putting things down that I wished he hadn't done. Actually, I wish he hadn't existed. I still hate him for what he did to my sister and then tried to do to me."

Once you recognize the fact that you have been in denial about a particular fact, you will no longer be in denial.

Acknowledging and Releasing Anger

When denial no longer works, anger often emerges. When you face up to how cruelly you were cheated out of your childhood, you will feel angry.

You may have a great deal of difficulty doing this. You associate anger with abuse because when your parents were angry, they abused you physically or emotionally. You may be afraid of losing control and behaving just like your parents did.

Maureen describes how she learned to associate anger with violence: "That's all I've known. Either things were quiet or they exploded into fighting. Everybody tiptoed around my father, because we were all afraid that if he got upset, he'd go into one of his rampages. I see today how I am still dreadfully afraid of anger—my own or anyone else's. I still sort of tiptoe around."

Another reason you have denied your anger is that since childhood you have believed that the abuse was all your fault. Since you believed you were the "bad" one, how could you justify being angry with someone who was not only bigger than you, but whom you saw as being "good" and "right"? If you got angry at all, it was at yourself. Your anger turned inward served to punish you for being "bad." This then led you to feel guilty and depressed.

Martha recalls how she used to deal with her anger: "When I was little I used to pound my head with the side of my fist if I thought I had been bad. And I heard that from my mom often enough. Nowadays I don't use a fist. I use words to beat up on myself!"

There are two important things to consider about your anger as it surfaces: First, *feeling* angry doesn't mean you have to *do* anything with it—you don't have to act it out or abuse someone. Feeling angry simply means you feel angry. Second, simply stating out loud, "I am angry," may help you acknowledge and release the anger. Hitting something soft and inanimate, like a pillow, as you say it may help achieve the release.

Exercise: Acknowledge and release your anger.

Go back to your "I wish my mom/dad hadn't . . ." lists. Pick one item, close your eyes, and think back to that scene. For instance, "I wish Mom hadn't yelled at me in front of my teacher at the school open house." Picture that scene, but picture it as if you were an adult witnessing the abuse of this helpless, vulnerable child. As that adult, pay attention to your body senses. Where do you feel your tension? A tight stomach, grinding jaws, a clenched fist, and a furrowed brow all suggest anger. Notice whatever you feel. If you do feel angry and you must let it out, you can do so by kneeling at the edge of the bed and hitting the mattress as you shout, "I'm angry!" Repeat this exercise once a week for four weeks, using two different items from your lists each time.

Journal:

Record your experience of this exercise each time you do it. Whatever happened for you is fine. You may or may not have felt angry. Perhaps you noticed some physical tension in your body in specific areas, or perhaps you mostly felt afraid. Those reactions, as well as anger, suggest you are paying attention to your body and becoming aware. A sample entry from Chris's journal:

April 16: "When I closed my eyes, I could see this little girl and her mom going through the classroom. I could tell the little girl was really excited about showing her mom some of her pictures. Her mom started talking to another mom, and the little girl came up and tugged on her mom's coat and tried to get her mom's attention. That's when the little girl's mom turned and yelled at her, telling her she was always such a pest. I'm watching this and can actually feel myself getting angry at the mom, and feel so sorry for the little girl. When I look at the mom, I want to walk up to her and tell her to lighten up with the kid!"

The whole point of moving past denial and learning to acknowledge your anger is to release it. If you stay in denial, you stay stuck with feeling angry and either turn it back on yourself or act it out on others randomly and unconsciously, unaware of any connection with the past. By recognizing your angry feelings and releasing them, you also begin to feel hurt and sadness. This paves the way for releasing your sorrow and accepting the loss.

Releasing Your Hurting Child's Sadness

Once you have allowed your anger to surface, just below it you will discern hurt and sadness. This is the reawakening of your Hurting Child. As you fully appreciate the fact that you have missed out on most of your childhood, you will begin feeling compassion for your scared and lonely Hurting Child. With compassion comes an awareness of the deep sorrow that this aspect of your Inner Child has had to carry throughout the years.

Craig describes how he used to fear his sadness: "I could get angry pretty easily, but I thought it was a waste of time to feel sad or to cry. I would think I was feeling sorry for myself. Well, one time I was yelling at my little boy when I really *saw* the look on his face, and I could see myself reflected in him! I really crumbled! I went to him and held him for the longest time, and we both sobbed and cried together. I felt sorry for him and what I had done to him, but just as importantly I felt sorry for myself, and it was okay!"

When you truly feel your sorrow, you permit the release of your Hurting Child's agony. By doing so, you also begin to free yourself from the anger and blame. The lost child inside you will cry out for comfort and relief, feeling deeply the pain of betrayal and isolation yet not knowing where to turn or what to do. You may indeed feel lost. You may need to withdraw from time to time in your sorrow. It's as if you are truly mourning a death—the death of your missing childhood.

Once she began to let herself feel angry, Erin, one of my patients, for the first time began to feel truly sorry for her Hurting Child: "It seems like the dam has burst. I've never cried so much in my life. I'll look at a little kid with his mom, and his mom will be loving him or doing something with him in a very caring way, and I start crying. I keep flashing on how my mom never used to do that with me. She was so cold. I haven't felt much like being around other people. Oh, I go to the bank and do my work, and I don't think anybody really notices, but when I come home I just want to be alone and usually end up writing in my journal and crying. Sometimes it's scary, but I have a real faith that this is good for me."

Exercise: Focus on the hurt.

Look back again to your "I wish my mom/dad hadn't . . ." lists. Choose one item, preferably the same one you first focused on when you worked with your anger. Close your eyes and bring the scene into focus, once again from the perspective of a compassionate adult watching someone else treating a child that way. Notice your feelings. Are you aware of any tension in your body? Anger? Sorrow? Now, shift the perspective by becoming that little child. Be aware of your feelings. Particularly let yourself feel your hurt and sorrow. Let yourself cry if tears come. Tears are one of nature's provisions for us to release our emotions.

Choose two items from the list and do this exercise once a week for four weeks. If you find that anger automatically leads you to feeling sadness, you can combine the two exercises, though it will still be helpful to focus on the sadness by itself.

Journal:

Record your experience each time you do this exercise. A sample from Chris's journal:

May 6: "Well, this gets more interesting. When I did the initial exercise on anger as an adult watching a mom in the classroom yell at her little girl, who was really me, I could really feel my anger toward the mom and felt sorry for the little girl. When I focused in on the little girl, I could *really* feel sorry for her. But when I switched to becoming the little girl, I felt numb and started getting distracted. So I stayed with it, and I could see the classroom and my mom, and then I could hear her yelling at me. I felt so humiliated and embarrassed and hurt. That's when I could feel my heart ache. My eyes puddled up slowly, and the trickle turned into a flood. It was like I was seven years old again!"

Because you are feeling so vulnerable and open at this point in your mourning process, support from others is invaluable. Support will help you to break down the intense feelings of isolation you may experience during this stage. You will find that you are not the only one who has experienced this kind of disappointment and hurt.

Sadness provides you with a release from your feelings of loss, so let the tears come. As you let yourself experience sadness, what normally follows is a time of clarity and peacefulness, a period of acceptance.

Freeing Yourself by Acceptance

Reaching acceptance is somewhat like finding a clearing in the jungle after you have been hacking away at a dense thicket of denial, anger, and sadness. Although I describe acceptance as the final stage, it is perhaps more helpful to view it as a resting point in the overall grieving process. Remember, grieving is a *process,* and the different stages will occur at different times. Acceptance, even more than the other stages, may be one that you will visit many times on the road to recovery.

As you mourn, you'll find that each time you reach this stage, your perspective on life will be lighter and clearer. It's as if you are shedding excess baggage each time you let yourself go through your grief about the loss of your childhood. Although the memories of your abusive past will always be there, they will have less and less influence on your present feelings and behavior. When you fully indulge in your griefwork, it will get a little bit easier to more completely accept the loss of your childhood. Thus, you will little by little free yourself to be more fully alive, to be more fully present in the here and now, to let your Natural Child come forth.

This feeling of being more alive has enhanced Sandy's life. "Even though I've been crying a lot lately," Sandy says, "I haven't felt as depressed as usual. Even though it's been painful at times, it's felt good to get all this stuff off my chest, because I feel lighter somehow. Why, the other day at a picnic, somebody asked me to play volleyball, and I did! That was unusual for me, but I liked it."

Exercise. Affirm the feelings of acceptance.

Consider for a few moments times in your life when you felt at peace, when you accepted life exactly the way it was and felt very present. Perhaps it was watching a sunset, or playing with your child, or painting a picture. Perhaps by this point you have allowed yourself to grieve and have felt the peacefulness and acceptance that often follow a good cry. As you think of these times, what happens with your body? How do you feel? Do you feel more relaxed just thinking of these things? How typical is this feeling?

Do this exercise at least once a week for the next six weeks, and as frequently as you wish after that. This exercise may coincide with others on griefwork.

Journal:

Write about any other thoughts or feelings you may have about acceptance or any other aspect of the grieving process. For example, here's an entry I made in my journal one night:

December 8: "I had come home after my daughter was already asleep and went in to say good night to her. I leaned down and gave her a good-night kiss on her forehead. She woke up and said sleepily, "Hi, Daddy." It warmed my heart. I don't remember my mother or father ever doing that. My eyes filled, not with tears of sadness, but tears of joy. I felt such a strong sense that everything about life was just fine and that all was well. I cherish those moments."

The more you practice these exercises, the easier it will become to accept your emotions, both positive and negative, as they become apparent. As you do, it will become easier to grieve the loss of your childhood, leading you to the next step in the healing program: learning to let go.

LETTING GO OF THE PAST: FORGIVING YOUR PARENTS

It's been said that "to understand is to forgive." You are not ready to understand until you have acknowledged your true feelings. Once you have let yourself feel the repressed anger and hurt toward your parents, you have set the stage for compassion. When you can begin to truly understand your parents and why they did what they did to you, you can forgive them. Most likely they suffered from abuse when they were children and were simply passing along what they had learned about how to treat children.

One of my patients, Carol, balked at the idea of forgiving her father. "I think I understand why he did what he did," she proclaimed. "I know his mother beat him a lot when he was growing up. I'm just not sure I'm ready to forgive him for it. I don't feel as angry anymore. I almost have to really try hard to get angry." We can sense the budding compassion in Carol's description, yet also sense her unwillingness at this point to let go mentally of her grudge.

If you are ready to work with letting go mentally of your past through forgiveness, do the following closed-eye exercise, which I often use in seminars and with patients.

Exercise: The circle of forgiveness.

Sit in a comfortable spot, close your eyes, and breathe deeply and slowly for six breaths, letting yourself relax each time you exhale. In your mind, take yourself to a meadow. Look around and see the grass in the meadow, the trees, the blue sky. Feel the slight breeze on your skin. The temperature is just right. Hear the sounds of the gentle breeze as it blows through the grass and trees.

Now, notice in the distance several figures coming slowly toward you. You feel relaxed and comfortable as they approach, secure in the knowledge that you are safe and no harm can come to you. As these people come near, you recognize them as familiar faces. These are people from your past or present against whom you hold some anger, resentment, or hurt. These are people you are ready to forgive. As they approach, they automatically form a semicircle around you, each one approximately 10 feet away. Now, go up to the person at one end of the semicircle, stand in front of him about three feet away, and look him in the eyes. You feel safe and protected as you do so. As you look this person in the eyes, say out loud to him, "(Person's name), I now forgive you for hurting me. I now release you completely. You have no power over me. Go your own way and be happy." Be aware of any emotions that are aroused as a result of this, and simply let yourself go through them.

Now, move to the next person, look him in the eyes, and repeat the process. Move around the circle, stopping at each person consecutively, and repeat this statement of forgiveness for each one. Powerful emotions may be aroused, which signal that you are truly releasing the past.

Once you have finished, say goodbye and watch as the figures move away. After a few moments, observe some other figures approach from the distance. Still feeling quite safe and protected, you notice that these are people from your past whom you feel *you* have hurt, and who may still carry with them hurt, anger, or resentment toward you. You need not include anybody in your semicircle whom you are not ready to face.

As before, these people form a semicircle around you. This time, however, one person at a time approaches you. The first person walks up to you and stops about three feet away, looks lovingly into your eyes, and says, "(Your name), I now forgive you for hurting me. I now release you completely. Go your own way and be happy." Once again, notice how you feel. Repeat this process with each person around you. Take your time with each one. When you have finished with everyone, say goodbye and observe any emotions as they depart.

Bring your awareness gradually back into the room you are in. Whenever you are ready, open your eyes. Repeat this exercise as often as needed.

Journal:

Record your observations of this exercise. Whatever your experience, it is exactly right for you at this time. Do not force yourself to forgive if you are not ready. A sample journal entry from *Kimberly:*

June 23: "Lots of Kleenex for this one. I was really surprised at my reaction with my father and mother. With my dad it was relatively easy, since I've worked a lot already on forgiving him. Where I was surprised was with my mom. I couldn't look her in the eyes to forgive her. I felt guilty and ashamed. When it got around to her forgiving me, the dam burst. I so much want her to forgive me, but I don't even think she's really still upset or angry or resentful anymore. I think it's just my own guilt, and I guess it's really up to me to forgive myself. That sounds kind of trite even as I write it, but it's really true."

Alice Miller writes elegantly about true forgiveness in *For Your Own Good: Hidden Cruelty in Child-Rearing and the Roots of Violence:*

> Genuine forgiveness does not deny anger but faces it head-on. If I can feel outrage at the injustice I have suffered, can recognize my persecution as such, and can acknowledge and hate my persecutor for what he or she has done, only then will the way to forgiveness be open to me. Only if the history of abuse in earliest childhood can be uncovered will the repressed anger, rage, and hatred cease to be perpetuated. Instead, they will be transformed into sorrow and pain at the fact that things had to be that way. As a result of this pain, they will give way to the genuine understanding of an adult who now has gained insight into his or her parents' childhood and finally, liberated from his own hatred, can experience genuine, mature sympathy. Such forgiveness cannot be coerced by rules and commandments; it is experienced as a form of grace and appears spontaneously when a repressed (because forbidden) hatred no longer poisons the soul. The sun does not need to be told to shine. When the clouds part, it simply shines. But it would be a mistake to say that the clouds are not in the way if they are indeed there.

> If an adult has been fortunate enough to get back to the sources of the specific injustice he suffered in his childhood and experience it on a conscious level, then in time he will realize on his own—preferably with-

out the aid of any pedagogical or religious exhortations—that in most cases his parents did not torment or abuse him for their own pleasure or out of sheer strength and vitality, but because they could not help it, since they were once victims themselves and thus believed in traditional methods of child-rearing.

Whether or not you ever completely forgive your parents, as you will see, you can give yourself the gift of your own set of internal "good parents."

REPARENTING YOURSELF

As a child, you decided that you were bad, based on the logic that your parents would not have treated you as they did if you were good. Although you could not have acknowledged it when you were a child and may still have difficulty doing so today, you carry inside you the internalized parental images of an abusive and depriving "bad mother" and "bad father," based on the parenting you received. These are the parental images to whom your Hurting Child readily relates.

Whenever you mentally beat yourself up, or do not take good care of your needs, your internalized bad mother or bad father is operating. You can sometimes hear the "voice" of this internal parent in your self-talk, identified by its disrespectful and abusive language and tone. For instance, a while back I thought I had been insulted when I hadn't been. When I found out the truth, I said to myself, "Boy, am I stupid!" repeatedly for several minutes. At first I was puzzled, but then I realized this was a message I had gotten from my father long ago. This was a "bad father" message. Not that my father was bad, but I still carried within me all his abusive messages.

As long as these are the only internal parental images known to your Inner Child, your Hurting Child will continue to think of herself as "bad," your Controlling Child will see the need to take care of you, and your Natural Child will stay buried. This is why it's necessary to reparent your Inner Child.

Unless you had some positive experiences during childhood with significant adults to whom you could turn, you are missing an internalized mental symbol of a more protective and loving mother and father. If you did admire certain adults while growing up, these have come to internally represent Good Mother or Good Father. You can now turn to them as an adult. You can turn to your Good Mother image for comfort, care, unconditional love and acceptance, and nurturing—all the things a good mother would provide. She would love you no matter what you did. You can turn to your Good Father image for guidance, protection, setting boundaries, and encouragement—all the things you imagine a good father would provide.

In recalling his childhood, Roy remembers his grandmother: "Grandma was always around, thank God! She was much softer and more loving than my real mom. She was in so many ways more of a mother than my own mother. I remember being upset one time—I must have been about seven—because my goldfish had died. I told my mother, and she was really cold. She said something about flushing it down the toilet, which horrified me. My grandma was there, and she came in and suggested we do a funeral, which meant a lot to me. It seemed she was much more understanding and patient." Rob's grandmother became a Good Mother representation for him, and he still refers to her memory when he feels the need for some comfort and nurturing.

You are reparenting yourself as you establish these internal symbolic representations of Good Mother and Good Father. For one of the final steps in your healing, the task is to create an internal family of father-mother-child, with the internal parents in control and continuously available and the Inner Child feeling safe, protected, and loved—free to be a child. As you develop an image of a steadier, more consistent quality of love and guidance, it makes it much safer for your Hurting Child to experience the intensity of its feelings. It also makes it far easier for your Controlling Child to surrender control, because there is someone else to take the reins. And, of course, your Natural Child can be much more freely expressive and creative, because the Good Mother/Father is available to surround it with love and protection.

There are three phases in reparenting yourself: first, you must release your original parents; second, create new internal parents; and third, adopt your Inner Child.

Releasing Your Original Parents

Your mother and father really did the best they knew how, considering the resources they had. Undoubtedly they grew up with abuse as a way of life and did not even think of what they received and what they gave to you as abusive. You may never feel sorry for them; you may never even like them. But you can empathize with them.

Releasing your parents, specifically releasing their hold over you as an Adult Child, is a gradual process. It starts with recognizing them as products of their own fragmented, injurious childhoods. It requires you to be consistently focused on your own healing process and to literally not "need" anything from them.

There are two things you can do to release your original parents. The first is to practice The Circle of Forgiveness exercise in Letting Go of the Past, the preceding step in this healing program. Repeat this exercise periodically, particularly when you notice yourself feeling hurt, angry, or resentful. Remember, it's these emotions that usually precede any true forgiveness or letting go of the past.

The second thing you can do is to talk with your parents, whether alive or not (see exercises that follow). To make this effective, you must begin to view yourself, not as their "child," but as their adult son or daughter. Like most parents, they may not think of you as a grown-up, so you have to let them know you are by talking to them like a grown-up who totally respects himself. As you think of yourself in this way, your perspective on your parents will begin to shift.

The first of these two exercises in releasing your original parents is designed mainly to help you focus on your feelings as an adult son or daughter. You may do this exercise even if your parents are deceased.

Exercise: Write a letter to your mother or father.

Do not write one letter for both; write to them separately. Do not censor your letter. Write about the abuse, about your childhood, about questions you have always wanted to ask. Let them know how you feel and who you are. Tell them how you have been affected by the abuse. It's important not to minimize or downplay your feelings. The writing is for your benefit, not theirs.

When you have finished, put the letter in an envelope, address it, and put a postage stamp on it. Set it aside for a day or two while you decide whether to mail it. If, after waiting, you are ready for your parent to read what you have written, then mail it. The decision is up to you. The primary value for you in writing the letter is to identify and clarify your honest feelings and thoughts with regard to your parents, with the opportunity available for sharing them with the appropriate parent.

Do this exercise at least once, then repeat it every four to six months as your healing and recovery progresses.

Journal:

There should not be any rough drafts of this type of letter since it's best done spontaneously and uncorrected, but you may want to make a copy for your journal. Also, record any observations about your experience of writing the letter. A sample entry after Jack wrote a letter to his father:

September 8: "He's such a man of steel, I doubt if what I said in the letter would touch him at all, but I went ahead and sent it anyway. He may not even let me know he got it. I sent him a Father's Day card once, and in it I wrote the words 'I love you' for the first time, along with some very sincere thank you's. He never said a word. Of course, neither did I. I'm determined this time to ask him if he got my letter. That makes me nervous just thinking about it, but I just have to do it. He won't be around that much longer, and I need to mend some fences with him."

Exercise: Talk with your parents.

In the past you have still unconsciously thought of yourself as their child and have related to them through your Controlling Child. Now you can consider yourself an adult son or daughter and view them through the eyes of an adult. The first few times you try this exercise, do not feel compelled to say anything. You may simply observe how you relate to them through your Controlling Child's role. When you are ready to talk with them, you need not think of it as a confrontation. Intense feelings may be felt and expressed, but it need not be done abusively on your part. Ask them about themselves, about your childhood. Tell them how you have been affected by the abuse. If you feel angry, hurt, or afraid, let them know. Let them know who you are at any given moment by stating honestly how you feel and what you think.

The main thing to keep in mind when you are talking to your parents is *do not expect anything from them.* If you expect them to change, you are bound to be disappointed. If you expect them to agree, you are in trouble. If you expect them to admit to the abuse, you may end up even more hurt and angry. They *may* change, but do not make that your goal. You should talk to them with the objective of simply letting your presence as a human being and as an adult son or daughter be known. Do this exercise with the premise that you will not change your parents. Talk with them as frequently as needed to further your own healing program. If your parents are deceased, do this as a closed-eye, imaginary process.

Journal:

Whether or not you talk more openly and honestly with your parents, for the next six weeks record your observations each time you are with them. You may notice how closely guarded you ordinarily keep your Natural Child and Hurting Child when you are in their presence. A sample entry from Dawn, who talked with her father about the incest that occurred when she was between the ages nine and twelve:

August 27: "I was surprised by his reaction, because he admitted he was wrong and that he shouldn't have done what he did. My reaction was really curious. I was pleased, but at the same time, I think I expected more of a fight or a fuss or something, because I was sure nervous going into it. He confessed, and we talked, and that was it. I have been making it such a big deal all these years by keeping my feelings about it hidden, I think because I felt guilty. To finally talk about it was surprisingly quiet and calm. I do feel some relief, though, like I don't have to carry it anymore."

Creating New Internal Parents

If you have someone from your past you can call on to represent your Good Mother and Good Father images, you are one step ahead in the process of creating new internal parents. If you do not, then you can find someone in your world to model these images after, or you can make up your own image. This exercise will help you establish new internal parents for your Inner Child.

Exercise: Form good parent images.

For your Good Mother image, think of someone you know or have known in the past, or someone you have heard or read about. This person possesses the qualities of mothering that you did not experience consistently from your actual mother: nurturing, protectiveness, softness. She is someone who listens to you and helps you express your feelings, someone whose touch is affectionate and whose mannerisms are gentle and caring. List all the women in your past or present who seem to have the qualities that you were missing from your mother.

What are some other qualities and characteristics that you wish your mother had? Forgiveness? Honesty? Sensitivity? Sensuality? Take out a sheet of paper and finish the following sentence: "A 'good mother' is . . ." in as many different ways as come to mind. Take your time and try to visualize your Good Mother image, hear the sound of her voice, and be aware of how you feel as you imagine her. She will likely be a composite of several people you have known, or she may primarily take on one person's features. Either way, when you finish your list of qualities, close your eyes for a few moments and let yourself be completely immersed in this Good Mother image. Don't worry if you don't fix on one particular image. The important point is to focus on good mother characteristics.

Next, think of someone from your past or present who represents the qualities of fathering that you would like to have gotten from your father but didn't—qualities such as steadiness, protectiveness, caring, and encouragement. Make a list of men you have known who seem to express the qualities that were missing from your father.

Take out another sheet of paper and complete the sentence, "A 'good father' is . . ." in as many different ways as possible with whatever comes to mind. Like the Good Mother image, choose or create someone for your Good Father. Perhaps you've always yearned for someone who showed interest in you, who was supportive of your accomplishments and was clear about his boundaries. Now you can have him. Close your eyes for a few moments after you complete your list and picture your composite Good Father in as much detail as possible, hear his voice, and notice how you feel as you imagine him nearby.

Next, take the lists of the men and women who represent the qualities of Good Mother/Father and post them where you will see them each day. Once each day for the next three weeks, study this list and bring to mind each of these men and women and the qualities they represent. Next to the list of people, post your list of the good parent qualities you have thought of. Study these attributes for a few moments immediately following your contemplation of the people. Close your eyes for a few moments and bring to mind a composite picture of Good Mother. Then do the same with a composite Good Father. The more consistently you do this, the more quickly you will internalize these images and thereby give your Inner Child greater protection.

Journal:

Write your observations throughout the process of creating your Good Mother/Father. A sample entry from Lucy's observations about her new Good Mother:

May 3: "She is soft, kind, and trustworthy. I can talk to her about anything. She has dark hair and a long, slender frame and laughs easily. She is a combination of an aunt I was once close to and a few other women I have known. I know I've made her up, but she's real to me, and I'm looking forward to talking with her more and more. I've already told her about one dumb mistake I made with my boyfriend, and she reminded me that it was perfectly okay for me to make mistakes, and that in spite of mistakes, I can still love myself."

Adopting Your Inner Child

Now that you have an internal image of your good parents, you will be able to help your healing by adopting your Inner Child. For the following exercise, choose either your Good Mother or Good Father image with which to work. We will use the term "Good Mother," but you can do this with either.

Find a comfortable, relaxed setting. Read through the exercise once or twice to familiarize yourself with it. If it seems helpful, tape the exercise and play it back as you do it.

Exercise: Call on your Good Mother.

Be aware of the steadiness of your breathing. Breathe deeply and slowly. Count your breaths from 1 to 4, stating the number silently each time you inhale. When you reach 4, start counting from 1 again. Do this several times, until you feel reasonably relaxed. Now, take yourself back to a time when you were younger and smaller, smaller and younger. When a clear image comes to mind, see if you can determine how old you are. Notice the details of the surrounding area, shapes, colors, textures. Does this look familiar to you in some way, or entirely new and different? Be aware of any sounds around you. Especially be aware of anything you are feeling at this time. Are you frightened? Hurting? Do you feel the need for comfort? Allow whatever feelings are there to simply be there, and let yourself feel them completely and fully. Once again, notice how old you are. Now, observe as you sense a presence in the room with you. You feel very safe and relaxed, and soon you notice the presence of your Good Mother.

Observe as your Good Mother approaches you, the child, and gently takes you in her arms. She sits down with you, holds you firmly yet gently, and begins to rock slowly and softly, humming a sweet melody as you relax comfortably in her arms, taking in all the love and care. Hear the soothing sound of her voice, nestled in the fold of her bosom, feeling very safe, warm, and protected.

Now, you become the mother. Feel the tiny body you hold in your arms. Feel the child's vulnerability and warmth, and notice how absolutely calm and relaxed she is with you. Caress her, love her, and protect her, for she is a tender, impressionable young child, needing your care and comfort.

Now, become the child again, and simply let yourself feel the loving surround you at this moment. Now, slowly return your awareness back to the setting you are presently in. Whenever you're ready, open your eyes.

Do this exercise the next day with your Good Father, then repeat the entire process three more times, spaced one week apart.

Journal:

Record this experience, and especially notice any changes in your day-to-day behavior. A sample entry from Patricia's journal:

February 21: "After doing the exercise with Good Mother, I felt so much fuller, yet lighter. Words seem so inadequate for this experience. I recognize now that my mother will never be what I want her to be, but now I can give *myself* that unconditional love and acceptance that I've always longed for. I've been trying to find it elsewhere—in men, at my work, from friends—but now I see how it first has to come from me. I think me and my new mom are going to get along just fabulously!"

With practice, you'll find it easier and easier to call on your internal mother or father to provide your Inner Child with what it needs at the moment.

As your inner parents develop, your Controlling Child will feel safer surrendering control. As your Good Mother and Good Father take an increasingly active part in your internal family, your Natural Child will feel safer making herself known as the most active and prominent of the three inner children. The dynamic interaction of this threesome produces a third internal image: you as your Natural Self. You find greater freedom and spontaneity in your life, compliments of your Natural Child, with an increased sense of peacefulness, protection, and love, compliments of your Good Mother/Father. And there is an increasing sense of integration between these different components, out of which the Natural Self emerges.

As the healing process continues to unfold and you feel increasingly secure in the expression of your Natural Self, in a very real sense you will grow up all over again. This time, however, you will grow up with loving, conscious parenting provided by your internal Good Mother and Good Father. Growing up again is the subject of our next chapter.

6

Growing Up Again

CHAPTER

*D*elores looked at the clock and saw that it was steadily and surely headed toward 8:00 P.M. The dance had already started, but she didn't want to arrive too early for fear of seeming too eager, so she drove around the block one more time. She regretted not having invited a friend to come along, then remembered that she had intentionally decided to do this on her own.

She got out of the car, nervously adjusted her dress and hair, then stood up straight and, with heart pounding, walked to the door. "You can do it!" she thought to herself. "Relax and have fun. You don't have to impress anybody. Just be yourself." With these thoughts she felt more relaxed. Once inside, she scanned the room for familiar faces. She soon found an old acquaintance, walked up to him, smiled, and unabashedly started a conversation. Soon another man, then another woman, joined them. Delores introduced herself and continued with the conversation. Pleased with how she was handling the whole situation, she soon began to relax and really have fun. She danced a few dances, met some interesting people, and even gave her phone number to a man she liked. Leaving the dance, Delores felt buoyant. She was glad she had taken the risk and was already planning her next social outing.

Like Delores, as you heal your Inner Child, you become more prepared to take emotional risks. In order to feel even safer in doing so, it will be helpful to develop some areas that were left untended when you were young. These areas have to do with how to act with other people, how to cultivate greater personal effectiveness. In this particular stage of your recovery, you will in a very real sense be growing up again, but this time with a different set of parents—your own internal good parents.

Childhood should be a time to learn and practice skills for getting along with others. But since you had to grow up fast, you didn't have much chance to learn basic interactive skills. Growing up again means learning as an adult what you didn't have a chance to learn as a child.

There are two ways children learn and practice interaction. First, they learn through play, where they have the opportunity through trial and error to find out what behaviors work best with others. If Johnny repeatedly demands that he and Susie play only the games *he* wants to play, Susie may stop playing with him. As a result, Johnny learns to be less demanding and more compromising.

Second, children learn interactive skills from their parents by imitating them and following their guidance. Children who see their parents relating constructively and peacefully with others, children whose parents provide them with gentle guidance for getting along in the world, are likely to do well.

Sadly, neither of these was your experience. You didn't have the opportunity to learn either by trial and error or by positive role modeling. You may not have played much at all. Because of your seriousness, you may not have had many friends while growing up. You spent much of your energy—and still do—struggling to maintain control over your buried hurt. Your parents themselves were probably less than adequate role models for getting along with others.

In *The Battered Child,* Dr. Ray Helfer describes how this process works:

> Every young adult can look back upon his or her childhood and identify specific incidents, or a whole series of incidents, which didn't "go" very well. We all can recall times when certain skills or tasks were learned poorly and when the modeling was less than it should have been. From learning to hold a golf club or learning to solve a math problem to learning how mothers and fathers interact with each other, the child learns many skills during these very critical years. The more incidents that didn't "go so well" and the more skills that were poorly learned, the more difficult interactions become as an adult, whether it be interaction with a golf ball, a math problem, or a spouse. . . . When childhood hasn't provided this training, an individual becomes poorly trained in many very important skills.

You *can* learn these skills as an adult, with some persistence and patience. It's like swimming: If you learned improper swimming techniques as a child and have used them most of your life, they are well-conditioned, ingrained behaviors. Your swimming methods, although they may save you from drowning, do not allow you to relax and enjoy yourself. Your bad habits will not change overnight, but you can replace them gradually with more effective skills.

In order to grow up again, you need to work on six major areas:

(1) Learning how to act, (2) Learning to play, (3) Acknowledging and expressing feelings, (4) Reaching out and making friends, (5) Setting boundaries, and (6) Learning to touch. This chapter will provide you with specific steps and exercises to help you work on these areas. There are lots of exercises, but the intent is not for you to be overwhelmed. Take each step one at a time and follow the exercises in sequence. You may work with more than one area at the same time, and you may pick and choose the areas most relevant to your needs. Decide which ones are most significant for you. As with the exercises in the previous chapter, recording your experiences in your journal will help you to more fully understand them.

"WHAT DO I DO NOW?": LEARNING HOW TO ACT

You have been searching for something that doesn't exist: For most of your life you've been trying to find out how to act "normal." The truth is there is no such thing as normal behavior. The term "normal" encompasses such a broad range of behavior that the term itself is meaningless.

Dr. Pat Allen, founder of the Want Institute and author of *Pat Allen's Want Training for Effective Relationships,* puts it this way: "Some people think only if you play golf are you normal. If you go to their church, you're normal. If you think the way they think, you're normal. Forget the whole idea of normal—it's a crippling, harmful concept. There are so many ways of living, of being in the world, it's impossible to say what's normal. Just figure that if you're on the outside and they haven't locked you up, you're normal!"

A far more constructive question than "What is normal?" is, "What is functional?" To determine whether something is functional, ask yourself the following: Will it work to get the job done? Will it hurt me? Will it hurt others? Is it practical? Your answers will go a long way toward teaching you what is functional. For instance, suppose you're at a party, you've had too much to drink, and you wonder if you should drive home. Though driving home may work to get the job done, it also poses a great risk of hurting yourself and/or others, and this is dysfunctional.

For more help in deciding what is functional, you can turn to friends, your own instincts, and self-help books.

Ask a Friend

It's important that you cultivate friendships with one or two people you can trust and to whom you can say just about anything. Choose friends who are willing to be honest with you about what they think is wise.

An example: Gina was feeling harassed by her boss. The boss had asked Gina to work late every night the previous week and implied that she'd be very upset if Gina didn't stay. Gina wasn't sure what to do, so she went to her friend Lucille and talked it over. Gina wondered whether she had the right to say no to her boss, whether she was being unduly sensitive to her boss's temperament, and what would happen if she said no. Of course, there were no "normal" answers to these questions, but after discussing it with her friend, Gina decided it would be functional for her to assertively say no to her boss's request and accept the possibility that her boss might get upset. Gina realized that she has a right to say no and to ask that her boss schedule overtime in advance.

To talk with a friend about these kinds of questions means you must admit that you don't know all the answers. This may be particularly hard for you if you are a Perfectionist. Whichever role you're in, to say, "I don't know what to do" takes courage and a willingness to seek help.

I recall talking with my good friend Bruce after my girlfriend and I had broken up. I had continued seeing this ex-girlfriend for a few weeks after we had separated but found it painful to be with her knowing that she was also seeing other men. Bruce not only listened to me compassionately, he also advised me to stop seeing her. It wasn't working, he told me; it wasn't functional in that it wasn't allowing me time to heal.

Asking a friend's advice doesn't mean you have to take the advice. You can be appreciative of the counsel yet not feel obligated to follow it. It must ring true for you if it's to work well. The exercise below will help you feel more comfortable asking a friend for advice.

Exercise: Ask for advice.

The next time you have any doubts about a decision, call up a friend, describe the problem, and ask her what she thinks you should do. Start by asking her opinion on less pressing decisions, such as whether to buy a certain item of clothing or whether to go to a social affair. You can then move on to asking advice about more involved decisions, such as whether to move, whether to buy a new car, whether to have a child.

Notice your feelings before, during, and after the request. Was the advice helpful? Was your decision functional? Perhaps you will become more aware of a broad range of possible choices, all of which can be considered functional. Ask a friend for advice at least three times in the next two weeks.

Journal:

Record your experiences and observations each time you ask for advice. Here is a sample entry from Susan's journal:

December 19: "I called up Toni and asked her whether she thought I should accept the invitation from Greg for New Year's Eve, since he's still kind of new to me. I have asked friends for advice before, but I had never called with that as the main purpose. I could tell Toni was glad I asked, because she gave me all sorts of advice—about Greg, and much more! It wasn't as hard as I thought it would be to do this, and I'm glad I did. I've decided I'm going to take Greg up on his offer!"

Trust Your Instinct

You were trained to deny and to ignore your "gut instinct," the messages of your senses, in early childhood. As part of your recovery, you need to learn to trust these messages once again.

The first step in learning to trust your instinct is to develop a keen awareness of what your senses are telling you. What do you see, hear, and feel? Are these particular areas of tension? The hyperalertness and watchfulness you developed in childhood to help you survive abuse can now be redirected to your internal environment, your sensory experience, to help you make decisions as to how to act.

One of my clients, Mary, is learning to use this kind of information to make decisions: "I went out on a date and the guy started pressing me to have sex. In the past I would have just gone ahead to please him and have him like me. This time, though, I noticed my stomach was all tight. It just didn't feel right. So I told him I'd like to wait, and he started acting really weird—cold, distant, aloof. He told me if I didn't want him, he'd go find someone who did. Then he took off. Am I glad I followed my instincts!"

The sense of something "not feeling right" that Mary describes is her gut instinct. Sometimes we call it our "inner voice," a "hunch," or "intuition." As you learn to quiet down and listen to your senses, your gut instinct will become more and more powerful. Rather than your mind being the primary instigator of your decision on how to act, your senses will be.

Exercise: Learn to listen to yourself.

Think back on the times you've followed your instinct. Maybe there was a time when you didn't take a particular job, or you decided not to date a particular person, or you introduced yourself to a complete stranger, all because your instinct told you to do so. What was the outcome? Now think of times when you didn't listen to what your instinct told you. What were the results of these instances?

For the next two weeks, pay particular attention to your instinct, especially if you have a decision to make. We conjure up many logical reasons that stop us from listening to our instinct. Sometimes we're just afraid to do what our instinct tells us is the functional thing to do. What reasons, thoughts, or fears occur to you in response to what your instinct tells you? What advantages, if any, might result from listening to your instinct?

Journal:

As you consider the above questions and pay attention to your instinct over the next two weeks, record your observations. In his journal, Gene describes listening to his gut instinct while making a major decision:

January 11: "Martha and I had been tossing back and forth whether to buy this particular house. Escrow was just about to close, but the more I thought about it, the less I liked it. Logically, just about everything fit with the house, and at first I really wanted it. But something was telling me that it wasn't going to be right. So I told Martha about my feelings, and she said she had been feeling the same things. I called the real estate agent right then and cancelled the deal. She was a bit upset, but I'm sure that was the right thing to do."

Read All About It

Self-help books and tapes can be immensely useful in giving you advice on what is functional. See the appendix "Suggested Readings".

For instance, one major area of concern for most Adult Children is how to raise emotionally healthy children. One excellent resource is the Gesell Institute's book, *Child Behavior from Birth to Ten,* by Francis Ilg and Louise Bates Ames. By reading this or any other good book on child development, you can base your decision on how to act with your child on reasonable expectations as to what the child is capable of. You will learn for example, that you can expect a three-year-old to have temper tantrums, so it's best not to try to control these. Instead, let them run their course without letting yourself get too upset. (More on this in Chapter 8.)

Exercise: Make a reading list.

Go to a bookstore or library and browse through self-help books. Take your time and read parts of any that attract you. Then, make a list of those you'd like to read. Number the books in the order you would like to read them. Set a goal of reading at least one of these books every three to four weeks—and then do it.

Journal:

Write down any helpful thoughts from these books, or write out your reaction to any material you read. A sample comment from Susan's journal:

September 14: "I started reading the book *Love Is Letting Go of Fear* by Gerald Jampolsky. He says in it that there are really only two emotions, love and fear, and it's up to us to choose which one we want to feel. I like it because it's so simple and straightforward. I'm beginning to see how when I'm angry, it's because underneath the anger I'm really afraid, but it feels safer to feel angry. I can also see how when other people are angry or upset, they are really afraid too. There's some truth to that, because I watched how my boss was huffing and puffing earlier today and I could see how he was really just afraid that this one account wasn't going to come through. When I realized that, I felt a lot of compassion for him rather than fear."

"LET'S HAVE FUN!": LEARNING TO PLAY

Play encourages your Natural Child's full and spontaneous expressiveness and helps your Controlling Child to relax and enjoy. You may be afraid that others will think you silly or childish when you play freely and creatively. Let them think what they may. Let go of your fears—and play! It's not as hard as it perhaps sounds, but it will require you to let go of control.

Letting go of control will be difficult at first. Your Controlling Child will try to inhibit any spontaneity, since she fears that if she lets down its guard, your Natural Child will be unprotected. As your recovery progresses, it will become easier for your Controlling Child to let go.

To learn how to play again, do the following series of exercises in sequence:

Exercise 1: Watch children as they play.

They can be your children, a friend's children, or children at the park. Sit back and spend a few minutes doing nothing but observing exactly how these children play. Drop all your preconceived notions and merely watch. Notice your feelings. What sort of games are they playing? Are some of the children more reserved than others? How do they involve other children in their play? Do any of them play alone? Do these children seem truly happy at play? With which children do you identify most closely? Follow this procedure until you can feel comfortable around children playing. You may wish to observe more than one time.

Journal:

Record your observations each time you observe children playing. A sample entry from Virginia's journal:

July 12: "Melissa and Kim were trying to recruit the younger girls for a game of 'House,' but the other girls weren't having any of it. They were playing on the swing, spinning it round and round to make themselves dizzy. As I watched the children playing, I noticed that I was smiling and feeling very peaceful. I also felt very wistful, but was thinking to myself, 'Virginia, you can't do that. How would it look for a 43-year-old woman to be doing such things?' I must admit, however, that the thought of playing like those children was very enticing."

Exercise 2: Play with toys.

If you have a child, you might start by playing with one of his toys. Choose one that looks intriguing. Spend a few minutes examining it. Do this a few times until you become familiar with the toy. When you're ready, play with it. Observe your internal reactions as you do. Record your feelings in your journal.

If you don't have any children, go out and buy a toy that looks appealing to you. If this seems too preposterous, then spend some time simply looking in a toy store until you feel more at ease. When you have selected a toy, take it home and play with it in privacy. Write down your experience in your journal.

I'm sure you can find a toy you'll enjoy. I have a real fondness for soap bubbles, for example. The shapes and colors always fascinate me, and I can play with them for hours. Perhaps a handball you can play with against the wall sounds appealing. How about a Hula Hoop? I dare you! Start with something that's not too intimidating for you, such as a yo-yo you can play with in private, then progress to more challenging toys. All it takes is some willingness to relax your control for a while. As you do, it gets easier.

Journal:

Record your experience. A sample entry from Ronald's journal:

September 18: "This was a bit of a stretch for me. I was going to skip all this playing with toys, but one day while I was driving around doing some errands, I passed a toy store. I decided to stop and have a look. I figured if anybody asked me, I could say I was shopping for my nephew. I went in and wandered around a bit. I saw a few things that looked interesting but figured I'd never buy them. Then, on the way out I saw some Silly Putty and decided to buy some. Well, I'm glad I did, because as funny as it sounds, I had a great time with it. I even made some transfers from the Sunday comics like I used to."

Exercise 3: Play with children.

Once you have observed children playing and have played on your own, you're ready for the next step: playing with your own children or with a relative's or friend's children. Play with them as if you were their age again. Start out with simple games like pat-a-cake and jump rope, then progress to more involved games like house. As you start feeling more at ease, you can experiment with more spontaneous play. When the children invite you to come into the sandbox and help them make tunnels and cities, go ahead. If they're playing on a Slip'n'Slide, put your bathing suit on and get wet. If they make silly faces at each other, make silly faces at them. Playing with children is a real opportunity for you to be creative and spontaneous. Plan to play with children on at least four different occasions before going on to the next step. In particular, notice how you feel during and after play.

Journal:

Record your experiences of each instance of play. Jackie recorded this entry:

October 4: "When Sheila first asked me to watch her four-year-old while she went to the doctor, I was a bit hesitant but agreed to do so anyway. I'm so glad I did, because we had a great time. I've never really played with a kid before, though I've been a baby-sitter. I stopped worrying about making a mess or leaving things untidy, and became a four-year-old myself. We painted and colored and played with her dolls. After doing this, I'm finding I now try to approach my life a little more often with this attitude of play."

Exercise 4: Play creatively.

Now that you have played with toys on your own and with children, think of other activities that you used to enjoy when you were a child or things you wanted to do when you were a child. These can be games, hobbies, recreational pursuits, or plain fun things to do. Some examples: go to the beach and collect shells, swing on a swing, play hopscotch, roll downhill in the grass, or climb on some rocks.

Take a sheet of paper and list some of the activities you think you might enjoy. Now, set a specific goal to do at least three of the activities on your list in the next four weeks. Be sure to specify a time; for instance, "This Saturday I will go to the beach and hunt shells." Happy hunting!

Journal:

Write out your goals and record your experiences in your journal. Jackie wrote as follows:

October 9: "One of my goals was to climb a tree. While I was walking through the park Saturday, I saw the greatest climbing tree, so I figured, 'Why not?' My boyfriend gave me a boost, and voilà, I was up! It was fun. The hardest part was getting past my inhibitions, my fears of what other people would think. Once I do something like this, I'm fine and it feels good."

Exercise 5: Play with other adults.

Once you have gone through the first four steps, begin to play with other adults. As you learn to play and begin to let go more and more of the rigid control you have over yourself, you'll feel more comfortable around other people and less fearful of looking foolish.

Choose a friend who has genuine affection for his or her Inner Child and lets her out to play often. This will help you feel supported in encouraging your own Natural Child to emerge. To discover the types of activities you can do with this friend (and others), ask yourself, "What kinds of activities have I enjoyed in the past? What activities have I wanted to do? What kinds of classes or recreational activities could I participate in?" Write out your answers in your journal. Set goals for accomplishing them in the next four to six weeks. Then, get going!

Journal:

Write out your goals and your experiences of accomplishing them. Dan described one of his goals:

November 1: "I joined a softball league run by the city. I probably won't know anyone on the team, I haven't played for years, and I'm not even sure I'll like it, but I'm going to try it anyway. The worst that can happen can't be all that bad, and I might even have fun and enjoy myself."

Exercise 6: Play as a way of life.

For the next week, find at least one way each day to be playful. If you work in a sales job, for example, perhaps you can engage a customer in some light banter by making a comment or asking a question. Share an observation about something that struck you as funny. Be willing to smile and to laugh as you talk. If you get a response, continue in the dialogue until you have to move on, then say your thank you's and goodbyes.

If you go for walks, walk because you enjoy it and have fun. You might try stepping on sidewalk cracks, or avoiding every other crack, or skipping along.

As you grow up again, it will become much easier and so much more fun to let go of a "this is serious" approach to life. Life is much too short to be taken too seriously.

Journal:

Each day this week, write about your experiences of playing. Kevin wrote the following:

August 14: "Today I was in the supermarket, and this lady was looking at the watermelons, so I asked her if she knew anything about picking out the ripe ones. She admitted she didn't, so we started talking about 'watermelons we have known' and creative things you can do with the seeds. We got pretty silly for a few minutes. It was a fun conversation—very lighthearted."

"I'VE GOT A FEELING": ACKNOWLEDGING AND EXPRESSING FEELINGS

Another crucial area in growing up again is learning to acknowledge and express your feelings. In *Grown-up Abused Children,* authors James Leehan and Laura Wilson stress the reasons why Adult Children have difficulty expressing any intense feelings:

Many former abuse victims report almost no experience of joy, exhilaration, or even satisfaction.

This behavior is understandable, perhaps even predictable, given that as children these people were often punished for being too exuberant. At best, parents frowned upon and discouraged the excessive activity associated with these children's joy of accomplishment. Even as they grew older and did not express their satisfaction so boisterously, they usually found that achievements were not met with praise or reinforcement, but rather became occasions for ridicule or physical beatings designed to "put them in their place." Two lessons were learned: joy should not be expressed, or even felt; and happiness is followed by pain. The ultimate lesson was that it is best not to be happy or to express or acknowledge any emotion at all.

To learn to acknowledge your feelings, you must pause from time to time and pay attention to what your body is experiencing. Be aware of any areas of tension. Is your heart pounding? Is there any tension in your facial muscles? By practicing paying attention to your emotional state, you will begin to notice sensations and emotions.

In your relearning period you will encounter two powerful myths about feelings that you came to accept as true. It will be necessary to refute these myths again and again.

Myth #1—Some feelings are good and some are bad. Feelings are natural reactions to situations and events we encounter. There are no "good" or "bad" feelings. Feelings simply exist.

Myth #2—Feelings always lead to actions. This is an extremely critical point, since this is what you witnessed in childhood. When your parents felt angry, they struck out physically and/or verbally. When they felt sad, they withdrew completely.

It will take some time to retrain yourself to distinguish between feelings and actions and develop more functional ways to handle your feelings. Be patient with yourself.

Four Basic Feelings

Emotions need not be complicated. There are only four basic feelings: anger, sadness, fear, and happiness. All other feelings are either variations or combinations of these four.

Anger is undoubtedly the most difficult feeling for you to express. You are used to denying your anger because it has meant hurt, violence, and destruction in the past.

It is helpful to recognize that you can feel angry without hurting someone or something. Anger need not be associated with violence. There are two important things to know about anger: First, the fact that you feel angry doesn't mean you're right—it simply means you're angry. Second, just because you're angry at others doesn't mean they have to change their behavior.

Sadness, unlike depression, is a temporary emotional state usually released through crying. I'm reminded of Jane Craig, the character played by Holly Hunter in the movie *Broadcast News.* As a busy television news producer, she still manages to set aside 10 minutes each day to think of sad things and cry!

Fear alerts us to danger and prepares our bodies for a survival response of fight-or-flight. Many of your present-day fears are based on survival responses left over from childhood.

Still, fear can signal when you are in danger. What you have to contend with as you grow up again are the conditioned, reflexive fear reactions that no longer serve a true survival function yet stop you from taking risks and growing.

Happiness is a feeling that your Natural Child certainly knows well, though you may have forgotten how to let yourself feel it. It's a feeling you will be able to experience to a greater degree and greater depth as you learn to allow yourself the full range of emotional experience.

Making Your Feelings Known

In order to accustom yourself to admitting and expressing feelings, do the following exercises in sequence (adapted from "Retraining and Relearning" by Ray Helfer in *The Battered Child*).

Exercise 1: Acknowledge that your feelings are okay.

Everything in your belief system says otherwise, so you must persuade yourself that your feelings *are* okay. "I'm upset, I'm frustrated, I'm angry, I feel good, I like you, I'm sad" are all perfectly acceptable expressions of feeling. Every morning for the next 21 days, say out loud: "I have a right to my feelings. My feelings are real. My feelings are okay." Repeat these three statements 10 times at each sitting, relaxing as you do and letting each idea sink in.

Put these sentences on several three-by-five-inch cards and put the cards in strategic locations throughout your house, in your car, and, if possible, at work. Then read them frequently as reminders. Your purpose is to inundate yourself with another way of thinking about having feelings.

At the end of each day for the next 21 days, sit down with your journal and as you reflect back on your day, write about the different feelings you noticed, such as: "I was angry at Joe for being late." "I felt good when my daughter gave me a hug." "I was pleased with how the project at work went." "I was nervous waiting for my wife to call." It's important that you write down *feelings,* not *actions.* "I yelled at the kids" is an action, whereas "I got angry at the kids" is a feeling statement. After you've written out the feelings, pause, close your eyes, and repeat 10 times: "I have a right to my feelings. My feelings are real. My feelings are okay." After working with this consistently for the next three weeks, you'll notice that you're giving yourself much more permission to have feelings.

Journal:

Write down the feelings you noticed each day and anything else you observe. After working with this first exercise on feelings for two weeks, Bonnie observed:

May 30: "It's beginning to sink in—I do have a right to my feelings. The other day some neighbor kids were teasing my little dog, and I felt very irritated. I even said something to them, and I really sounded angry. In the past I would have politely asked them not to tease the dog, in hopes that they would get the message. I think my anger got through much more quickly."

Exercise 2: Name your feelings.

Identify what you are feeling, put a name to it, then express it either verbally or nonverbally. Use the guidelines above for the four basic feelings. Listen to what your senses are telling you. If your brow is furrowed, your stomach and your shoulders are tight, and your teeth are clenched, you're feeling either angry or scared. If your shoulders are slumped down, your mouth is drawn, you're moving slowly and deliberately, and your concentration is poor, you're probably feeling sad. If you're not sure what to label a particular feeling, take a chance and see if the label fits.

Next, begin to express your feelings to others. This will feel scary, but it is a critical step in learning to feel relaxed with your feelings. The more you practice naming and expressing your feelings, the easier it becomes. When you're pleased with something your mate does, tell him; for example, "I like it when you listen to me without giving advice." When your child does something that you feel angry about, you can say, "Danny, when you don't come inside after I've told you twice, I get angry, and I want you to come in now!"

For the next 21 days following Exercise 1, record your feeling expressions from the day in your journal each evening. Follow up by repeating 10 times, "I have a right to express my feelings. My feelings are real. It's okay for me to express my feelings."

When you express your emotions, be specific. If you're too general others won't know what you're talking about. For instance, if you say, "I don't like it when you talk that way," or "I like it when you're a good boy," the listener isn't clear what it is exactly that you like or do not like. Instead say, "When you raise your voice really loud and call me names, I don't like it," or, "I like it when you help your sister pick up the toys."

Journal:

In addition to recording your feeling expressions, write about any related experiences. Charlotte described an experience after doing this exercise for a week:

October 2: "I was visiting with Mom today, and she was nagging me about getting a boyfriend. Usually I sit quietly and listen to this stuff, but today I told her I didn't like it when she kept telling me this and that I was getting angry. Afterwards I felt immediately guilty, but then in my mind I kept saying to myself, 'I have a right to express my feelings. My feelings are real. It's okay for me to express my feelings.' It helped a lot, and I told my mom I didn't want to hurt her, but I just needed her to not keep telling me what I should do."

Exercise 3: Identify others' feelings.

As you give yourself permission to acknowledge and express your own feelings, you're ready to take the next step, which is to identify and name the feelings of others. Observe their nonverbal behaviors. What do their facial expressions tell you? Their body postures? Eyes? Tones of voice? Observe with your eyes, your ears, all your senses. Offer a statement as to what they are feeling. For example, "You look pretty upset today." "You seem rather tense." "You look happy!" "You seem like you're kind of sad."

Although it will be difficult, don't worry about being exactly right or about the other person agreeing with you. If you say, "You look sad," and the other person denies it, there's no need to argue the point. Or if you say, "You look tired," and the other person says, "Well, no, not exactly. I'm just worried about this tax bill," give yourself credit for getting close if not right-on. By saying something about his feelings, you have at least opened up the conversation. Listening closely and naming another's feelings immediately puts the conversation on a more personal plane, so it will give you an opportunity to generate a more personal relationship.

It's important that you be very patient with yourself and practice, practice, practice! Listening is a highly refined skill, one that you build up slowly, at times through trial and error. For the next 21 days, focus on identifying and naming other people's feelings.

Journal:

Each day, chronicle your experiences with identifying and naming others' feelings, as Lois did with her husband in the following example:

March 5: "I've been a little too quick to jump on Chuck for not doing enough around the house on his days off. When we talked about it earlier tonight, I decided to try this feeling exercise with him. I had to bite my tongue a couple of times, but I did it. I found out he's really tired of my getting on his case, and that he doesn't feel appreciated. I have to be honest and admit I don't tell him how much I do appreciate what he does, so I'm going to make a point of doing that. And I think he really felt like I was listening to him, so it made it easier for him to talk."

"YOU'VE GOT A FRIEND": REACHING OUT AND MAKING FRIENDS

The more people you meet, the more likely you will be to make friends. It is important during this growing-up-again phase to practice reaching out and making contact with others. As you do, you'll find that some of the folks you meet may turn into valuable friends.

It's important that you learn to trust others and that you do so gradually. As you learn to trust your own instincts, it will be easier to discern whom you can trust. You'll also develop ways to work out difficulties as they surface in relationships. You can learn to view friendships much more realistically and not as all-or-nothing enterprises. Friendships are always changing, evolving, growing, and dying, and some of the changes come as a result of resolving differences rather than running from the conflict. You will triumph in your friendships when you can welcome change as inevitable rather than denying or avoiding it.

To Make a Friend, Be a Friend

To develop friendships, you must learn how to be a friend. What is it in friendships that you appreciate? How can you reach out and make friends? The next five exercises, followed in sequence, will help you do this.

Exercise 1: Listen closely and actively.

One of the nicest things that friends have to offer is their full attention. Not their advice, not their distance, not their complaints, not their corrections, but simply their undivided attention and willingness to listen. To be a friend, you need to cultivate this skill and practice it regularly.

To listen closely, you must bring your attention fully and completely to the other person. This means focusing on what the other person is saying, rather than on what *you* want to say. Most people think that listening means waiting until the other person is finished talking so they can talk!

To practice listening closely and attentively as you are conversing with someone, imagine yourself as the other person. What is she feeling? Can you picture yourself in her situation? What is she really saying? Make eye contact in an easy, relaxed manner. Be open by sitting or standing up straight, uncrossing your arms, and crossing your legs toward the other person. As you're listening, nod. Small nods do not mean you agree, they mean you're paying attention.

Pay attention to the other person's nonverbal cues and, most important of all, put your own agenda aside when you are listening.

For the next seven days, at least two times a day, practice using these attentive skills for three minutes in any conversation. Is it difficult to maintain concentration? Does the other person respond favorably? How do you feel doing this? Are you comfortable or uncomfortable?

Journal:

Enter your observations in your journal, as George did after experimenting with this exercise:

August 9: "This one was a lot harder than I expected. I tried it with Tina today, and I kept getting distracted. I found I have this tendency to think way ahead and to interrupt her when she's talking. I told her about it, and she agreed. So I guess I'll have to try a little harder."

Exercise 2: Paraphrase.

To listen actively, you need to paraphrase, or restate, what the other person is saying. When you paraphrase, you find out if the message you received was in fact the message the speaker intended to send. This helps keep the communication clear and understood.

You can paraphrase *content,* or you can paraphrase *feelings.* You can paraphrase content by highlighting a key word or phrase, with a slight questioning intonation at the end of the word or phrase, such as:

TOM: I can't wait to get to the horse races! My favorite horse is racing today.

TERRY: The races?

You can also paraphrase content by restating the main idea as you've received it but dropping the questioning intonation, as follows:

SUSAN: There's been just too much fussing and planning about our vacation. We should just take off on Saturday and go wherever we feel like.

JEFF: You'd rather be more spontaneous about this trip.

If you're accurate in your paraphrasing, the speaker will tell you so. If you're not accurate, the speaker will correct your interpretation. In either case, you've accomplished your objective, which is to clarify the message.

PATRICIA: Whenever we visit your mother's, we end up staying the whole day, and I don't get any of the work done around here.

SAM: You don't like going to my mother's.

PATRICIA: No, it's not that. I like going there, I just don't get any work done around here.

Another way to listen actively is to paraphrase feelings. Remember the four basic feelings and listen for which ones most closely describe what the other person is feeling. Tell the other person your guess about what she's feeling:

LINDA: There just doesn't seem to be enough time during the day to do all that I want to do.

FRANCIS: You feel overwhelmed.

LINDA: Yeah, and then I think that I'm not spending enough time with the kids, or doing enough for them.

FRANCIS: You feel bad because you think you're neglecting your children.

Notice that in the above example, Francis has *restated* the feelings, not repeated them word for word.

For the next seven days, at least twice each day, paraphrase either content or feelings in communications with others. Note how you feel when you're trying this skill. Note the speaker's response to your active listening.

Journal:

Make a note of your experience with this exercise each evening. Carol wrote about an experience with her nine-year-old son:

August 25: "Louis lost his hamster yesterday, and I knew he was feeling bad about it, but he wasn't saying much. When I was fixing dinner he was sitting with me, and the subject of his hamster came up. I just listened, and paraphrased his feelings about the loss, saying, 'You sound upset.' I'm somewhat surprised at how much he opened up, and how much that hamster meant to him."

When trying this skill, it's critical that you reward yourself with a mental pat on the back—first, for making the effort, and second, for coming close at all to correct active listening. If it's a new skill to you, it will take time and practice to make it a regular part of your communication repertoire, so go easy on the self-criticism and heavy on the self-praise.

Exercise 3: Share yourself.

Sharing information about yourself contradicts your childhood training and feels risky to you. You think it best not to get personal with anyone. But you're going to have to get personal if you're going to make friends. As you reveal information about yourself, this prompts the other person to open up with you.

Feelings are the most personal level of sharing yourself. Whereas facts tell the listener what's going on inside your mind, feelings tell the listener what's going on inside your heart. By sharing feelings, you bring the communication to its most personal level. Examples of feelings are:

"I thoroughly enjoy helping people find the kind of house they need."
"I hate shopping, and I feel really frustrated about having to go."
"I am completely intimidated by computers."

For the next seven days, share at least one feeling in each conversation you have. Note how you felt when you did it. What sort of response did you get? What was the scariest part about doing this exercise? With whom was it the most difficult? The easiest?

Journal:

Record your experiences with this exercise. Heather observed in her journal:

January 25: "This one wasn't too difficult, though I did find it was easier to do with some people than others. It was easiest with other girl-friends, and hardest with my father. That doesn't surprise me because I never did feel at ease talking with him about my feelings anyway."

Exercise 4: Socializing.

The next step is to get out and meet others so you can make new friends. This may not be easy at first, but as your Natural Child emerges it will become easier.

An excellent resource to help you in reaching out and making friends is *Conversationally Speaking,* by Alan Garner. Many of the skills described in this section are discussed more thoroughly in Garner's book, and it will be a handy companion as you develop your skills.

In this socializing exercise you take specific, successive, small steps toward the goal of feeling comfortable socializing with others. It's important that you take each step in sequence and at your own pace. Allow yourself several weeks to go through the entire process, and use your journal to record your experiences.

First, write out a list of all the different places you can think of where you have an opportunity to meet and talk with other people. You can ask others for ideas as well.

Next, think of a scale from 1 to 10, with 1 being the easiest and 10 being the most anxiety-provoking. Go through your list and next to each item put a number that corresponds with the degree of discomfort you imagine you would experience if you were to socialize with people in that situation. Then rewrite the list, arranging it in a hierarchy from least uncomfortable to most uncomfortable. One of my clients, Tina, arranged her hierarchy as follows:

Work = 2
Market = 4
Classroom = 5
Ticket line = 6

Park = 7

Dance = 9

Next, take each situation and think of specific circumstances within that situation and rank them. Tina broke down "socializing in the classroom" into:

A. Talking to someone I know during the break = 2

B. Talking to the teacher during break = 5

C. Speaking up in class voluntarily = 6

D. Talking to someone I don't know during break = 7

E. Speaking up in class when called on = 9

After you've broken down each situation into smaller substeps, set a goal for yourself of accomplishing one item each time you are in the situation. Start with the easiest and head down the list. If you get too anxious at any one step, return to the previous item on the hierarchy and repeat it until you feel at ease. Be sure to breathe deeply and relax every step of the way.

Tina started with the easiest item on her list, "Talking to someone I know during break," and did this during three class meetings in a row. Then she moved on to "Talking to the teacher during break."

"It made it easier to do one item at a time," Tina observes. "That way I could go at my own pace and feel more relaxed."

Next, practice mental rehearsal and positive self-talk about the specified goal. With your eyes closed, see yourself accomplishing your goal. Breathe deeply and slowly as you imagine this scene. Walk yourself through the desired behavior in your mind, and as you do, use positive self-talk. For example, as Tina visualized her desired goal—to talk with someone new during a class break—she would say to herself, "Now I'm walking up to this other woman in class. I'm smiling as I do, saying 'Hello' and introducing myself. I feel relaxed and confident and it shows. I'm talking to her about the class. I feel very comfortable, and she is very receptive to our conversation. We talk for a few minutes, and then break is over. I'm pleased with how relaxed I am and feel good about talking with her. I say goodbye, return to the classroom, take my seat and feel satisfied that I've accomplished my goal."

Now take your vision and do it for real. Take one step at a time and reward yourself for small successes. As with the other steps, record your experiences in your journal.

Continue in this way for the next several weeks, setting a goal each week for socializing. If you stay with this for as little as three weeks, you'll begin to notice a difference in your level of comfort while socializing. You'll actually start having fun while you're doing it!

Journal:

At each point in your socializing, record your comments. Tina wrote the following:

June 18: "Today I talked with the teacher in class. He was really sweet, and I felt much more relaxed than I thought I would. The day before, I visualized doing this, and I'm sure it helped. It turns out he's from Grand Rapids, too. We didn't find anybody we knew in common, but it was great getting to talk with him. And now on to the next challenge!"

Friendships, like most living things, grow best when they are nurtured and cared for and allowed to rest occasionally. With your present friends or with new friends you develop during this phase of your recovery, make it a point to periodically contact them, even if it's just to say hello.

One of my friends, Priscilla, is great at this. Even though she and I may not see each other for several months at a stretch, inevitably we talk over the phone every few weeks. Either she or I will call, and we'll have a pleasant, friendly chat. Each time this happens, I'm pleased and know that our friendship is affirmed.

Another way to make contact is through the long-forgotten art of writing letters. When was the last time you received a letter from a friend? When was the last time you wrote one? If a friend has done something special for you, or was just there for you when you needed him, tell him thanks through a letter or note.

Exercise 5: Make regular contact.

This exercise will help keep your friendships alive and well.

For the first step, write in your journal the names of any friends whom you have not contacted at all recently. Make a commitment to contact these persons within the next few months.

Next, on a calendar or a schedule, write in big letters, "CONTACT A FRIEND" every two weeks for the next six months. This is a way of reminding yourself to do so at regular intervals. Then, when that time comes, think of a friend you'd like to contact in some way, and do so. The contact can be a phone call, a letter, a thank-you note, or a social engagement such as dinner or lunch.

Journal:

Write about your experiences making contact with friends. Joyce describes one experience:

November 4: "When the note came up on my calendar to contact a friend, I had been thinking about my old college roommate Ruth Freeman, whom I haven't talked with in years. So I called her. Was she surprised to hear from me! She's married for a second time and now has two children. We had a great talk and made a promise to keep in touch more regularly."

In a very real sense, by reaching out and making friends, you are developing a new "family" to replace or enhance your original family. As Richard Bach states in his book *Illusions:* "The bond that links your true family is not one of blood, but of respect and joy in each other's life. Rarely do members of one family grow up under the same roof."

"JUST SAY NO!": SETTING BOUNDARIES

An absolutely critical issue for you in growing up again is learning to set boundaries. You grew up in a family where the psychological and physical boundaries were enmeshed and confused and where protection was lacking. If your Inner Child is to feel safe as you go through your recovery, it's essential you learn to say no and set limits that serve you.

In the past you didn't feel you had much of a choice except to accommodate others, to honor their boundaries and needs while denying your own. By establishing your boundaries more clearly, you stop yourself from feeling victimized by others and give yourself much greater freedom, choice, and personal power.

Fears of Setting Boundaries

In setting boundaries, you first need to set aside some fears and considerations. The first is your strong need to be liked. Most everyone wants to be liked; we find it gratifying when others like us. However, you believe you *must* be liked, and that it would be terrible if someone didn't like you. As long as you believe this, you will be fearful and uncertain about setting boundaries.

Although it may be desirable that someone like you, it is not absolutely necessary. You can function and do quite well whether or not you get someone to like you or approve of you. You must learn to be good to yourself by setting boundaries and saying no even though you will feel uneasy at times taking this risk. It will take you a while to convince yourself that it's safe to say no.

One of my patients, Victoria, describes how difficult it has been for her to say no: "I never said no to my mom or dad, and I carried that over into my adult life. I always feel so guilty even when I just think about turning someone down. I really am afraid of what they'll think or that they won't like me."

A second consideration is the fear that if you say no, you will be abandoned. This fear is common to all, yet heightened for you because of your abusive past. One of the most primal fears anyone has is of being left alone. For you, it triggers memories of having been left alone and abandoned in childhood.

The truth is that now, as an adult, you can only abandon yourself. As long as you give someone else the power to declare you okay or not okay, you risk potential feelings of abandonment when this other person does not approve. When you *know* you're okay and do not need someone else's approval to feel okay, then you cannot truly be abandoned.

Besides, how likely is it that *everyone* will abandon you? Can you get along without a given person's attention or approval, or even presence? This other person is another human being, and there are five billion others in the world with whom you can be friends if this one is incapable of respecting your boundaries.

A final and important consideration is your fear of being abused. If you attempted to set boundaries in the past and were verbally or physically abused as a result, you may be reluctant now to set boundaries. By accommodating others automatically, you avoid the imagined retaliation.

Whether or not you are in an abusive relationship, the conditioned fear of retaliation and abuse is powerful. As you practice setting boundaries, you'll no doubt notice your heart pounding and your muscles tensing. Realize that this is a conditioned fear from childhood and perfectly understandable. Realize also that your reaction will be less and less intense the more you practice setting boundaries.

Exercise: Why can't you say no?

Think back on a situation where you said yes even though you wanted to say no. What were some of your specific thoughts? What fears or considerations stopped you from saying no? What were the consequences of your not setting boundaries? How could you handle this differently the next time? Observe several of these situations as they come up over the next two weeks.

Journal:

As you consider these questions and make your observations, write any pertinent comments in your journal. Ray described his repeated difficulty with saying no:

April 28: "On many occasions I've said yes to something, only to back out at the last minute. Sometimes if I agreed to do something I would, but I would be angry and resentful the whole time. My biggest fear of saying no is that other people won't think I'm a nice guy, and of course I couldn't stand that."

How to Say No

There are two effective ways to say no: a simple preference statement and an empathic refusal.

A preference statement—in this case, a negative preference statement—is clearly stating what you don't want. For example: "No, I'd rather not." "No, I don't want to." "I don't care to."

You may follow any statement like this with a brief explanation if you wish, but you don't have to. It's your right to not explain or justify your decision about your boundaries. You do not have to make up some excuse in order to state your limits.

An empathic refusal is a two-part statement consisting of an empathic statement followed by a negative preference. An empathic statement is one that offers the person making the request some acknowledgment of his feelings, circumstance, or opinion. It is not simply, "I understand," but instead is truly responsive to what the other person has said. You then follow this with your negative preference statement. If you choose, you may offer a brief explanation. You may also choose to effect a compromise solution. For instance, you may not be willing to loan your car to a friend, but may be willing to give him a ride.

Some examples:

(1) BOB: Will you help me out this Saturday? I've got to move a bunch of boxes from my storage bin to my garage before noon, and my back's been giving me problems again.

ALLEN: Ouch! That'll make lifting a real problem for you [empathic statement]. However, I can't make it this Saturday [negative preference]. I've already promised my son that we would go to the zoo [explanation]. How about next Saturday [compromise solution]?

(2) MARK: Oh, come on, Charlotte. Let's go to bed. It's been a long time since we made love, and I've really missed you.

CHARLOTTE: Well, Mark, I'm sure you've been pretty lonesome [empathic statement], and I've missed you too, but I don't want to go to bed with you [negative preference]. I just don't feel right about doing it [explanation/feeling statement].

(3) GABRIELLE: Sandy, I need a place to stay for the next few weeks. My boyfriend and I broke up, and I don't have anywhere to go.

SANDY: Well, Gabrielle, I can see that you're in a tough situation and it's sure no fun not having a home [empathic statement]. However, I just can't [negative preference], because I don't have enough room at my place for another person [explanation]. You can sleep here tonight and tomorrow night, but you'll have to find somewhere else after that [compromise solution].

Exercise: Set boundaries.

Look for opportunities to set boundaries, using either a simple negative preference statement or an empathic refusal. These can be simple situations, such as someone's asking you to sign a petition, to more difficult situations, such as your husband's asking you to stay at home instead of working. Practice on simple situations first. What thoughts interfere with your setting boundaries? What thoughts help you set boundaries? How did you feel after you said no? What was the other person's response?

Journal:

Record your answers and observations each time you have an opportunity to set boundaries. Do so for the next several weeks, especially those times when you do refuse. Grace recalls in her journal a significant time when she said no:

June 22: "Last night on the phone my mom asked me again—or should I say, hinted, cajoled, pleaded with me—to come over this weekend. Right now, I need to be away from her and my dad. I told her so. I wasn't too empathic about it, but it got the job done. I might have even been a little harsh, because I was angry when I said it. But at least I feel good that I'm on the right track."

Dealing with Pushy People

Sometimes others will not respect your boundaries. In this case, you can use a tool called Broken Record.

With Broken Record, you repeat your refusal over and over again, no matter what type of pressure or manipulation the other person throws at you. You may respond to what the other person is saying, but you do not get distracted from your main objective, which is to say no. If the other person is manipulative enough, he will try to get you to feel stupid or guilty in hopes that you will give up and say yes. Just stay as relaxed and calm as possible and keep reiterating your refusal, as Paula does in the following example with a door-to-door magazine salesman:

> SALESMAN: Hello, and how are you? I am in a program sponsored by the American College Students Achievement Organization to earn money for college. To help me, all you have to do is to subscribe for six months to the magazine of your choice from this list here.
>
> PAULA: No, thanks, I'm really not interested.
>
> SALESMAN: Are you sure? We've got some great deals here. The prices for these subscriptions are anywhere from 20 to 50 percent less than the cover price.
>
> PAULA: I'm sure they're a great deal, however, I'm not interested.
>
> SALESMAN: Well, do you read at all?
>
> PAULA: (staying calm) Yes, I do, but I'm not interested.
>
> SALESMAN: You could sure help me out by taking even a short subscription to one magazine. It'll really help me stay in school.
>
> PAULA: I'm sure it would, however I'm really not interested.
>
> SALESMAN: Well, okay, if that's how you feel. Goodbye.
>
> PAULA: Goodbye, and good luck with your sales.

Notice that Paula stays calm throughout; she simply outpersists the salesman by using Broken Record.

With Broken Record, you'll feel more comfortable setting your boundaries and sticking by them.

Exercise: Use the Broken Record technique.

You may have the opportunity at some point to deal with a door-to-door salesperson or with pushy friends or acquaintances. These are excellent opportunities to practice your assertiveness. When such an opportunity arrives, use Broken Record. Stay calm and persistently refuse, no matter what devices the other person uses.

Another way to practice is to role-play with a friend. Ask your friend to play the pushy salesperson and to try selling you his product in as many different ways as possible. Using Broken Record as in the above example, refuse.

Journal:

Whether in practice with a friend or in real life, whenever you have a chance to respond with Broken Record, do so and note your experience in your journal. Teresa wrote about her experience:

July 17: "I had a fun time with Richard practicing this Broken Record technique. He played a ten-year-old boy selling a newspaper subscription, and he tried every trick in the book to try to make me feel guilty. Though it was hard to keep a straight face because he looked so pathetic and acted the part so well, I held my ground and didn't get into justifying my no."

"HOLD ME!": LEARNING TO TOUCH AGAIN

For Adult Children of abusive parents, touching and being touched are major issues. For you, touch has come to mean something other than gentle, loving physical contact, something other than innocent physical pleasure. You may find that you avoid touch as much as possible, or that when you do touch, you have conflicting feelings about it.

If you were physically beaten, you've learned that touch equals pain. Ray Helfer in *The Battered Child* describes how this happens:

> Consider what happens when touching hurts *most of the time*; smells about the house bring on very negative feelings, *most of the time*; mom's eyes show the threat of a swat; when the child listens to mom and dad talk he becomes afraid, since the messages he hears are threats, screams, and anger. Over and over, day after day, the child is bombarded with negative sensory messages, messages that truly force the senses to "shut down."

The child learns that it is far safer not to listen, not to look, and not to be touched, for when these senses are used, he hurts much more often than he feels good.

A similar consequence of sensory shutdown results from too little touch or a steady diet of tense, anxious touching from a parent who herself has conflicting feelings about touching. In the case of emotional abuse, it was very confusing for you to rely on the touch of someone who mistreated you emotionally and verbally, so here, too, you learned to shut down your senses and deny your need for touch.

If you were sexually abused, touch meant a violation of your body's boundaries. Since touch is such a significant part of a sexual intimacy, the boundaries between sexual touching and nonsexual touching are understandably confused for you. This, plus your tendency toward all-or-nothing thinking, leads you to equate touch with sex. It's very difficult to trust someone touching you, since it has been so intricately associated for you with abuse, disappointment, and exploitation.

Maria recalls how distrustful she has been of anyone's touch: "For me, touch with a man meant sex. My father crossed that line early on in my life, and I've never known any different. For me a simple hug would be confusing, because I figured that if I let a man hug me, then I had to go to bed with him."

Part of growing up again is learning to feel comfort and pleasure in touching and being touched, both in nonsexual and sexual ways. The first priority, however, is to feel relaxed and comfortable with nonsexual touching. This is the primary focus of this section, since it is such a vital foundation for any pleasurable sensory experience. Once you have gained some mastery with nonsexual touch, it will become easier to enjoy sexual touch and pleasure. (When you are ready to explore sexual touching further, read *For Yourself* and *For Each Other,* both by Lonnie Barbach, as well as *The Joy of Sex* by Alex Comfort.)

For Touch's Sake

It's helpful to discern differing kinds of touching. In an article entitled "Close Encounters" in *Psychology Today* (March 1988), Stephen Thayer quotes psychologist Richard Hesling's five categories of touching:

FUNCTIONAL-PROFESSIONAL touches occur when the person who touches is performing a professional function, such as a doctor, tailor, or hairdresser. These touches are impersonal.

SOCIAL-POLITE touches are best reflected in the common hand-shake. These types of touches are formal and generally used for saying hello or goodbye or expressing appreciation or congratulations between business associates or between strangers and acquaintances.

FRIENDSHIP-WARMTH touches express personal concern and caring, usually between extended family members, people at work to whom you are close, and closer neighbors. These types of touches are "friendly touches," such as a hand on the shoulder.

LOVE-INTIMACY touches occur between close family members and friends, and are expressions of deeper affection and caring. Included in this are hand-holding and hugs of all types. All of the touches up to and including this one are nonsexual.

SEXUAL-AROUSAL touches are ones that occur in erotic-sexual contacts.

Of the five types of touch, only one is sexual. The rest indicate differing degrees of friendship and intimacy. It's sad but true that in our American culture, according to some researchers, gentle, loving touch between friends and family members occurs at a strikingly low rate. Perhaps this is why we have bumper stickers to remind us: "Have you hugged your child today?"

Since touch has been shown in a vast number of studies to be of great importance to emotional and physical health and well-being, it is worth your time and effort to teach yourself to be more at ease with touch as part of your recovery.

To Touch and to Be Touched: A Program for Sensory Recovery

The particular program described below may be the most difficult part of your recovery. Touch is a vital part of growing up again, yet it raises issues of intimacy, trust, and sexuality. Though this sensory recovery procedure is designed to be a 12-week program, it is important to proceed at your own pace and to give yourself plenty of time. You will confront some discomfort, but the program is designed in such a way that it will occur gradually. As with any of the programs or exercises in this book, work closely with your journal in recording your observations and responses.

Some of the exercises here were adapted from an article entitled "Retraining and Relearning," by Ray Helfer in *The Battered Child*.

Exercise 1: Touching objects.

For the next 14 days, touch objects each day that are part of your everyday experience and that are not frightening. These can be things with which you are familiar yet with which you haven't engaged your sense of touch. Things such as a towel, a glass figurine, a silky cloth, a fur coat, or a feather are good ones with which to start. Close your eyes for a few moments and become absorbed with your sensory experience. How does it feel? How would you describe the texture to someone else? Is it cold or warm, smooth or bumpy, soft or hard? Continue to feel the object as you ask yourself these questions. Do you like how it feels? How does it make *you* feel? Smell it. If possible, taste it.

Touch many different kinds of objects throughout the next three weeks, each time noticing your experience. In addition, for about 5 to 10 minutes each day, take several objects, some of which you have already touched, set them in front of you, and close your eyes. One at a time, touch each of the objects slowly and carefully. Be aware of how many different kinds of sensations you're able to pick up. Play some soft, pleasant music as you do this, and do it in as quiet a place as you can. This will help you associate touch with pleasure.

Journal:

Write your observations each day for the two-week period. Kelly describes one of her experiences in her journal as follows:

March 27: "I think I'm beginning to get the point of the exercise. Earlier today I put a few things on the kitchen table while no one else was around. There was a rose petal, a pair of furry earmuffs, an orange, an empty coffee can, and a swatch of denim. I took a few deep breaths, then began the exercise by touching the rose petal. It was so silky smooth and still had a lot of the fragrance in it. For some reason I got some powerful images of dancers swirling amidst multicolored lights that I could not only see but feel. The furry earmuffs were exquisite, very sensual. I never thought of earmuffs before as sensual. I continued with the other objects, and each one prompted a powerful sensory reaction."

Exercise 2: Touching animals.

Now you can move on to the next step, which is touching animals, such as a dog or a cat. Go ahead and touch one. Close your eyes and notice what your sense of touch is telling you. Does the animal respond to your touch? What does it feel like? How do you feel when you do this? Do this every day if possible for the next two weeks.

Journal:

Write about your experiences each time you try this. An example from Kelly's journal:

April 9: "This one was a pleasure. My kitty, Q.B. Jackson, must have thought he had died and gone to heaven. I made it a point to pet him a few minutes each day, and I really enjoyed it. He's such a lover and a furball to boot. Every once in a while I'd feel so appreciative of the fact that here was this living creature, and we were each giving something to the other. I don't think I've ever enjoyed petting Q.B. quite so much as I have this past week."

Exercise 3: Touching a child.

If you have a child, make it a point to touch him. This may seem absurd to you, because you already do so. But in addition to the kind of touching that's done purely for the care and maintenance of the child—holding, hanging onto his hand, bathing him—touch him simply to express your affection. You may feel somewhat silly at first, but it will get easier. A good place to start is to touch his hair and face when he's sleeping, closing your eyes as you do so. If he awakens, tell him you love him and were just checking on him.

From here you can find other opportunities to touch him appropriately. Start with small steps. At night spend a few minutes sitting next to him while you're both watching television, stroking his hair, arms, back, or feet. Both of you can learn to enjoy this. If he asks why you want to do this, tell him the truth: that you're practicing touch. Do this for at least a few minutes every day for the next 14 days and record your experiences in your journal. (It's only fair to warn you that this could become habit-forming for both you and your child!)

Journal:

Record your experiences each time you do this. Let's follow Kelly's progression with these exercises:

April 18: "I hadn't realized how much of my touching with Jason is for maintenance. Today at the market while we were standing in line, I put my arm around his shoulder and stroked his hair. He seemed to enjoy it, then slowly pushed himself away after a few moments of this. Tonight after he had fallen asleep, I went in and kissed him on the forehead, and lightly stroked his hair and forehead. He woke up slightly and turned over, so I asked him if it was okay to touch him like I was doing. He nodded his head then went back to sleep. What a joy it is to share with him in this way."

Exercise 4: Touching yourself.

Now on to an even more challenging exercise—touching yourself. For the next 14 days, spend 5 to 10 minutes each day touching your body. You will be likely to feel nervous and experience some resistance because of earlier childhood messages. If at any point during the process of self-touching you get too distressed, simply back up to a previous step in the program or put it aside for a while. Because our bodies tend to have sensory memories, if you were physically or sexually abused this exercise may trigger some repressed memories. As is true at any point during your recovery, if your feelings become too unpleasant or overwhelming, find a competent therapist to help you work through these reactions. At the very least, talk with a trusted friend.

Remember, however, that you have a right to touch yourself—it is your body. It was designed to feel all sorts of sensations, and by touching yourself, you are reminding your body that it is capable of feeling many different sensations. Move slowly, and each time you do this exercise, go only as far as you can easily tolerate.

Start by closing your eyes and *very gently* touch yourself on your face, hands, and arms. Experiment with different ways of touching yourself. Try lighter and heavier strokes. Express tenderness with your touch. Move slowly, then try a faster movement. Observe your experience as you do. What kind of touch do you find particularly pleasant? Was there any kind that you didn't like? How did you feel doing this exercise? Did any distracting thoughts come up, like, "You shouldn't touch yourself like this"? Try this exercise at least once a day for several days.

Once you have accustomed yourself to doing this, the next step is to take off all your clothes in the privacy of your room and extend your touching to the rest of your body. At first you may feel some anxiety, but go ahead and do this exercise. Experiment with a variety of ways of touching yourself—slow, fast, hard, soft. Don't include your genitals at first. After a few times, include genital touching, but don't make this the focus. You may experience sexual feelings during any portion of this exercise, but keep your focus on the total sensory experience, of which your sexual feelings are but one aspect. As with all other feelings, let your sexual feelings pass through you if they do occur.

Feel free to touch yourself in different ways and notice how your body responds. As you touch yourself, say out loud, "I give my body lots of love. It's okay for my body to feel good and for me to feel pleasure. I am good to my body and it responds with vitality and health." Immerse yourself in the pure experience of touching your body rather than listening to the negative dialogue that may be taking place between your ears. Your body is a miracle of nature and you can appreciate that fact through this exercise.

Journal:

Writing in your journal during this sequence of exercises will be especially useful, since you may have some strong reactions. Kelly described one of her experiences as follows:

April 30: "I finally tried the one without my clothes. I think the worst part was leading up to it. I kept thinking that I could never do this, but finally one day when Hal and Jason were gone, I did it. I kept hearing my mother's voice in my mind saying, "Don't touch yourself that way!" and I'd get nervous, but I went right ahead and didn't give the voice much attention. I found I really enjoy light touch—I don't think I ever got much of it. In fact, I don't think my mom or dad touched me much for touch's sake."

Exercise 5: Touching others.

This next step involves touching someone else over the next 14 days. As usual, record your experiences and feelings in your journal. One way to start is to touch friends and associates appropriately on the shoulder or forearm as a way of greeting them or saying goodbye. You can gauge from their reaction whether they are receptive to your doing so. If they are not, do not be alarmed. It tells you more about their level of comfort with touch than about your doing something wrong. Simply pull back and forgo touching them.

The next step, if and when you are ready, is to practice giving hugs to your closer friends and family members. Remember, although these hugs are nonsexual, others may not feel comfortable receiving them. Respect the other person's physical boundaries when it comes to any kind of touching or hugging. You might even ask them beforehand, "Do you mind if I give you a hug?"

If you have a mate or intimate partner, you can practice more intimate caressing and touching. Start by caressing his arms, hands, and face. If he wonders what you're up to, tell him. You may then offer to give him a back massage. While doing so, be particularly aware of the different types of touch you give to him. When you are ready, you can give him a full body massage. You may even end up making love after the massage. Whatever type of touch you are giving to someone else, stay as focused as you possibly can on the sensory dimensions of your touch.

Journal:

Note your experiences with touching others. Kelly wrote:

May 14: "I've always enjoyed hugs, but I've never felt comfortable hugging my dad. Yesterday, when we visited my parents, before we were about to leave, I gave my dad a hug. It was just a brief embrace, and it took a lot of courage on my part to do it. He wasn't quite sure what to do with it, so he sort of put his arms on my shoulders when I hugged him. I was a little bit shy about doing it, but he was even more so. I liked it, though, and I could tell he did, even if he felt a little uneasy."

Exercise 6: Receiving touch.

This final step is the culmination of all the others and may be the most difficult. For this step there is no set time within which to work. Being able to receive the touch of another is a gradual learning experience, and with your attention and willingness, it will take place over time. When you were a child, someone touching you meant hurt or pain, and inviting another's touch now means being vulnerable and less in control than if you were doing the touching.

Find someone you like and who is nonthreatening, perhaps a child. Have her touch you on the arm or hand, or possibly your hair. Close your eyes as she touches you and notice what you feel. Then write out your observations in your journal, being as specific as possible about what you felt. Repeat this process a few times. If you get too anxious, back off for a while, then try again. Each time, record the experience in your journal.

Next, find an adult you like and with whom you feel relatively safe. The hardest part will be asking an adult to help you out with this exercise. Have him touch your hands, arms, and perhaps your face and scalp. Notice how you feel, and record these reactions.

After you have experienced the preceding two exercises a few times, get a sensual, nonsexual, massage. You can have an intimate friend or lover give it to you, or you can get a professional massage. Let whoever is giving you the massage know what degree of pressure and what kind of touch you enjoy, and during the massage, let the massager know what feels good. Like any of these touching exercises, a massage may trigger flashbacks. If this happens, don't be alarmed. Talk these over with a friend or therapist as soon as you can. During the massage, be sure to breathe deeply and slowly, particularly if you find yourself tensing up. Repeat this massage exercise at least twice.

Journal:

Record your observations about any facet of your experience of receiving touch. Kelly's husband, Hal, gave her a massage:

June 18: "At first I was a bit stiff, worried about whether Hal was enjoying giving it or not. I kept taking slow, deep breaths, and eventually found I could relax a bit. Whenever Hal did something that felt good, I told him, 'That feels good.' Pretty soon it got to be a game, where he'd ask me if a particular stroke felt good or not, and I'd moan and we'd both end up laughing. I thought the massage might feel kind of good, but I didn't expect it to be that much fun!"

With perseverance, you will find that receiving touch can be a very pleasurable, rewarding experience. You will find that by practicing this type of touching, you will learn to be much more relaxed being vulnerable with someone else. Remember, the goal of all these steps is to retrain yourself to associate touch with pleasure rather than with fear and pain.

As you practice these various exercises, you'll find yourself well on the road to recovery from your childhood abuse. Your Hurting Child will have been acknowledged and cared for, your Controlling Child will have begun to relax control, while your Natural Child will blossom forth under the loving influence of your internal Good Mother and the guidance and protection of your Good Father.

Next, we will move into the integration phase of your recovery, where your inner family will coordinate together more fluidly in your Natural Self.

7

CHAPTER

Integration

*B*etsy listened closely to her husband, Dennis. He wanted to make an offer on a house, despite the fact that they couldn't afford it. In the past, she basically went along with whatever Dennis wanted, never making a fuss. But lately, she had been learning to be increasingly assertive. Betsy realized that she had to be honest with Dennis about this decision on the house.

Her heart quickened and she could feel her whole body tense up. At first it was hard to look at Dennis and start talking, but she forced herself to do so. She told him that she did not want to buy the house because they could not afford it. He listened, then swore once and left the room. Betsy felt a rush of guilt and "bad girl" feelings and started to cry. Then she reminded herself that she had done the right thing in her eyes and did not need to feel guilty. She did not have to stay stuck in the role of Caretaker. Dennis would have to work out his own feelings. Betsy was willing to talk with him some more but felt considerable faith in her judgment. She realized that she had no control over Dennis's behavior, but only her own boundaries and needs. Life had not become perfect, but Betsy looked back on the past few months with much contentment. She had come a long way.

Like Betsy, you have discovered many things about yourself throughout your recovery. You have found that not only are you increasingly aware of your feelings, you can trust them more readily. It's getting easier and easier to express yourself. You have grieved the loss of your childhood and have for the most part let go of your past. Your Inner Child has substantially healed from its suffering. You have developed your own set of good parents to help comfort and guide you. You are learning how to play again and have been practicing setting your physical and psychological boundaries. You are learning to enjoy the simple pleasures of touch.

Now your recovery evolves naturally into its third step: Integration. Here you blend all of the previously disparate elements into a unique whole called you. Your inner "children" will operate more cohesively together, with your Natural Child leading the way. Working in unison with your internal Good Mother and Good Father, a new you—your Natural Self—emerges with greater strength and solidness. The physical, emotional, and spiritual aspects of your experience synchronize more closely together than ever before.

Each of the five areas covered in this chapter will augment what you have developed so far. They will not only help you complete the process of recovery, but will give you a framework for living beyond your previous survival mode, with integrity and without abuse.

Each section includes exercises, and your journal will continue to be useful in recording the exercises and your responses. I would recommend that you do each exercise, but if that is impossible or undesirable, choose the ones you consider most relevant for your integrative needs.

NO MORE SPLITTING

Integration means that the various disowned parts of your personality become reunited. The fragmentation you have experienced most of your life need no longer dominate your existence. You can own and accept the different expressions of who you are—the angry part of you, the loving part, the shy part, the various aspects of your Inner Child, your inner parents—allowing each to take its appropriate place in your psychological makeup.

Your Natural Self

The core of your being is your Natural Child, which has emerged from your subconscious as you have moved through the Healing and Growing Up Again phases of recovery. Your Controlling Child and your Hurting Child remain but have become less influential in your day-to-day living. As you have become increasingly integrated, these three aspects have blended fluidly and easily, with your Natural Child being the most prominent. You experience this transition as greater spontaneity, openness, and freedom of expression.

Jeremy describes how the appearance of her Natural Child has affected her: "I had forgotten how to play and was all caught up in the seriousness of life. The other day I was out taking my evening walk when I came across some neighborhood kids playing stickball. I stopped to watch for a while. The ball came my way, and I threw it back to one of the children. Andy, the boy who caught it, asked me jokingly if I would like a turn at bat. I surprised myself when I said, 'Sure!' and took a turn with the stick. I did pretty well, too, considering I haven't done something like that for years."

Since you have become your own parent, your Inner Child comes under loving care and protection. Your symbolic inner parents are allied in their efforts to take good care of you, with your Good Mother providing unconditional love, nurturing, and acceptance and your Good Father providing guidance, protection, and setting of boundaries. In their presence, your Natural Child blossoms. Correspondingly, your Controlling Child relaxes her control and your Hurting Child feels assured that safety and protection are available when needed.

This dynamic, shifting interplay between your Natural Child and your inner good parents allows your Natural Self to emerge. Your Natural Self is not fixed and immutable; she is alive and continuously adapting to the situation at hand, balancing external demands with your needs and limitations. It is the outward manifestation of your Natural Child, with your good parents always nearby to serve as protectors and consultants. You experience this integration as an inner harmony and cooperativeness between the various facets of your personality, with the core of your being clearly at the center. Even though you may "fall off the wagon" sometimes, it gets easier and easier to return to a state of balance.

Joyce describes her experience of this aspect of integration: "Life is just generally a lot smoother. I find it easier and easier to let go of things. Yesterday I was arguing with my ex-husband over the phone, and after I hung up on him I thought, 'What's the point of this? Here I am trying to make him wrong just so I can be right. I really don't want to keep that kind of tension going.' So I called him back and apologized for arguing. We were able to talk quite a bit more honestly after that."

Your inner Good Mother and Good Father symbols may be called on from time to time within your inner family. For instance, if you experience a disappointment or a good friend moves away, it's natural to feel some sadness and loss. You can "mother" yourself, giving yourself the nurturing and the comfort you need to grieve this loss. It's as if you were actually holding the child inside, empathizing and saying, "It's okay. I'm here for you. I know you're hurt." Mothering yourself may include contacting friends for support and emotional nurturance. It may be as simple as taking good care of your body: when tired, you rest; when hungry, you eat.

Deanne described how she has made this way of treating herself more intentional lately: "The real mother I knew wasn't very kind or very loving, but in the past couple of years I've been able to treat myself a lot better than she ever treated me when I was growing up. These days I even think, 'I need some mothering,' whenever I'm feeling emotionally needy or drained."

Your inner symbolic Good Father serves a different sort of function. He guides, directs, sets limits, encourages, and sometimes offers tough, nonabusive love. It's the fathering you wish you had had as a child, and you can now give it to yourself. The more firmly established this image is in your consciousness, the more at ease you feel with your own boundaries and the more self-discipline you will have.

Jeff talks about the fathering he gives himself: "I was feeling discouraged about an engineering project I was working on. I was procrastinating, finding other things to do. Finally, I said to myself, 'Look, just sit down at the drawing table and do it. It will come to you. Be patient, think about it, but sit down and do it!' I was very firm with myself, but very loving—something really new for me, because usually I just kind of mentally pound at myself and feel guilty, then end up doing a less than satisfactory job. This time I got the job done on time, and I was very satisfied with the results."

The following exercise will help you get more acquainted with each of the different facets of yourself.

Exercise: Your points of view.

In your journal, write a paragraph from the point of view of your Controlling Child, Hurting Child, Natural Child, Good Mother, and Good Father. Use the first-person "I" form and describe each as though they were a separate person. For example, "I am my Controlling Child. I try to keep everything calm by pleasing everyone. I get very upset when things don't go just right." Then, do the same for your Natural Self, describing her as a blend of these different parts. At first you might feel a little silly or embarrassed doing this, but don't worry. You will find it helpful getting to know the different parts of yourself.

How old are each of the "children"? Do you notice your Natural Self emerging? Do you like each of these different parts? Do you accept each as being an aspect of yourself? Which part is the hardest to describe? Which one is expressing herself right now? What is the value in your overall makeup of each part? Be aware of any feelings that are evoked as a result of writing from these vantage points.

Next, take some crayons or colored marking pens and draw pictures of each part of yourself in as much detail as possible. Which did you draw as the biggest? The smallest? How do you feel towards each one? Next, draw a picture of yourself as your integrated Natural Self. Is your Natural Self a synthesis of these other parts or something entirely new? To what extent do you already experience and express the qualities of the Natural Self?

Journal:

Use your journal to write out the statements from these different aspects, to do your drawings, and to record any other observations related to this exercise. You may wish to do each drawing on the same page as the description of that aspect. Some vignettes from Carolyn's journal:

February 18: *"My Hurting Child:* I'm afraid. I'm still not sure I trust anyone with my feelings, but it's getting a little bit better. I still hurt a lot, but I'm glad Carolyn's finally taking better care of me.

"My Good Mother: I am quiet, soft, and I listen very well. I don't say much, but when I do, it's the right thing to soothe Carolyn's pain. I like laughing too, and enjoying life for exactly what it is. I am glad I can be there for Carolyn. She deserves me.

"My Natural Child: I like to have fun. I really 'go with the flow,' and don't let things disturb me for too long. I am a greater part of Carolyn these days, and she lets me come out more often. I do not feel afraid, but trust that she will take good care of me. I've been hiding for a long time, so it's good to be out and see the sunlight again."

Letting Go of Your Role

Once you are no longer split and have turned over control to your Natural Self, you will no longer need the rigid protection of your Controlling Child. If you adopted the Perfectionist role, you will find that you can now more readily tolerate things being disorganized and ambiguous. If you have been a Caretaker, you will find that you can *care* for others now without having to *take care of* or rescue them. If you've been an Invisible One, you will find that being seen and known is less intimidating than you thought. If you took on the role of Rebel, you will find less need to act out and will discover ways to channel your intense passion more constructively.

As you increasingly operate from your Natural Self, you will find you can play a number of different roles. The key word here is *play*. When an actor plays a role, he may get very involved in it. The role may even overlap with the actor's personality. Still, he remains aware at all times that he is playing a role. You will find that as you integrate more completely and consistently, you will treat the different expressions of yourself as roles, while remaining aware at all times of who you really are at your center.

When your roles are integrated, they will not be fixed and rigid like the one you adopted to survive your childhood. You'll have much greater flexibility and choice in expressing different aspects of yourself, and you will relate to others more honestly and directly.

One of my patients, Sally, recalls, "I always rescued people, giving them what they needed no matter what it cost me. Lately I've realized how I give myself away when I rescue, so I've been doing much less of that. When my roommate Bill first moved in, I made him breakfast, cleaned his room, made his bed. It got so that he expected this from me. After a while he started coming on to me sexually. In the past I would probably have given in because I figured the man needed it. But this time I told him no and stopped being his maid. He was a little taken aback and I even felt a little guilty, but I told him how I felt and decided that he would have to take care of his own feelings."

No matter what role you play at any given time, when you see yourself as *playing* these roles rather than *being* these roles, you realize that roles are something you *do* rather than something you *are*. Everything you do in life, including your roles, is put into proper perspective when you operate from the awareness of your Natural Self.

This exercise will help you further shed your particular role. If you see yourself playing more than one role, do the exercise for each role. Have fun with this exercise.

Exercise: Roles and role reversal.

In your journal, describe as accurately as possible the fixed, rigid role to which you are accustomed. Note different examples of how this role manifests itself in your behavior. For example, if you are a Perfectionist, you might write the following: "I'm always punctual. I get upset with other people when they are late. I've got to have everything put away and in its place before I go to bed at night or I can't sleep. I work past closing time at the office and take work home with me."

Next, describe how you might behave if you were playing the exact opposite role. For example: "I'm always late for appointments. I don't care if others are late. I never do the housework, and my home is always a mess. I leave work on time and relax and have fun." Notice how you feel as you write these things. Do you in fact sometimes play this role? What fears or considerations does this arouse in you?

Finally, once each day for the next 14 days, spend five minutes acting "out of character." If you're a Perfectionist, let the dishes go one night. If you're a Caretaker, when a friend calls to tell you his tale of woe, tell him you're too busy to listen. If you are an Invisible One, smile and say hello to a stranger. If you're a Rebel, agree with someone's suggestions rather than countering with your own.

Journal:

Each day, record your observations of this role contrast. Here's a sample from Rachelle's journal:

July 25: "When I am playing my role: I'm always loving, sensitive, kind, and caring. I watch out for other people, and I'm always there when you need me. Whenever someone wants something from me, I do my best to give it. I am selfless, and my feelings don't really count. Other people always come first, because their feelings and needs are much more impor-tant. I can handle my feelings. I don't need anything from anyone else.

"And now, the opposite of this role: I really don't give a damn about anyone else! I should always come first. My husband and my kids should wait on *me*. I'm completely selfish and it's okay. It's every man or woman for himself or herself. I'm very insensitive and out for #1. (Boy, if I could just do this sometimes!)

"Acting out of character: Today I asked Rick, my eleven-year-old, to get me a glass of water. It was a lot harder than I thought it would be. My heart was actually pounding when I did, I felt *so* uncomfortable! What a relief when he did it. I don't know what I would have done had he said no."

Owning Your Feelings

When you split off parts of yourself, you split off the feelings associated with them. In healing and growing up again you have learned to be aware of your feelings and to identify and express them. An important part of the integration process is to take this one step further and own whatever feeling you experience. This means that you first acknowledge the feeling, accept it, experience it 100 percent, then let it go. Owning your feelings doesn't mean you have to act them out or necessarily even let anyone else know you're feeling them. It simply means you no longer pretend that you do not feel what you feel.

One way to encourage ownership of your emotions is to exagger-ate them. In this exercise, the point is to overstate what you are feeling so that strong emotions become less intimidating. You may feel inhibited at first, but stay with it and give it a try.

Exercise: Exaggerate your feelings.

Each day for the next 14 days, take five minutes, sit down in a private spot, and notice what you are feeling. If you don't feel anything at the time, think back on a recent situation. Next, increase or exaggerate whatever it is you feel. Be particularly aware of any body sensations. If your muscles are tense, tense them up even further. If your jaw is clenched, clench it even harder (but not hard enough to hurt your teeth!). If you are smiling, smile even bigger. Now, try expressing your feelings even more. Make some kind of expressive sound. If you're angry, hit the bed and growl. If you're happy, hum or sing. Let yourself feel and express this emotion as strongly as you possibly can. Your only boundary is to avoid hurting yourself or anybody else in the process.

Journal:

Record your experiences and reactions. A sample from Todd's journal:

September 3: "Tonight I noticed I was feeling a bit sad, so I thought back on how Janice had stood me up. I lay down on my bed. My body felt heavy, so I tried to make it feel even heavier. I curled up in a fetal position, and the more I thought about it the more I wanted to cry. Finally the tears started, and I started sobbing. When I first started the exercise, I thought it was kind of stupid, but I really was able to feel sad. I even tried moaning for a while, but then I started cracking up. I must admit, I did feel better. I didn't know I could make myself feel something to that degree."

TAKING PERSONAL RESPONSIBILITY

Any time you fail to take personal responsibility, you feel a familiar sense of helplessness and powerlessness. Continuing to treat yourself as a victim is a sad, losing game. It is based on the false assumption that what was once true in your childhood remains true today: that you can do nothing about your situation.

Disavowing your personal power is a lot like walking out in the rain unprotected, knowing full well it's raining, yet complaining because you're getting wet. You can't stop the rain, but you can either choose to get out of the rain or, as you'll see in the following section, you can choose how to feel about standing in the rain. In either case you're taking personal responsibility for your choice.

It's important to note that taking personal responsibility does not mean taking the blame or feeling guilty. It has nothing to do with blame or guilt. Instead, it is an unqualified recognition of the fact that you are the captain of your own ship and you choose how to sail it. You make your own choices and decisions. No one else can make you do something or make you feel bad, though sometimes it may seem otherwise. You are at the center of your own life, creating your own experience every moment. Whenever you think of yourself as being governed by external circumstances or controlled by your past, you feel powerless and victimized, but you need not perpetuate your self-victimization anymore.

Harriet is increasingly recognizing this theme in her life: "I was sitting in a restaurant waiting for some service, and I started to feel angry because the waitress was ignoring me. It occurred to me that I didn't have to sit there and take this kind of treatment, nor did I have to get terribly upset over it. So I got out of my seat, went up to the waitress, and asked her if I could place my order. She was a bit snippy, but came and took my order. In the past, I think I would have just sat there and fumed, feeling very sorry for myself but not thinking I could take care of myself the way I did."

Asking for What You Want

A simple yet incredibly powerful way of taking personal responsibility is to ask for what you want. Instead of directly and honestly expressing our preferences, we often hint, imply, cajole, manipulate, whimper, or simply hope that others will guess what it is we want. Then we get angry because they didn't guess our preference. All the while we feel powerless and victimized.

You may find, as do many Adult Children, that asking for what you want is difficult. You may fear that others will say no or will think you pushy, needy, or demanding. While these are all possibilities, remind yourself that none of these feared consequences would be the end of the world. You would survive and probably learn something from the experience. Most likely, however, when you ask for what you want, you will get it.

There are many ways to ask for what you want, but it's usually as simple as asking, "Could you please pass the salt?" Here are some examples:

"I'd like to get your help moving some things Saturday. Would you give me a hand?"

"I want you to meet me for a few minutes after work. Would you be willing to?"

"Could you give me a hug?"

"The music is really loud. Will you please turn it down?"

There are two things to remember about asking for what you want. First, it's best to start out by making small requests. That way you're less likely to feel intimidated, since you're not risking as much. It's a lot easier to ask for change for a dollar than it is to ask someone to marry you! Second, it's important to sound casual when asking. Others will be much more at ease and receptive if your tone is friendly and conversational than if your voice is somber and heavy.

By taking care of your wants and needs in this way, you take responsibility for yourself and thereby facilitate your integration. The following exercise will help you focus on this very important skill.

Exercise: Ask for what you want.

Once each day for the next 14 days, ask for something you want. Start out small and increase the size of your requests gradually. Ask for help, information, or something material. Honor your right to ask, and respect the right of others to decline. Notice any thoughts or fears that come to mind when you make requests.

Journal:

Each day, record your experiences before, during, and after doing your asking exercise. Here's a sample from Tricia's journal:

January 17: "I was feeling sort of needy, so I picked up the phone and called my girlfriend Sylvia. We talked for a while, and I noticed I was sounding rather sad. I think I was hoping she would ask me what's wrong— she often does when I sound that way. But she was too caught up in her excitement about this coming weekend and either missed it altogether or chose to ignore it. Anyway, once I noticed how I was sounding, I snapped out of it and went right to a direct question. I told Sylvia I wanted to spend some time with her before she left for the weekend, that I was feeling like I needed to talk to her about a few things. No great surprise—she said, 'Sure,' and we set up a time to meet. It was really refreshing to come right out and ask her for what I wanted."

No More Victimization

You have taught people how to treat you. If you rarely talk to anyone, don't return smiles, and don't acknowledge others' existence, you train them to leave you alone. If you constantly berate yourself and treat yourself disrespectfully, you train others to treat you the same way. If you do not take care of your own needs and wants, you train others to treat you as helpless and powerless—as a victim.

As you proceed with your integration process, you will find yourself increasingly dissatisfied with your role as victim. And when you stop treating yourself like a victim, others will stop treating you like one. By setting boundaries, asking for what you want, and expressing your feelings, you will teach other people to treat you with the same respect you grant yourself.

Paul describes how assuming responsibility for his limits worked with an ex-girlfriend: "Wendy and I had agreed to be friends after we broke up, and even though she had a new boyfriend, we'd get together over lunch or coffee. I noticed that whenever she wanted to see me, I'd be there for her, but when I wanted to see her, she was always too busy. After realizing how one-sided it was, I stopped seeing her as much and started saying no when she asked to see me."

Making Choices

As you take greater personal responsibility for your life, you'll recognize that you always have a choice. You never have to think of yourself as a victim again. If you don't like your situation, you have the power to change it. You don't have to listen politely to the salesperson at the door; you can say, "Thanks, but no thanks," and shut the door. You don't have to visit your parents every Sunday—you can tell them you're busy. If you're miserable at work, you don't have to stay at that job. You're free to do what you'd like to do.

In *How I Found Freedom in an Unfree World,* Harry Brown puts it very simply:

> I've often been bored by someone telling me over and over again how his spouse mistreats him, how his friends take advantage of him, how his boss abuses him, how his lover "uses" him. *Why does he permit it?* Why doesn't he terminate the relationship rather than allow the same person to "exploit" him over and over again? . . . You don't have to be involved with cheaters, frauds, cheapskates, liars, demanding people or anyone else you don't like. It's up to you to choose the people you'll deal with.
>
> Friendships don't have to be excuses for continual demands. And love affairs don't have to include constant arguments for sacrifices. If *your* situation does, it's because you've chosen to permit it.

If you don't like the situation, you are free to change it. If you do, however, there will be consequences. If you quit your job, you will be out of work. If you don't visit your parents every Sunday, they may be upset with you. If you break up with your lover, you may be lonely for a while. Your choice to do something about the situation might lead to such reactions, but you would survive them. And even when you choose not to change the situation or you cannot change the situation, you *always* have an option to change what you think and how you feel about it.

CHANGING YOUR THINKING

You can dramatically increase your control over your feelings by working on your thinking. It may seem to you that events determine how you feel. An acquaintance turns down your invitation, your landlord hikes your rent, you're late for an appointment, and you hit a traffic snarl—you respond with particular emotions. It seems as though these emotions automatically result from the events.

If you look deeper, however, you will see that it is your *beliefs* about events, and not the events themselves, that make you feel the way you do. Epictetus, an ancient Greek philosopher, once observed, "Men are disturbed, not by things, but by the views they take of them." And Shakespeare wrote, "Nothing is good or bad, but thinking makes it so." For example, when an acquaintance turns down your invitation, your feelings will be dramatically different depending upon which of these two things you tell yourself:

(1) "How horrible! How humiliating! I just can't *stand* being rejected!"
(2) "It's possible he really is just too busy this month. Maybe I'll try again—maybe not."

Extreme anger, hurt, or depression result from irrational thoughts. Two of the most common types of irrational thinking are *catastrophizing* and *demanding*.

"Ain't It Awful!": Catastrophizing

Catastrophizing is telling yourself that things are likely to go wrong and that if they do, the results would be dire. You have probably heard your parents catastrophizing, and now you do it too:

"It would be horrible if my husband divorced me."
"How awful it would be if I lost this account."
"It would be terrible if my business failed."

Catastrophizing causes your heart to beat faster, your adrenal glands to dump adrenaline into your bloodstream, your blood to flow away from your brain and increasingly toward your muscles, preparing your body to fight it out or run away. Catastrophizing causes your body to react as if you were in danger even though you're not, and the anxiety that results can be highly uncomfortable and debilitating. (Remember the last time you catastrophized about giving a speech? You were barely able to talk!)

Your first step in countering catastrophizing is to realistically assess the likelihood of the events you fear. Chances are they're not really very likely. As Will Rogers said, "I've had a lot of problems in my life—and most of them never happened." Marriages do break up, people do lose accounts, and businesses do fail, but the chances that these things will happen to you are a lot less than you might think when you catastrophize.

I remember when my new computer, purchased only a few days earlier, started acting funny. I was upset, and I got even more angry when I imagined taking it back to the store and asking them to fix it. I envisioned a scenario in which they would say I had broken it, and I would let them know how angry I was and how shoddy their product was and insist on seeing the manager, then the owner, until I got the problem solved. Just thinking about it made me angry. I got to the store prepared for all this to ensue, and when I presented my complaint, the salesman said, "No problem. We'll have it fixed in a few hours." Of course, I had to act as if I had expected this response all along!

Once you realize that the disaster you fear is very unlikely to occur, tell yourself that. For example: "It's really pretty unlikely he'll divorce me over this. He didn't threaten to. We've had fights before and nothing has happened." Then take a deep breath, exhale, and notice yourself calming down.

Second, realize that the events you dread would not be so dreadful even on the off chance that they should occur. You would certainly not enjoy being rejected, or losing a client, or having a business fail, but it would not be the end of the world. You could try again—and maybe even do better the next time. Thinking rationally, you might say these possibilities would simply be "unfortunate" if they were to occur; you could survive.

Exercise: Escalating the catastrophe.

This exercise can be used any time you are catastrophizing. The first few times you do it, write out your escalation in your journal. Take a situation, either real or imaginary, in which you are feeling excessively afraid—for instance, an interview for a job you would very much like to have. Ask yourself the simple question, "What's the worst that could happen?" and imagine some potential disaster. Then ask yourself if you could survive such an outcome. If the answer is yes (it usually is), then consider some possibility *even worse.* Continue imagining worse things until you have escalated to the point where it becomes ludicrous.

Journal:

Write out this exercise in your journal. Gary tried escalating about asking someone for a date:

September 29: "If I asked April out, she might say no. She might not remember me. She might even laugh in my face. Worse, she could tell all my friends that she turned me down, and even call my mother. She might even call my boss and tell him what a creep I was for asking her, and he would fire me. Of course, I'd have to leave the state because of the embarrassment and humiliation—and all because I asked her out. What a joke!"

As you can see, escalating the catastrophe to its most absurd conclusion often brings you to a more rational perspective of the situation. Then you can ask yourself, "Realistically, what's the worst that can happen?" and see that even if the feared event does occur, it will not be nearly as disastrous as what you had fantasized. As someone once said, "There are only two rules in life you need to follow. First, don't sweat the small stuff, and second, it's all small stuff."

"I Have To!": Demanding

If you use demanding self-talk, you are insisting that things "must," "should," or "ought to" be the way you would like them to be. You are following rules and regulations your parents passed on to you or you made up for yourself.

"Men should make the first move."
"People should be friendlier."
"My children must show me affection."
"I have to be making more money."

Coupled with catastrophizing, demanding keeps you alone, rigid, alienated, paralyzed, and miserable.

Jill is typical. She had been taught by her parents that men "should" be the ones to approach her first, "should" be the ones to ask her out, "ought to" pick her up, and "must" pay all expenses. Jill's demanding self-talk even told her she "must" give no hint to men that she was even interested in them, "must" not smile even after she was approached, "must" accept whatever arrangements they offered if she wanted to go out with them, and "must" not display any physical affection until the third date.

Jill came to me complaining that she was lonely and miserable and was regularly rejected by the few men she met. Never did it occur to her that her rigidity and slavish obedience to the rules her mother had taught her were causing her to sabotage her life.

When you find yourself demanding, ask yourself: "Why *must* this be the way I would *like* it to be? Where is the proof that it should be this way? Who made up this crazy rule anyway? Why do I have to go on following it even though it never brings me any happiness?" You will find that your parents, teachers, or friends made up the rule and passed it on to you, or you may have made up the rule when you were a child, often as a way of keeping out of harm's way. In any case, you will find no "proof" that you must follow that rule—and lots of reasons to drop it.

You can begin to consistently challenge these outmoded rules by using more rational self-talk, such as, "It's true my mother taught me to be passive and that by being passive and aloof I saved myself from my father's abuse, but following that rule has brought me nothing but loneliness, so I'm going to drop it." Then go ahead and do what you want to do—and feel good about it.

One way to modify demanding self-talk is to change your demands to preferences. Life would be much smoother if we treated our preferences as just that—preferences—rather than demanding we have our way.

The following exercise will help you change your demanding thinking to preferential thinking.

Exercise: Modifying your demands.

Take out three sheets of paper. At the top of the first, write "I should. . . ." At the top of the second, write "She (or He) should . . .", thinking of a particular person, such as a spouse, lover, friend, parent, or child. At the top of the third put "Life (or the world) should. . . ." Then, on each piece of paper, write the numbers 1 through 10 down the lefthand side. Now, complete each sentence at least 10 different ways for each list. Some examples:

> "I should be more loving."
> "I should be a better father."
> "I should make more money."

> "She should stand up to her mother."
> "She should do a better job cleaning the house."
> "She should want to have sex when I do."

"Life should be fair."
"Life should be easier."
"Life should give me more of what I want."

Even if you find that some of these statements sound absurd as you're writing, write them anyway. After you have completed each group of 10 sentences, find a private, quiet place, and read each sentence out loud. As you do so, notice your thoughts and feelings.

Then, go back and reread each sentence out loud, this time substituting for "should" a preference statement. For example, instead of "I *should* be more loving," "I'd *prefer* to be more loving." Instead of "Life *should* be fair," "I would *rather* have life be more fair." Observe closely your feelings and thoughts while doing this exercise.

Journal:

Record your observations. Leslie wrote the following:

July 12: "This exercise was extremely helpful. I tend to be a perfectionist, and I really could see how rigid some of my beliefs are about how I should be and how other people should be. I noticed particularly how I do this with my son. 'I would prefer that Roger do well in school' is a lot different from 'Roger should do well.' "

Three Irrational Beliefs

Like most Adult Children, as part of your catastrophizing and demanding ways of thinking, you probably hold tenaciously to three specific irrational beliefs. These beliefs will wreak havoc with your emotions as long as you continue to think they are true.

Irrational Belief #1: "I have to have everyone's love and approval or I'll just die."

If you cling to this belief, you give away your power and make everyone else your judge. If someone doesn't love you, you decide you are not lovable. If someone doesn't like you, you are not likable. If someone disapproves of an action you take, it must be wrong. Holding this belief is bound to make you continually frustrated and depressed.

Other people's opinions are not the "truth"—they're only their opinions. And opinions differ on virtually any subject. Many of my friends don't find hiking enjoyable, but I do. Some think it's a waste of time to spend an hour a day exercising at the gym, but I enjoy it. Several wonder how I can stand counseling adults who were abused as children, but I like it. Everyone is entitled to his or her opinion, and I can listen to it and take it into consideration. But I need not let others' opinions completely determine what I believe.

I recall working with a 50-year-old woman who placed inordinate weight on her parents' opinions. Terrified of their consistently negative opinions, she remained unmarried and seldom accomplished anything for fear they would find it wanting. After several sessions with me, she came to the following conclusion: "My parents are just two elderly Baptists who live in a retirement community twenty miles away. If they weren't my parents, I'd attach no weight whatsoever to what they say; I probably wouldn't even listen to them. Their opinions are just that—opinions— not truths. They have thirty-one flavors of ice cream at the store because different people have different tastes . . . and it's time I started telling myself that and not letting fear of their opinions run my life." After declaring her independence from her parents' opinions, this woman has gone on to have what she considers the most happy and productive years of her life.

The following exercise will give you a set of affirmations you can use regularly to counter your tendency to believe that you must have other people's approval.

Exercise: Declaration of independence.

Twice each day for the next 14 days, repeat these statements out loud: "I am independent of anyone else's approval. I am the best judge of my own actions." Say this affirmation 10 times in a row at each setting, pausing after each statement to observe any reactions. Do not pay a lot of attention or spend much time with any reactions; simply return to the affirmation and say it once again.

Journal:

Record your observations of this exercise. Be aware of any changes after using this affirmation process for a few days. Julianne observed the following:

December 9: "There's less resistance to the idea that I don't need other people's approval nor do they have to even like me or what I do. I'd prefer it, but it's not necessary. I found the biggest stumbling block to accepting this is that I don't completely trust my own judgment, even though I'm 38 years old."

Irrational Belief #2: "I have to do everything absolutely perfectly."

If you hold this belief, chances are you accomplish very little because you are waiting for the "perfect" time in which to make the effort—and it never arrives. If you do get started, you probably quit easily as you measure your progress by the yardstick of your impossible standards and conclude that there's no use going on. Even when you do complete a project, you get little satisfaction. You see only the flaws in it and judge yourself and your efforts harshly. Since you judge everything you do by a standard of perfection, you always fail—and this has led you to have low self-esteem. This particular belief, while more dominant in the Perfectionist role, is by no means exclusive to that role.

To counter this harmful belief, remind yourself as often as necessary that nothing in this world is perfect—and neither are you. You'll just have to settle for being imperfect and living an imperfect life in an imperfect world. Decide to do a "good enough" job on most projects—go for the B rather than the A. You'll find that way you'll get things done, you'll get them done far faster, and they really will be good enough.

A patient named Arthur recalled: "When I held out for the perfect woman, I had no woman. When I held out for the perfect job, I had no job. When I held out for the perfect apartment, I ended up living at home. Now that I've accepted that life is imperfect and have realistic standards, I have all those things I never had before—and I'm really pretty happy."

Exercise: Nobody's perfect.

Sometime today, deliberately do a mediocre job of something. Prepare soup with too much water, write a letter without making a first draft, leave part of your house messy.

Journal:

Record your experience of the exercise. Marty observed:
February 11: "I left the house cluttered last night. It almost drove me nuts. I kept reminding myself that I didn't have to be perfect, that this exercise was good for me, that I needed to start loosening up with my perfectionistic standards. And I found out the world didn't come to an end and that life goes on in spite of the fact that there were newspapers all over the living room and dirty dishes still in the sink."

Irrational Belief #3: "Life should be fair and should go according to my plan."

If you demand that life conform to this belief, you will always be frustrated. When you don't get the job or the raise you insist must be yours, when you get hurt in a car accident that is not your fault, when people less "worthy" than you find love, you become angry and upset. As Wayne Dyer observes in *Your Erroneous Zones:*

> Fairness is an external concept—a way of avoiding the taking charge of your own life. Instead of thinking of anything as being unfair, you can decide what you really want, and then set about devising strategies for attaining it, independent of what anyone else in the world wants or does. The simple facts are that everyone is different, and no amount of your bitching about others having it better than you will bring about any positive self-changes. You'll need to eliminate the other-references, and throw away the binoculars that focus on what others are doing. Some people work less and get more money. Others get promoted out of favoritism, when you have the ability. Your spouse and children will continue to do things differently from you. But if you focus on yourself rather than compare yourself to others, then you will have no opportunity to upset yourself with the lack of equality you observe. The backdrop for virtually all neurosis is making others' behavior more significant than your own. If you carry around the 'If he can do it, so should I' sentences, you'll be running your life on the basis of someone else and never create your own life.

In countering this belief, ask yourself, "Why should life be any different than it is? Where is the proof that it should be any different?" You will find no answers, no proof. Life simply is how it is. Demanding that it should be easier to get a job or a raise or to find love doesn't change a thing. Demanding that the past change is futile. To make progress in life, you need to deal with things as they are. Then you can move forward. As the Serenity Prayer from Alcoholics Anonymous puts it: "God grant me the serenity to accept the things I cannot change, the courage to change the things I cannot accept, and the wisdom to know the difference."

Exercise: Doing what you can.

Make a list of everything in your life and in your world that you believe is unfair. If you're not sure about something, include it on your list. Now, go back through the list and see which items you feel upset about. Of these, which ones are you willing to do something about? Which ones *can* you do something about? What specific thoughts lead you to feel upset? Are these thoughts *demands* or *preferences* that life be different? If they are demands, change the statements to preferences, and note how you feel. It's possible to have strong preferences and strong feelings about something without upsetting yourself about it. Next, of those items you have strong preferences about, what can you do about them? What are you willing to do about them? Create a plan of action and follow through on it.

Journal:

Record your list and any observations about your experience of doing this exercise. A sample from Dave's journal:

June 3: "Two hot buttons for me were child abuse and environmental concerns. I still get upset about child abuse, but I'm beginning to sort out my upset from the fact that whether or not it's unfair or I don't like it, children do get abused. I realized from this exercise that I can do something that may help reduce it, so I'm going to write a letter to the National Committee for the Prevention of Child Abuse and get some information and see what else I can do. As for the environment, I've already started doing things about that, like separating metal cans from the rest of the garbage and taking shorter showers. I realize that I can do something every day about it, and do it with conviction, with passion, *and* without upset. Quite a difference."

SPIRITUAL REGENERATION

> *Indeed we are running away all the time to avoid coming face to face with our real selves, and we barter the truth for trifles.*
> —WAY OF THE PILGRIM

The program outlined thus far will help you recover physically, mentally, and emotionally, and integrate all you have learned into new ways of being and new ways of doing. By following this program, your awareness will keep expanding and your perspective will keep broadening. Like many Adult Children at this stage of integration, you may find yourself naturally evolving into your spirituality.

In *Recovery*, Gravitz and Bowden observe that as we explore our spirituality, we become aware that:

> . . . we have the potential to reach higher levels of consciousness and well-being. We do not have to accept a limited reality; we can actively promote our spiritual development. . . . [Through spirituality] a change

in the overall quality of our subjective experience is possible, and a new and varied responsiveness to life can follow.

As your spiritual awareness increases, you will likely become increasingly aware of higher levels of consciousness—a "higher self"—and a deepening sense of connectedness with other people and with a "higher power" that is not separate from yourself.

The acknowledgment of a higher power is the backbone of most 12-step programs, all of which were fostered by the successful 12-step program of Alcoholics Anonymous. Some recognition and acceptance of a higher power, something that represents the oneness of the universe, is an important part of the 12 steps.

Whether you have a religious background or no religious sentiments, you may choose to embrace this spiritual awareness. Spirituality is nondenominational, and, while it may include the practice of a particular religion, it can be said to transcend any specific religious beliefs. If you were disillusioned with religion at one time, you may find in examining your experience that it was not the spiritual aspects but the rigidity or inconsistency of the people involved that led to your disillusionment. If and when you are ready, take another look at what you believe based on your own experience of your spirituality, rather than what you were led to believe was true. Always trust in your own experience of the truth.

To encourage your spiritual regeneration and bring it to full flower, let's focus on three different aspects of your spirituality: stillness, living in the present moment, and love.

Being Still

> *Nature never makes haste; her systems revolve at an even pace. The buds swell imperceptibly, without hurry or confusion, as though the short spring days were an eternity. Why, then, should man hasten as if anything less than eternity were allotted for the least deed? The wise man is restful, never restless or impatient. He each moment abides where he is, as some walkers actually rest the whole body at each step, while others never relax the muscles of the legs till the accumulated fatigue obliges them to stop short.*
>
> —HENRY DAVID THOREAU

It is only when you are still that you can see clearly, that you can discern the finer qualities of being within you. When you are agitated, you can't see things for what they are. If you look into a clear pool of water, you can see the bottom in some detail. If you disturb the water by throwing a stone into it, it becomes much more difficult to make out the details just a few inches below the surface. Only when the water is calm once again can you see clearly.

In *Magic at Our Hand,* Nancy Rose Exeter describes the connection between stillness and the quality of being:

> The ability to live in the still point springs from a respect for being, for what flows out of being, for one's own simple presence. We have tended to assume that everything happens in . . . what shows, where results are visible. We discover that there is a magic in being, that our very presence is significant. It is not just what we say or do. It is often in our silences that something can be offered that is true and valuable, that is a blessing. Out of Being flows the magic of manifold creation—all the color, the excitement, the nuance and beauty, that can be part of human experience.

With practice you can experience and express this quality of stillness consistently in your life, thus opening the door to greater alignment with your core of being, with spirit. Many people find that meditating regularly is one way to get in touch with this quality of stillness and incorporate it into their lives. By practicing the following meditation regularly (adapted from *How to Meditate* by Lawrence LeShan), you'll find it gets easier and easier to make stillness a part of your daily life and to return to this stillness when you most need it. Start by doing this meditation 15 minutes each day at least five days a week. When this becomes easier, increase the time in five-minute increments until you are meditating for 30 minutes each day.

Exercise: Breath-counting Meditation.

Find a quiet place in which to sit. If you wish, play some soft, pleasant music in the background. Close your eyes and notice your breathing. Be aware of the rise of your chest as you inhale and the falling of your chest as you exhale. Notice the steady rhythm of your breathing. Know that as you inhale, you breathe in the needed oxygen that nourishes your body, replenishing the blood through your lungs; and know that as you exhale, you breathe out the carbon dioxide that is waste to your body, and that this becomes nourishment for plant life. Thus another circle of nature is complete.

Be aware of distracting thoughts or sensations. As these occur, simply notice them, then return your attention to your breathing at each and every opportunity. Remain focused on your breathing and count each exhalation. Count up to four, then repeat. Aim to involve your entire being in the counting. With your first exhalation, count "one"; then breathe in. With the next exhalation, count "two," then breathe in, and continue until you have counted four breaths, then repeat. Your attention may wander from your counting to other thoughts, impressions, or sensory perceptions. If your attention does wander, firmly but gently bring it back to your breathing. If you find yourself *thinking* about your counting or about anything else, rather than simply counting, bring yourself gently back to the task of counting each breath. It may be helpful to set a timer for whatever length of time you have designated so you don't have to think about that.

Journal:

Record any observations regarding your experience with this exercise. Charlene writes of her second try with this meditation:

May 24: "It was wonderful! The first time I was a little too nervous, having never done anything quite like this before. But this time I just thought, 'Oh, what the heck!' and tried it. My attention wandered quite a bit at first, but eventually I lost track of everything else except for counting my breathing. I just finished a few minutes ago, and I feel very relaxed and very peaceful."

Living in the Present Moment

Another important facet of spiritual regeneration is to remind yourself of one simple yet profound truth: All that truly exists is here in this present moment. Your experience *right now* is the only true reality. The imaginings of your mind may make you forget this simple fact, yet nonetheless it is true. The past doesn't truly exist—all that does exist are your *present memories* of the past. The future exists only as a mental image, a hope, a dream. Actual living takes place only in this present moment.

In *On Eagle's Wings,* Lord Martin Cecil makes this point:

> Nothing ever does happen in the future and nothing ever has happened in the past; the only happening is in the present moment. And yet people everywhere are so wrapped up in the past and future that the present moment tends to be overlooked. Yet this present moment is the only moment of reality; everything else is imagination. Now is the only time we can live. We can't live in the past, although some attempt it, and we can't live in the future. We live now or not at all. To the extent that we are drawn out of the present moment we begin to die, because there is no experience of life anywhere else but now.

The point is not to live *for* the moment, but to live *in* the moment—to appreciate each moment and to treat it as special. As you do so, this will support your integration process. Only when you live in the moment can you appreciate its fullness.

Returning your attention to the here and now whenever it wanders allows you to let go of nagging doubts and worries very quickly. One of my favorite stories is from *The Way of the Peaceful Warrior,* by Dan Millman:

> Two monks, one old, one very young, walked along a muddy path in a rain forest, on their way back to a monastery in Japan. They came upon a lovely woman who stood helplessly at the edge of a muddy, fast-flowing stream.
>
> Seeing her predicament, the older monk swept her up in his strong arms and carried her across. She smiled at him, her arms around his neck, until he put her gently down on the other side. Thanking him, she bowed, and the monks continued on their way in silence.
>
> As they neared the monastery gates, the young monk could no longer contain himself. "How could you carry a beautiful woman in your arms? Such behavior does not seem proper for a priest."
>
> The old monk looked at his companion, replying, "I left her back there. Are you still carrying her?"

More than just a philosophy, this attitude can be a way of life, one that supports your integration. It encourages you to pay attention to the real world, to whatever is happening right now. Practice your focus in the exercise below.

Exercise: Focus in the present moment.

Set your book down after reading this and look around you for five or ten minutes. Listen to your breathing and your heartbeat. Notice the different sensations you are experiencing at this moment, both inside and outside your body. Notice the colors, shapes, and textures of the various objects around you. See if you can look at these objects without mentally labeling or describing each one. Your attention may wander from the experience of the present to random thoughts about the past or future. If so, don't be alarmed. Simply focus on something in your immediate environment; if that doesn't work, focus on your breathing. As you are observing, repeat the affirmation "I am here now" about 12 to 15 times, pausing each time to allow the impact of these words to sink into your psyche.

Practice this exercise at least five minutes each day for the next 14 days. You may find some similarities with the focusing exercise in Chapter

5, but at this point your experience will undoubtedly be quite different. Did you find it difficult to stay in the present? Did you tend to have thoughts about the future? The past? What did you notice when you were fully present?

Journal:

Record your experience of this exercise daily. Laurel described what happened for her after the fifth day:

November 9: "For some reason colors seemed a little sharper today and I found I was distracted a little less by my thoughts. I still think an awful lot about the future—I guess that would be called worrying. But I found it's getting easier to stay in (or at least closer to!) the present moment when I'm at work or when I'm out during the day. It's a lot more relaxing that way."

Loving

If you have everything but love, you have nothing. If you have nothing but love, you have everything.
—ALAN COHEN IN *THE PEACE THAT YOU SEEK*

You have tended to think of love as something you feel when you are in an intimate relationship, or what you feel for your children, or for your cat. Typically, being "in love" has meant focusing your loving feelings on only one person at a time. As you have progressed with your recovery and released many of the remnants of your abusive past, you may have increasing periods of openness, peacefulness, and a more expansive experience of love.

As you have perhaps discovered, love can be much broader and deeper than being "in love" with someone. It can be a more comprehensive and unrestricted feeling of caring and respect for other people and for all of life. The more you love, the more you appreciate how we are all interwoven into this larger tapestry of life. The more you love, the more love there is in your life.

This is a result of an inviolate law of life: What you sow, you will also reap. The more you give your love away, the more it returns to you. By treating others lovingly and respectfully, you will get similar treatment in return. You can express your love in many different ways—do a kind deed, smile at a stranger, or express your sincere appreciation to a friend for being in your life. As you make these expressions a more consistent part of your life, you will find that not only are people usually responsive, you are in turn receiving more love.

Tina described her experience: "I find that people really are affected by me when I'm open and friendly. The other day at a bus stop, I struck up a conversation with a 78-year-old lady who was on her way to a senior citizens' center. She was so sweet and so alive, it made me feel good to spend the time with her. We ended up riding the same bus, and laughed and talked the whole way."

Love Is Letting Go of Fear. In order to love in a more all-inclusive way, you need to do only one thing: give up your fear. In *Love Is Letting Go of Fear,* Gerald Jampolsky suggests that there are really only two emotions, love and fear, and that we can learn to choose love in any given situation. It is only fear that stops us from releasing the natural, vibrant life force, or love, that resides within us and is available for expression every moment. You may hide your fear behind anger and abusive thoughts, but it is there underneath the bravado. And beneath the fear is love. Once you choose to release your fear, you can let love radiate. To release your fear, release your judgments and openly receive whatever life has to offer. To love in this way, approach every situation you encounter trusting that life knows what it's doing. By your unconditional participation in life, you have nothing to fear and everything to love.

One of the most poetic, elegant statements about the nature of expansive, all-inclusive love comes from the Bible, in 1 Corinthians 1–8:

> Love is patient and kind; love is not jealous or boastful; it is not arrogant or rude. Love does not insist on its own way; it is not irritable or resentful; it does not rejoice at wrong, but rejoices in the right. Love bears all things, hopes all things, endures all things. Love never ends. . . .

Exercise: Thoughts about love.

List some situations (other than in an intimate relationship) when you have felt something like all-inclusive love. For example, I feel it when I'm in the desert looking up at the stars, or when I watch my children sleeping, or when I share a personal conversation with a friend. When have you felt this quiet kind of joy? What were the circumstances? Was it with another person or alone? What triggered this feeling? What thoughts encourage this sort of feeling?

Now list some situations in which you experienced fear. What were you afraid of? What helped you deal with that fear? If there were people or things you were angry with, what fear lurked behind the anger? What do you most fear that stops you from loving?

To what extent do you experience love in your life, giving or receiving? List some specific things you could do to have more love in your life. Try different ways of expressing love to people you know and to others you happen to meet. Experiment a bit, and see what kind of reactions you get and how you feel.

Journal:

Make your lists and record your responses to these questions and any other observations you have about love as an aspect of your spiritual regeneration. Nora described the following thoughts:

January 7: "I got stopped by a policeman yesterday who gave me a ticket for speeding. My first reaction was anger, which I instantly realized was in turn a reaction to my being afraid. I was afraid someone would see me getting the ticket, afraid that the ticket was going to cost me a lot, and afraid that my insurance rates were going to go up. So I thought this would be the perfect place to try this letting-go-of-fear stuff. I did, and it was actually quite easy. I just decided I didn't want to be afraid, that I had nothing to fear, and it wasn't the end of the world. I was friendly to the policeman, really loving him, and he was friendly right back. He still gave me a ticket, but on it he wrote that I was going just five miles per hour over the limit. That's the first time I've ever felt good about getting a traffic ticket!"

As your higher self emerges, you will likely find it increasingly important to change any thoughts or actions that promote fear rather than love, respect, and acceptance. You may find that anything less than love and respect becomes unacceptable. You should not idealize love to the point where expressing it becomes a rigid rule, but instead simply make lots of room for it in your life. As you awaken spiritually, your love will evolve naturally. As your fear dissipates, your capacity for loving expression will expand tremendously. This is not only recovery from your childhood abuse, it is truly a regeneration and restoration of your Natural Child, of the magic that has always resided within you but that you had forgotten along the way.

As has been said, recovery is not a destination but a journey. It is a process, one in which you will be involved to some extent for the rest of your life. Integration is a stage of the process where you have put together in new form all the work from prior stages. As you reach this integrative stage, do not be alarmed by periods of fragmentation—expect them. These periods of uncertainty will get briefer and less intense each time; they serve as indications that you are about to integrate your experiences in some new way. Periods of integration will recur throughout your life, lasting longer and feeling more substantial each time. Each time you integrate, you will be building on the past stages of recovery in new and dynamic ways, with increasing clarity as to your identity and purpose.

Your recovery will serve to break the cycle of abuse within yourself. Now let's focus on what you can do to break the cycle with your children and your children's children.

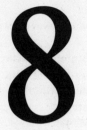

Breaking the Cycle: The Next Generation

CHAPTER

I won't go without my ball!" Frank was late for his company picnic, and his seven-year-old was staging a sit-down strike to get his way. "Come on, Erick," Frank said, "we have to go now!" Erick sat shaking his head, saying "No!" Frank, feeling more impatient and irritated, said, "There'll be other things there to play with. Let's go!" Erick said "No!" again, and Frank could feel his stomach tighten and his jaws clench as he walked up from behind Erick with his hand raised, thinking, "I'll show him!"

Just before he reached Erick, Frank stopped himself and took a deep breath. At that moment he recalled a time when he was seven years old and had gone to the beach with his dad. They had frolicked in the waves and built sand castles. When his father announced it was time to go, Frank protested, "Not yet!" Without warning, his father slapped him across the face, knocking him into the sand. His father shouted that he was a bad boy and ordered him into the car. Frank remembered hating his father, hating that day, and hating his life. He still hated his father for the humiliation and hurt. And he was *not* going to repeat that with his own child. At these thoughts, Frank lowered his hand, bent down, and sobbed with sorrow and relief.

If you have children or plan to have children, inevitably you will face challenges like the one Frank faced with his son. This chapter can help you develop better parenting skills.

Being a single father and guardian angel for my two little angels, nine-year-old Nicole and six-year-old Catherine, I can appreciate the joys and hazards that go hand in hand with being a parent. I love my daughters' precious innocence and will do everything in my power to protect it and their trust in life. I am in awe of their natural expressiveness and see in them my own sometimes forgotten Natural Child. I cherish the opportunity to provide for them the kind of fathering that I didn't get when I was growing up.

Yet there are times when I lose my temper, or am impatient, or treat my children with something less than the love and respect they are due. And whenever I do these things, I worry that I am extending abuse into one more generation.

I'm sure you have also worried about perpetuating the abuse you suffered by passing it on to your own children. At the same time, deep in your heart you have felt a desire and a commitment not to pass on the abuse. Through your dedication to your recovery process, you *can* break the cycle.

Although many adults who were abused do not mistreat their children, statistics show that those who were abused as children run a greater risk of becoming abusive parents. You need not be alarmed, because the good news is that *you* are not a statistic. There are many things you can do to lessen your risk, the first of which is to educate yourself. The more you understand yourself and the dynamics of abuse, the more you can change your dysfunctional attitudes and behaviors.

Raising children is not an easy job, especially today. It requires an incredible amount of tolerance, fortitude, flexibility, adaptability, and support. It requires you as an Adult Child to take good care of yourself, to be completely invested in your own recovery so that you can supply the role modeling and limit setting that are necessary aspects of parenting.

Breaking the cycle starts with you. By taking personal responsibility for yourself and all that you bring into the world, you benefit not only your children but everyone around you. More than that, every time you make contact with any another man, woman, or child, you have an opportunity to offer that person caring and respectful treatment rather than abuse. Every time you forgive yourself and treat yourself well, you break the cycle of abuse, little by little. Every time you treat your child with respect, every time you honor your child's dignity as a human being, you put a little more love into the world.

One way you can do this is to get better at parenting. Doing your recovery program and working on the parenting skills in this chapter will help tremendously. Don't try to be a perfect parent, because that is an impossible goal. Instead of perfection, aim for improvement. Your parenting won't change overnight, so you need to be very forgiving. Your commitment to the steady practice of parenting skills will help you become a better parent—and a better person.

The two greatest challenges you face in raising your children, no matter what their ages, are expressing love and maintaining order and respect.

EXPRESSING LOVE

The love you got from your parents was either inconsistent or nonexistent. Your parents' behavior is a poor model for the way you want to express love to your child. Kris describes her experience: "I was raised by two very nice people who just weren't emotionally connected with me. I felt lonely and needy a lot of the time, and my needs were never really met. I've just recently had my first baby, and—I know this sounds terrible—I don't feel like touching her, talking to her, or cuddling her. I'm slowly getting used to it, but it's really hard. I don't remember either my mother or father ever touching me, and they hardly talked to me. I'm determined to have it different with my baby, though I'm just not always sure how to go about it."

Parents like Kris can gradually change unworkable patterns of parenting and find many ways to express love by concentrating on three areas: *noticing what's right, talking with your child,* and *touching for touch's sake.*

Notice What's Right

> *What's right is the point; what's wrong is beside the point.*
> —LLOYD MEEKER

So it is with expressing love. To express your love, you must first notice what's right, what your child does that you like. Noticing what's right requires that you look actively for the positive actions your child takes and then say something positive about them.

Watch for Positives. You must observe your child's behavior closely, looking for specific actions that you like. It's important to pay close attention and focus on the positive. This will help you see your child in an attractive light. You need to view your child as likable and lovable before you'll want to start giving love.

Exercise: Observe positive actions.

For the next week, observe your child closely every day, looking for things he does that you like. In your journal, write down at least 10 *specific* things he does each day that you find positive. If your child smiles when you enter the room, write that down. If your child opens a door for you, fixes you a muffin, does the dishes, or compliments you, write it down. If your child sidles up to you or sits on your lap, write that down. If your child plays happily with you or with other children, rides a bike skillfully, brings home a paper with a good mark, or says good night to you, write that down. And even when your child doesn't perform well, admire the effort and risk involved in drawing a picture or learning to write, and make note of it. Remember to look for the small things in particular and to be as specific as possible.

This exercise may be difficult, particularly if you were raised by critical parents and have tended to be critical of your own children. Don't worry about it. It will get easier. With practice and close observation, you should have no difficulty finding at least 10 actions to write down each day.

Read and reread your lists often. No matter how you feel toward your child at any given moment, when you dwell on the positive you'll find your feelings getting warmer and more loving. While you are scouting for positives, be aware of any negative thoughts that come to mind. There's no need to deny them, just don't dwell on them. Let these negative thoughts come and go, then go back to finding something positive to think about.

One of my clients, Bob, did this with his daughter. His observation: "The first time I did this exercise, I couldn't find a *single* positive thing to write down about Melissa. But I kept at it, looked and looked and saw that I liked the warmth of her voice when she says, 'Hello, Daddy.' Then I noticed that I liked her posture and her smile. 'That rotten kid isn't so bad after all!' I said to myself with a laugh. Being positive, being critical, they're kind of like muscles. My critical muscle was strong, and now I'm helping build my positive muscle—and I'm liking what I see!"

Say It Loud and Clear.   Now that you have practiced watching for positives, the next step is to say something about what you have observed. Sharing those positives, or complimenting, is an excellent way to express your love and appreciation for your child. Your child craves your praise and will grow and mature in the light of your acceptance.

The key to effective complimenting is to praise specific actions, achievements, or expressions. It's important that your comments be directed to the child's *behavior* rather than to the child herself.

"You did a fine job of watering the plants. You gave them just enough water."
"Thanks for helping me wash the dishes—they look so clean!"
"You cooperated so nicely with Katy today—thank you!"
"You read that whole book in one day? Great!"

Refrain from making any sweeping generalizations about your child's personality and character. For example:

> "You are such a good child!"
> "You are always so kind."
> "You are so helpful and nice."

Generalizations like these do not tell the child what specifically you liked about her behavior and so do not let her know how best to gain your approval and attention in the future. They also tend to encourage all-or-nothing thinking, leading her to conclude that if her entire personality and character can be "good," then it can also be "bad."

In praising actions and achievements, start with the ones you listed in the preceding exercise. Practice turning your list into compliments. Suppose your list includes the following:

(1) Made her bed without being asked.

(2) Picked up toys before bed.

(3) Got an A on spelling exam.

(4) Tied her shoes by herself.

(5) Smiled as I walked into the room.

Here's how you might turn these into compliments:

> "Thanks for doing such a good job of making your bed—and I hadn't even asked you!"
> "Thanks for helping me out by picking up all your toys!"
> "Congratulations on your A!"
> "What a big girl you are! You tied your shoes all by yourself!"
> "You know, I really like it when you smile that way."

To heighten your compliments, address the child by name. All children enjoy hearing their names; it makes them feel important. They will pay more attention to any message that includes their names. It is best if your compliments express sincere feelings. It's also important to express your warm and tender feelings regularly, rather than offering them only infrequently.

> "Cindy, when you make your bed without my asking, it makes me feel really good."
> "Jason, I really liked the way you picked up all your toys!"
> "I'm very proud of you for singing in the school play, Beth!"

When you make the effort, you can always find something to compliment your child on. Even when your child fails, you can praise effort or improvement. Consider these examples:

Instead of saying . . .	You could say . . .
Too bad you still can't ride without your training wheels.	Hey! You made it a full 10 feet!
Boy, it doesn't look as if you'll ever make a sale.	I admire the way you're trying again and again.
When I was seven I could read better than you.	Your reading is really getting much better!

In addition to direct compliments, there are three additional ways you can praise your child:

1. *Relayed compliments:* Whenever you hear something positive about your child, instead of just smiling about it to yourself, pass the word to the child. For example: "Your teacher tells me you're already reading at the third-grade level, Kit. I'm proud of you!"

2. *Third-person positives:* Let your child overhear you tell another parent or a teacher something positive about him. Or say something positive about your child in the presence of one of his friends who is likely to pass it on.

3. *Indirect positives:* Let your actions demonstrate your love and respect. When you and your child are going for a drive, open the child's door first. When the two of you are talking, kneel down to the child's level, make eye contact, and devote your full attention to the interchange. When you are trying to decide what to make for dinner or where to go out to eat, ask for your child's opinion. With a younger child, present two or three alternatives and ask for preferences.

Exercise: Compliment your child.

After watching for and writing down positives for a week, practice complimenting your child once each day for the next week. Remember to be specific, include the child's name, and follow up with a feeling. Be sure you don't praise your child too much, too soon. If your child has seldom received compliments in the past and you overdo it all of a sudden, he will find it difficult to accept them. The third week, compliment your child twice each day. The fourth week, compliment him three or four times each day. By then, complimenting him should be a regular way of expressing your love.

Journal:

Record your experiences and observations of your child's response over the next few weeks as you practice this exercise. Jody wrote about her experiences with her 12-year-old daughter:

May 22: "It's been a lot of fun working with this on Angela. I noticed that she doesn't react right away to my compliments, but I can tell that she likes them. Lately she's taking more initiative and I think it's a direct result of hearing more positives. I came home earlier today, and she had vacuumed the house and done the dishes—without my asking."

Talk with Your Child

Talking with your child involves two relatively simple aspects: asking questions and active listening. Following the tips below will help you feel well-grounded in talking with your child.

Ask Questions

PARENT: What did you do in school today?

CHILD: Nothing.

Sound familiar? Though parents frequently attribute such answers to their children's being secretive, often the blame really rests with the questions the parents are asking.

To encourage your child to open up, you need to ask more *open-ended* questions. Open-ended questions generally begin with "How," "Why," "Tell me about," or "What." Then ask for explanations and elaborations rather than just one-word answers. Indirectly, your questions express your love for your child and your interest in what she has to say. For example:

> "How did you get the idea to do a science project on worms?"
> "Why do you want to go to Camp Hiawatha this summer?"
> "Tell me about the speech you gave today."
> "What was the best thing that happened in school today?"

Avoid questions that are too open-ended. Questions like, "What's new in school?" or "Tell me about your trip" ask for so much information that the child, exhausted at the thought of fully answering, will generally respond closed-endedly ("Nothing," or "There's nothing to tell"). It's better to focus on one project your child is doing or to ask for the highlight of a trip.

Larry described how this worked with his daughter, Allison: "I used to ask Allison, 'What's new in school?' every day. And when she'd say 'Nothing,' I'd get mad and accuse her of keeping secrets. That didn't work, but I found that by changing tactics and asking her for the highlights of her day, we have had some really fabulous conversations. Today, she told me all about a bird that flew into the classroom and about the teacher's funny efforts to catch it."

Active Listening.   To communicate with your child, it's more important to listen than it is to talk. To listen effectively, use the active listening skills you learned in Chapter 6.

Here are some examples of how active listening works with a child:

CHILD: Billy hit me!

PARENT: You're mad at Billy.

CHILD: Yeah, I was just trying to help him catch a butterfly. I don't want to be his friend anymore.

PARENT: You hope you don't see him ever again.

CHILD: That's right. He's a dodo bird!

CHILD: I start driver's training tomorrow.

PARENT: You seem worried.

CHILD: Yeah, well, I've never driven before.

CHILD: Bobby asked Christal to the dance.

PARENT: You're upset he didn't ask you.

CHILD: No, but I didn't want Christal to get him either.

CHILD: My teacher skipped me seventy pages in my reading book!

PARENT: You're really pleased!

CHILD: Yeah, I'm getting to be a good reader, just like you said I would!

When you begin active listening, you may have a tendency to ignore or downplay your child's feelings. Your child's feelings won't go away just because you don't acknowledge them. Quite the opposite—feelings that aren't acknowledged tend to intensify. Demonstrating your understanding through active listening, on the other hand, will tend to have a cathartic effect, for both you and the child.

Exercise: Actively listen to your child.

Make it a point to use active listening with your child at least once each day for the next two weeks. Observe closely your child's response.

Journal:

Record your observations in your journal. Roger wrote the following when he used active listening with his nine-year-old son:

April 26: "Active listening really opened the floodgates. The other day Paul came to me after he had lost his baseball mitt. I said to him, 'You feel bad because you lost your mitt.' In the past I might have screamed at him for losing it, but this time I remained calm and reflected on his feelings. What a difference! He began telling me how afraid he was to tell me things like that because I used to get so angry. We had a great talk, and I even told him about my father and how he used to beat me regularly. I felt so close to my son after that. It seemed like I discovered a new child I'd never known."

I recall a time when my daughter Nicole had a very frustrating day where nothing seemed to go right. When I went to tuck her in she was obviously on the verge of tears. All it took was my saying, "You've been feeling sad," and she burst into tears as she nodded, and sobbed for several minutes as I held her and reminded her that it was okay to be sad.

Touch for Touch's Sake

Touch is essential for your child's healthy development and is a loving way to share your affection. Touching can help the two of you deepen your relationship and strengthen your feelings of connectedness. Because of what touch has come to mean to you, however, you may be intimidated by the prospect of touching your child.

Although your nonsexual touching of your child will be mutually gratifying, the primary purpose should be to satisfy your child's needs for affection, not your own. Your needs for affection are best met through contact with other adults. Consequently, you must observe certain boundaries in touching your child, the most important of which is not to sexualize your touching. Neither of you should kiss the other on the lips or touch genitals. If your child is five or older, the two of you should not be sleeping together, except possibly when the child is ill or having nightmares. Such actions may inadvertently stimulate your child sexually and can result in sexual preoccupation and experimentation long before your child is psychologically equipped to deal with the consequences.

It is, however, very important to provide for your child's need for appropriate touching and physical contact. If touching is something new to your relationship with your child, it's best to start small. Begin by touching your child's shoulder or head as you pass or when you hear some good news. Say, "That's terrific!" and touch her affectionately on the arm or head. An equally appropriate touch is to shake your child's hand when you get some good news. "You got a home run, Doris! Congratulations!"—then stretch out your hand and shake. Work up to giving embraces to show your love and affection.

Other examples of appropriate touching include cuddling on the couch while you're watching television, stroking your child's hair while waiting in line at the supermarket, holding hands while you are walking somewhere, holding her when she's upset or afraid, and embracing when you say hello and goodbye. My daughters and I sometimes exchange foot rubs as we sit together at the end of the day. As with many of these ideas, begin touching slowly and gradually until you become more comfortable. None of the touching will be a direct expression of your love, and yet all of it, somehow, will be.

Exercise: Affectionate touch.

For the next 14 days, make it a point to touch your child affectionately and appropriately once or twice each day. If you have already done the touching exercises in Chapter 6, this exercise will be an extension of those.

Journal:

Observe and record your experience and your child's response to your touch. Emily wrote about her experiences with her four-year-old daughter:

June 30: "Teresa has been eating up all this affection, and I'm learning to enjoy giving it. I've been working this program for about a week, and today she came up on her own and gave me a big hug. I was really moved. I stopped working at the computer and held her for the longest time. It was one of those quiet moments I will always treasure."

MAINTAINING ORDER AND RESPECT

The second most important challenge in raising a child is maintaining order and respect. Do not strive for perfection—you'll never be able to maintain perfect order with a child in your life. Children get sick, rebel, do not pay attention to what you tell them—and it's better to expect these kinds of things and deal with them than to try to eliminate all misbehavior or disorder. To do otherwise would be asking too much from your child and from yourself as a parent, thereby setting yourself up for frustration and failure. Strive for a reasonable amount of order, but allow for periods of disarray.

Like many Adult Children, you may have found yourself falling into abusive behavior patterns in your effort to maintain order. Your spankings may have on occasion gotten out of control. You may have said mean and spiteful things to your child that you later regretted. If you have had experiences like these, the first step to becoming a better parent is to forgive yourself. You did the best you could, given your background. The second step is to resolve not to physically harm or verbally abuse your child ever again. Corporal punishment works only for the short term, while the real message it teaches your child is, "When you get mad—hit!" Verbal abuse only tears down your child's self-esteem. The third step is to develop some alternative parenting methods.

The following sections will offer four ideas to help you maintain order while keeping intact an operational base of love and respect.

Have Reasonable Expectations

It's important to have reasonable expectations for your child based on age and stage of development. For instance, it is unrealistic to expect a six-month-old baby to stop crying because you're tired of listening. It is unrealistic to expect a three-year-old to always play cooperatively with other children. It is unrealistic to expect a six-year-old to clean the entire house perfectly. When you appreciate that a child's developmental capabilities vary with age, your response to a two-year-old's misbehavior will be considerably different than it would be to a seven-year-old's.

Psychologists have studied child development to such an extent that we now understand what we can reasonably expect from a child at any given age. To learn more about this vital subject, I recommend you read

Child Behavior from Birth to Ten, by Frances L. Ilg, M.D., and Louise Bates Ames, Ph.D., or any other good book on child development.

"Catch" Your Child Being Good

Most of us ignore our children when they play cooperatively, read quietly, and study diligently. We yell at them when they are noisy, when they swear, and when they come home late.

This is poor strategy, according to behavior modification principles. Actions you reward will tend to increase in frequency. Actions you punish may decrease unless your child is seeking attention, in which case he may continue them, consciously or unconsciously preferring punishment to no notice at all. Actions you ignore will tend to decrease.

Given these findings, it makes sense to praise your child for playing quietly or for studying—to "catch" your child being good. By the same token, it makes sense to ignore behaviors you don't like. This does not mean you should ignore behavior that threatens to harm your child or destroy property. In such cases, you need to take firm action without being abusive. For example, if your child is unscrewing a light bulb or playing with fire, you will have to stop him and firmly tell him that particular behavior is dangerous and unacceptable, though punishment isn't necessary.

Many Adult Children believe that if they praise their child, she will become lazy and rest on her laurels. They assume the attitude that "enough is not enough" and endlessly find room for improvement. Children who receive only negative feedback, even for their victories, often become exceedingly cautious and begin seeing themselves as inadequate. After a while, they may give up—or they may give up on the person who has been criticizing them.

Even when your child isn't doing what you want, you can best encourage change by ignoring the undesirable behavior and complimenting every small step you see on the way to desirable behavior. For example:

Instead of saying . . .	You could say . . .
You left your truck on the floor again.	Thanks for picking up your train set and your cars. I really appreciate your help!
You're in the fifth grade and you still don't know what 350 divided by 5 is?	Great! You got 19 out of 20 division questions right!
Yuk! You burned my eggs again!	(At another time) Wonderful, your eggs are getting better and better!

Determine the Consequences

There are two ways of using consequences to shape a child's behavior: You can allow the natural consequences to take effect, or you can impose consequences.

Natural consequences.   Natural consequences are the natural order of things. Gravity pulls us down, time marches on, the sun comes up in the morning. Allowing your child to face the natural consequences of his actions will save you endless aggravation while at the same time getting your point across better than words ever could.

Instead of repeatedly urging your child to be on time for school, for example, allow her to be late and to experience the natural consequences. The discipline the teacher imposes may be enough to correct that behavior.

Evelyn describes her experiment with natural consequences: "It was like a miracle! I had to almost tape my mouth shut the first time I tried it, but it worked. I told Ronnie he'd have to start being in charge of getting to school on time. And there he was, at 7:30, at 8 o'clock, watching TV—and his school starts at 8:20. I didn't say anything—just 'Let me know when you're ready.' At 8:30, he told me he was ready to go and I drove him to school, just like I always do and no faster. 'Oh boy, am I gonna be in trouble!' he said. 'Why'd you let me be late?' I reminded him that it had been his choice to be late. 'Won't you write me a note?' he pleaded. I calmly said no. I didn't lecture him or argue with him—I just let the consequences take their course. That night, Ronnie told me his teacher had given him a dirty look and had kept him in during recess. The next day he got himself ready on time, and that has been the case ever since."

Instead of announcing again and again that dinner is ready, do it once and let the consequences of late arrival be a plateful of cold food. Instead of urging your child over and over to eat more, let the child decide how much to eat. If the child doesn't eat enough, let the natural consequence of temporary hunger teach the lesson.

When using this technique, beware of warning your child repeatedly of the consequences: "You know, your teacher is going to be angry at you," "You're going to be hungry," "Your food will get cold." When you do, your words instead of the consequences become the focus of your child's attention, and she may not truly get the message.

Usually when parents begin to use this approach, they feel a strong urge to "save" the child from the consequences. It's important to resist this urge and let the consequences unfold naturally. If you rewarm your child's food or write an excuse for the teacher, the child will not take the consequences seriously. Why should she if she never has to face them?

Imposed consequences.   Letting your child experience the natural consequences of actions can act as a powerful deterrent against their repetition. But sometimes relying on natural consequences isn't appropriate. You certainly wouldn't want to let your child experience the consequences of wandering into the street or leaning out of a window or playing with knives. In such cases, you may have to *impose* consequences.

When your child rides her bicycle in the street, for example, you may at first tell her it's dangerous and you want her to stay on the sidewalk. If she rides in the street again, you may take the bicycle away—the logical consequence of its being ridden in the street. "Since you are not willing to stay on the sidewalk," you might say, "you may not play with your bicycle at all." If your child is younger than six, take the bike away for a relatively short time, usually no more than a few minutes. As the child gets older, the length of time can increase, but the maximum should never exceed one or two days, and then only if the child does not heed earlier warnings.

When your child disturbs you by playing too noisily, you may at first ask her to play more quietly. If that doesn't work, you may say, "I have asked you to play more quietly and you haven't done it. I want you to go to your room." Once again, the younger the child, the shorter the time. For a child of four, five to ten minutes is adequate time to get the point across.

Notice that in these examples, the imposed consequences flow logically from the child's actions. There would be no logic in making the child go to bed early or denying her a favorite TV show for making too much noise or riding her bike on the street. Such consequences would not do as good a job of conveying the lesson you want to teach.

Take Time Out

When tension is running high in your family, when your children are fighting, when you are about to spank or slap your child, declare a "time out." That may mean sending the child to a separate room for a cooling-off period or sending yourself to your room. The point is to somehow get away from each other before the tension gives way to abuse. It gives you and your child time to calm down and gives the child some thinking time.

Time outs can also be effective imposed consequences for unacceptable behavior. For younger children, the shorter the time out the better. For a child of three or under, a time out longer than five minutes is excessive because they lose the point of the consequence. For a child four to twelve years of age, time outs can increase in length but should never be more than 30 minutes. For teenagers, withdrawal of privileges seems to be generally effective as a modified time out.

Alex, one of my patients, reported: " 'Time outs' have been a lifesaver for me. I'll often want to slap the kid or yell at him—I get so mad. I have done those things, but after I do, I hate myself, I feel like a bully, like an s.o.b. for hitting a little child. Half the time I can hardly remember the 'terrible' offense that brought about my anger. Lately with time outs, instead of striking out, I say, 'Go to your room for a ten-minute time out,' and it gives me time to calm myself down and get over that rush of anger. It gives my body a chance to think about his actions, too."

Once the time out is complete, it's helpful to ask the child if he understands why he was timed out. If he doesn't, or if he does but won't say, *briefly* explain the reason. With a younger child especially, explaining helps him understand exactly what he was timed out for. It helps him see that the discipline resulted from his *doing* something unacceptable, rather from his *being* unacceptable or bad.

Look for Win-Win Solutions

Like most parents, you probably think conflicts with your child must be resolved with one of you the victor and the other the vanquished. Here is a typical example in which the parent wins and the child loses:

PARENT: Dear, please put on your jacket before we leave.

CHILD: I don't want to.

PARENT: But it's cold outside and I'm worried you'll catch cold.

CHILD: It's not so cold. If you're cold, *you* wear a jacket.

PARENT: I have a jacket. Dear, get your jacket, please. I'm asking you nicely for the last time.

CHILD: No.

PARENT: There'll be no television tonight unless I see that jacket on your body right away—and I mean it!

CHILD: Okay, okay. I'll get the jacket.

The parent may seem to have won here, but really both parent and child have lost. The child resents the parent for using strong-arm tactics.

Further, the parent's goal will probably not be accomplished—the child is likely to rip off the jacket once the parent is out of sight.

Suppose the child were to win this argument:

PARENT: Okay, have it your way. Don't bring your jacket and get a cold.

Both parent and child lose here, too. The child would probably become more and more demanding and unmanageable in the future in dealing with the parent, other authority figures, and other children.

Using the win-win method, parent and child join together to search for a solution acceptable to both. Instead of demanding, the parent uses active listening to reflect the child's views. The parent then invites the child to look for a win-win solution:

PARENT: Dear, please put on your jacket before we leave.

CHILD: I don't want to.

PARENT: It's cold outside and I'm concerned you'll catch cold.

CHILD: It's not so cold. If you're cold, *you* wear a jacket.

PARENT: Sounds like you really don't want to wear your jacket.

CHILD: I don't. And I won't.

PARENT: You and I have a conflict. I want you to wear your jacket, since I think it's really chilly outside and I'm worried you'll catch cold. You say it's not cold and you don't need it. Can you suggest a solution that would make us both happy?

CHILD: How about if I carry my jacket, but just put it on if I get cold?

PARENT: Would that be okay with you? You'd be happy about that solution?

CHILD: Yeah, it'd be okay.

When you search for solutions that satisfy both of you, nobody has to lose. Your child does not resent having a decision forced on her, for she has participated in the decision-making process and has agreed to the outcome. And your child's skills at arriving at intelligent solutions have been strengthened.

OUR GENERATION'S COMMISSION

We are fortunate to live at a time and in a society where there is an increasing awareness of the mistreatment that has been perpetrated on those most vulnerable and helpless of people—children. We are discovering how abuse has been handed down from generation to generation, and how damaging the effects have been to the self-esteem and emotional health of those of us who have survived.

As you recover from your childhood abuse, you will sweep out any abusive attitudes and behaviors that persist in your present-day experience. Then you can work on viable, nourishing alternatives to replace the old attitudes and ways of being. What a wonderful gift to give to yourself, to your children, and to your world—your own healing and recovery!

Your legacy and mine, our generation's commission, is to steadily increase and expand our love and respect for ourselves, for our children, and for all other human beings. Then we can end this destructive cycle of abuse and return to a more natural state of trust and innocence.

As a parent and as a man, I know clearly that the responsibility for ending abuse begins and ends with me. I have an opportunity to offer love and respect instead of abuse each and every moment, in each and every situation. You can also declare this your personal goal. The more of us who are willing to accept this commission, the greater the chances for our children and our children's children to thrive with one another in an atmosphere of mutual love and respect.

God loves people who don't know how to be anyone but themselves;
that's why He made children.
And that's why He leaves a little child in each of us.

APPENDIX 1:

SELECTING A THERAPIST

If you have decided to seek professional help, here are some guidelines for finding a therapist who is compatible with your particular needs. To start, you might ask for a recommendation from your medical doctor or from a friend. If that's not possible, call a local professional organization, such as the American Psychiatric Association, the American Psychological Association, the American Association of Marriage and Family Therapists, or the American Society of Clinical Social Workers. If that doesn't work, pick three names of therapists from the phone book and call each one, asking the questions outlined below.

Regardless of how you select a prospective counselor or therapist, do not hesitate to ask him *any* questions you may have about himself or his approach, methods, and philosophy. You want someone who will help you and not abuse you, and asking for this kind of information is one way to take care of yourself and your needs. Here are some specific questions you can ask to help find the right counselor:

1. What are her qualifications, training, and experience? Is she licensed or certified to do what she claims she can do? All states have regulations concerning counseling and therapy. You can check with the appropriate state agency to find out about licensing and certification laws. When you ask about qualifications—or anything else—the counselor should not be defensive or evasive.

2. Does he have experience and training in working with the specific problems of Adult Children of Abusive Parents? Ask about his treatment philosophy and approach with this type of client.

3. Do you feel safe with her? You may not always feel completely comfortable in therapy because of the issues you're working on,

but you should feel relatively safe even in your discomfort.

4. Does he seem to be hearing what you are saying? It's important to find someone who can truly listen and reflect back to you your feelings with reasonable accuracy.

5. Does she have a proper mixture of genuine caring for you as a person and a "gentle toughness" to push you at the right times to do your recovery work? You do not need a counselor who is abusive or reprimands you; you do need one who shows you respect, accurate empathy, and is willing to challenge you to stretch yourself and grow.

6. Is the therapist or counselor clear about his own boundaries? Be suspicious if he asks you to dinner or makes any other unusual requests of you. The therapist should be there to serve your needs, not his. He should not socialize with you outside the office and should not be sexually intimate with you under any circumstances. If you are ever in doubt about the appropriateness of your counselor's behavior, report your concerns to the proper professional organization or your local state agency that licenses such professionals.

7. Has the counselor progressed sufficiently with her own recovery so that she has perspective on your recovery? No counselor is perfect or ideal, but it is important that she be well along the path of her own recovery in order to serve you effectively.

8. Does he encourage or recommend the use of other resources outside of therapy, such as books, support groups, friends, and community activities? Therapy should incorporate other elements if you are to benefit maximally.

Do not expect to trust your therapist or the therapy process right away. Trust is not easy for you to give, and it will take a while for you to feel comfortable sharing personal information and feelings.

Your therapy may at some point include joining a therapy group run by your therapist, or the therapist may refer you to a group run by someone else. Group therapy can be one of the most powerful tools to break down your sense of isolation and help you see that you are not so different from others.

Despite what you may have heard, there are no quick fixes. Change takes time, and this is true even if you get involved in therapy. Growing is a lifetime process, and seeing a counselor when you feel the need will facilitate that growth.

APPENDIX 2:

SUGGESTED READINGS

Here are some books I have found personally helpful and have recommended many times to clients, students, and friends.

Adult Children of Alcoholics, by Janet Woititz. Hollywood, Fla.: Health Communications, 1983.
   A brief, well-organized exploration of the subject.

Betrayal of Innocence: Incest and Its Devastation, by Susan Forward and Craig Buck. Los Angeles: J. P. Tarcher, 1978.
   Must reading if you were sexually abused in childhood.

Child Behavior from Birth to Ten, by Frances L. Ilg, M.D., and Louise Bates Ames, Ph.D. New York: Harper & Row, 1955.
   One of the most definitive books on child development, this will help you have reasonable expectations for your child's behavior at any given age.

Co-dependent No More, by Melody Beattie. Minneapolis: Hazelden, 1987.
   An excellent guidebook for anyone who has ever been addicted to a relationship.

Conversationally Speaking, by Alan Garner. New York: McGraw-Hill, 1988.
   The most concise and comprehensive book on communication skills available. Very practical and useful.

For Your Own Good: Hidden Cruelty in Child-rearing and the Roots of Violence, by Alice Miller. New York: Farrar, Straus, Giroux, 1983.
   A detailed and fascinating look at how child abuse has been perpetuated through the ages, and how what has passed for child-rearing has really been abuse. Don't miss the analysis of Adolf Hitler.

Healing the Child Within, by Charles L. Whitfield, M.D. Deerfield Beach, Fla.: Health Communications, Inc., 1987.
   An intelligent and readable overview of the "Child Within" concept.

How to Meditate, by Lawrence LeShan. New York: Bantam Books, 1986. A
very practical, common-sense description of different types of meditation.

If You Really Loved Me . . . , by Jordan and Margaret Paul. Minneapolis:
CompCare, 1987.
   A well-written and thoughtful guide to resolving conflicts with parents.

"It Will Never Happen to Me!", by Claudia Black. New York: Ballantine
Books, 1981.
   For those whose abuse is related to having grown up with an alcoholic
   parent, this book highlights some of the problems common to children
   of alcoholics.

Love Is Letting Go of Fear, by Gerald Jampolsky. New York: Bantam Books,
1970.
   Just as the title says, this book explores how you can consistently experience more love in your life.

Magic at Our Hand, by Nancy Rose Exeter. Loveland, Colo.: Foundation
House Publications, 1988.
   A simple yet elegant book portraying the natural order and beauty of life
   available for us to recognize and embrace.

Outgrowing the Pain, by Eliana Gil. Walnut Creek, Calif.: Launch Press,
1983.
   The first book ever published designed specifically for adults who were
   abused in childhood.

Recovery: A Guide for Adult Children of Alcoholics, by Herbert L. Gravitz and
Julie D. Bowden. New York: Simon & Schuster, 1985.
   A well-written, comprehensive guide in question-and-answer form, this
   book covers in considerable detail what it's like to grow up in an alcoholic
   or dysfunctional family.

The Road Less Traveled, by M. Scott Peck, M.D. New York: Touchstone
Books, 1978.
   A classic groundbreaking work on spiritual and psychological growth,
   this book contains some timely and timeless messages for your spiritual
   recovery.

Way of the Peaceful Warrior, by Dan Millman. Tiburon, Calif.: H. J.
Kramer, Inc., 1984.
   This is one of my favorite stories, based on Millman's emotional and
   spiritual training with a mentor named Socrates.

Your Erroneous Zones, by Wayne Dyer. New York: Avon Books, 1977.
   This book spells out how your habitual negative patterns of thinking
   keep you miserable and upset, and gives you ideas on how to change your
   thinking and free yourself.

APPENDIX 3:

RESOURCES

Reading this book can be a valuable first step toward your recovery. You now understand a great deal about the nature of childhood emotional abuse, what you need to do for recovery, and how to raise emotionally healthy children. You may at some point want additional help and support. The purpose of this list is to provide direction in finding that help.

Check your phone book for a section titled "Community Services." If you can't find such a section, call your local library and ask if they carry a publication listing community services. If this fails, call any public service agency and ask about other services offered in the community. They will likely know of these services or at least direct you to an appropriate information resource.

It's important to get support for your recovery, so don't hesitate to do so. Take an active role in your healing and recovery. A good place to begin is by attending a meeting of Adult Children of Alcoholics. Don't be put off by the name—many who participate in their meetings had parents who never took a drink, and you will be welcome. For information, send a self-addressed, stamped envelope to:

National Association for Children of Alcoholics
31706 Coast Highway, Suite 201
South Laguna, CA 92677
(714) 499-3889

Groups are generally conducted by the people who attend and are free of charge. No records are kept of attendance at these groups. A small number of counselor-led groups are also available on a fee basis.

If you are a victim of sexual abuse, consider contacting either of the following two groups. VOICES in Action offers meetings, conferences, and a bimonthly newsletter. Pamphlets on "How to Choose a Therapist" and "How to Confront Your Perpetrator," as well as a survival kit, are also available. For information, write:

VOICES in Action
P.O. Box 148309
Chicago, IL 60614
(312) 327-1500

Incest Survivors Anonymous is a self-help program following the 12-steps and 12-traditions model originated by Alcoholics Anonymous. Meetings are held weekly in various communities. For information, contact:

Incest Survivors Anonymous
P.O. Box 5613
Long Beach, CA 90805-0613
(213) 422-1632

If you feel overwhelmed by your parental responsibilities or know someone who does, call Childhelp USA at (800) 4-A-CHILD. A professional counselor will provide immediate assistance and will refer you to groups and organizations in your area that can provide more assistance. Childhelp USA also runs the Village of Childhelp, a residential treatment center for severely abused and neglected children ages 2–12. For more information, contact:

Childhelp USA
6463 Independence Ave.
Woodland Hills, CA 91367
(818) 347-7280

If you are a parent who has abused your child, the husband or wife of such a parent, or a victim of abuse who now needs parenting skills yourself, consider attending a meeting of Parents Anonymous. Parents Anonymous offers member-led as well as therapist-led discussion groups and maintains a 24-hour hotline that you can call if you find yourself becoming abusive with your child. For more information on Parents Anonymous, and for meeting times and locations in your area, write:

Parents Anonymous
22330 Hawthorne Blvd., Suite 208
Torrance, CA 90505
(800) 352-0386 (24-hour hotline)

(You should note that in many states, counselors who lead therapeutic programs are required by law to report to the authorities any admissions parents make that they have abused or are abusing their children.)

If you have sexually abused your child, you may be referred to Parents United, which provides crisis and long-term support for families in which incest has occurred. They provide weekly professional counseling and lay therapy groups and arrange for medical, vocational and legal counseling for families. They will encourage your child to attend Daughters United or Sons United groups for children aged 5–18. For more information, write:

Parents United
(Daughters United/Sons United)
P.O. Box 952
San Jose, CA 95108
(408) 280-5055

If you finding drinking or drugs interfering with your functioning, attend Alcoholics Anonymous. Most AA meetings consist of people sharing their experiences, strength, and hope with the group. Some meetings also feature lectures. AA has helped millions of people stay sober and lead more productive lives. Problem drinkers often feel alone in their pain. In AA, you can see that your problems are similar to everyone else's—and that there are answers. All programs are anonymous; no last names are used. Most groups are exceedingly supportive of members. It's a good, safe place to talk out your problems and gain encouragement and support. For the location of the nearest AA meeting, consult the white pages, or contact:

Alcoholics Anonymous World Services, Inc.
P.O. Box 459, Grand Central Station
New York, NY 10163
(212) 686-1100

If you are related to an alcoholic or have a friend who has an alcohol problem, consider attending Al-Anon meetings. If you have a child aged 12 to 20 whose life is adversely affected by someone else's drinking, consider suggesting that he or she attend Alateen groups. In some areas, Alotot groups are available for children under 12. All are free and all can be immensely helpful. For more information, contact:

Al-Anon Family Group Headquarters
1372 Broadway
New York, NY 10018

If you are nonreligious or find the spiritual emphasis in AA objectionable you can contact Secular Organization for Sobriety (SOS) by writing:

Box 15781
North Hollywood, CA 91615
(818) 980-8851
(212) 302-7240

In addition, group therapy can be of tremendous benefit at any stage of your recovery. See Appendix 1 on finding a therapist, and check around for a group that will fit your needs.

Hiding your problems does not work, and seeking refuge in alcohol, drugs, or any other addiction merely masks the original problems and adds new ones. You are not alone, so why try to recover alone? There is tremendous power in the support of others and in supporting others. Take a risk and contact one or more of the groups described above, and attend more than one meeting. Expect to be somewhat uncomfortable at first, but after a few times you will begin to feel more relaxed. I'm sure you will be glad you took this most important step in your recovery from your childhood abuse.

INDEX